For Mom—
Enjoy! I love you!
Casey

I'm Listening with a Broken Ear

Vicky Kaseorg

ISBN-13: 978-1463711047

Dedication

This book is dedicated to my family- my husband who let us bring a crazy, half dead dog home, my daughter who has a heart the size of the universe for all living creatures, my sons who never questioned why we should try to rehabilitate this wild animal. Without them, Honeybun would not be alive today.

I am particularly indebted to the rescue farm that helped us in the rehabilitation of the dog who is the heroine of the story. They asked that their rescue farm and the names of the volunteers be changed, to prevent truckloads of unwanted pets from being discarded on their doorstep. However, if you would like to make donations to that remarkable "last chance rescue", please email the author at vicky.kaseorg@gmail.com, and I will help you find them.

Philippians 4:13

I can do all things through him who strengthens me.

CHAPTER 1

Character Revealed

"I will lead the blind by a road they do not know; by paths they have not known I will guide them." *Isaiah 42:16*

"I am not going to look," I tell myself while driving by the parking lot, staring ahead. If I don't see her, she isn't there. Eye muscles can be mutinous, of their own volition looking at things no one really has the heart to see. She's still there. Drat. My traitorous eye notices that the emaciated dog has not moved in the two hours since I first saw her. Careening around the U-turn, I skid into the parking lot.

"What are you doing?" asks Asherel, grabbing at the water bottle as it crashes to the floor.

"I don't know," I say to my 11 year old daughter, "But I can't just drive by."

The car settles near the little fox like dog. Swollen teats hang on a belly so thin that every bone threatens to poke through her mangy skin. An eye mournfully weeps, and angry cuts and sores spatter like broken glass on her face and legs. One ear droops, the cartilage likely damaged in some fight. Ticks cover her inner ears. She struggles to get up and run as I open the van door, but in the 90 degree heat, she is too dehydrated and hurting to move. She appears close to death. Just what I need on this twenty item checklist day.....What am I doing here? This dog is going to die before my daughter's heartbroken eyes. Move on and don't look back. You can't save the world.....

Filling an old cup with water, I ease inch by inch out of the van. I first saw the dog two hours earlier while on a run during Asherel's tennis lesson. I threw her some dog biscuits, but the dog had scuttled away, so I continued on my run, and hoped some kind stranger would help her.

That stranger will not be me. The world is full of discarded dogs. I have no time, little money, and no desire to be waylaid on this busy day. Where are her puppies she has so obviously birthed not long ago? If *they* materialize, I will be undone. Offer her water and then skedaddle. This sad creature is neither my problem nor my fault. The person who abandoned her however, should be hung from his toenails over a beehive. I am a good and kind person and *my* intentions are honorable. I love God, my country, and apple pie, and have great compassion for this dog. I will pray that just the right person will stop at just the right time. Feeling much better for this sacrifice, I bow my head in pious thought for this little dog.

With these charitable musings, I creep closer to the little dog. Again, she tries to get up and hobble away, but then sinks listlessly, painfully back down. For half an hour, I scrunch closer on my bottom, cooing to her the whole time. Each time I sidle faster than the pace of a three legged cockroach, the little dog threatens to stand. Hurry up and slow down, I mutter to myself.

I don't have time for this!

A few long, disgruntled sighs hiss out of my caring soul, and I squelch the urge to just make a wild grab for the poor beast. Asherel watches from the safety of the van, where she is banned until I know the dog is safe….though of course the dog is *not* safe. I know nothing about the dog. All I know is that she is in pain, abandoned, and near death, on a blistering hot day, bereft of recent puppies. A finger of cold water on her fevered muzzle would probably feel good, and might prolong her life for five more wretched minutes.

When close enough to touch her, I sit beside her motionless for a few minutes telling her, "Good dog!" I glance at my watch, moving only my eyeballs. Hurry up with this gaining trust thing or for sure the chicken will not be defrosted in time for dinner. And I will be in serious danger of missing American Idol. This is not just selfishness. Asherel likes American Idol too, and it is an important family bonding time.

Our mutual gazes fixed on those inspiring young singers teach us a great deal about perseverance against all odds.

You have five more minutes to drink up, dog, and then, we are history. My daughter's character development is not to be trifled with.

She watches me, the whites of her eyes showing like a solar eclipse. Not sensing aggression, I slide the cup of water in front of her. She looks at me, then sniffs the cup, and drinks until it is gone. After a third refill, she is done, licks her lips, and looks at me. I reach out and pet her. Of course, Asherel is then begging to get in on the action. I acquiesce.

"Overcautious" is the charitable way of describing my lunatic fears of horrible things malignantly lurking in wait for my beloved children. My college boys have managed to scamper away but my daughter, Asherel, is still in my protective clutches. I am not sure why I let her approach this potential carrier of germs that could lead to several excruciatingly painful shots in the abdomen to counteract the onslaught of rabies.

"You may come close, but please look out for rabies. If you start to froth at the mouth, you realize we will have to put you down." Asherel nods.

She approaches, walking stiffly in a shuffle, and lowers herself beside me. We both stroke the little dog and croon to her. Asherel is crooning, anyway. I am actually calculating how much longer it will take to demonstrate compassion, as motherhood and childhood training are serious business and should not be rushed. As soon as we reach that threshold at which the critical lesson is fully absorbed, we will scurry off to my chicken and television.

We are in the parking lot of a grocery store, just across the South Carolina border. Miserably noting that the dog is not yet taking her last breath, the least I can do before leaving her to the mercy of God is give her a last meal.

"You wait here while I prowl for cheap dogfood," I say, rising, "Don't let any strangers kidnap you."

"Yes mother," says Asherel.

Little cans of gourmet dog food are on sale, pop top kind. This is clearly a message from God. God is frugal as clearly demonstrated by all the verses in the Bible about saving souls. God knows we have little money, so He is providing reduced price dogfood, and then that kind and benevolent soul He is preparing to come whisk the little dog away will arrive. After buying several cans and returning to the dog, I look around. Where is the stranger that will take this sweet dog off our loving, but very busy hands? Thus far, Samaritans are in short supply.

The dog seems content with Asherel, who is still murmuring to her in a voice only the angels and dogs can hear. She is peacefully stroking her mangled coat. In contrast to a thick fox-like ruff of gorgeous soft fur, the rest of her coat is patchy, mangy looking, with large areas of no fur. Engorged ticks cover the inner recesses of her ears. An old rusty choke collar is around her neck. No tags. She feels feverish, and her teats have fluid dripping from them.

What am I doing- fully *not* equipped to handle this? Why am I feeding a dying dog gourmet dogfood when she can't come home with us? We have no money to save this creature so soft and sweet, with a dirty nose begging to be kissed.

As the dogfood can pops open, she cocks her ears. One is straight up, like a fox, the other parallel to the ground. Broken. Stirring the food with my finger, I hold it out to her. Daintily and gently the starving dog licks my finger. Carefully, sweetly, she licks fingerful after fingerful from my hand. She eats three canfulls of food and then licks her chops and her paws and looks at me. She is remarkably clean for all of her maladies. Her haunches have patches of red clay crusted on them, but her front paws are washed and neat.

There is no easy solution. Animal Control is one option but if they collect her, she'll be killed within an hour. Who can I pawn her off on?

My husband Arvo started his own company a year ago in the mortgage business, about ten seconds before the whole industry crumbled. It has been a lean year, with almost no income. Asherel is home schooled, as were her two older brothers, who are now in college. The last thing we have any right to be taking on is a homeless dog with obvious health issues. We already have a dog, with enough nutty issues of his own. Upon calling the humane society, they tell me I can certainly bring the dog, but a sick dog will probably not be accepted. Their available cages are filled with healthy dogs. The receptionist gives me a list of nearby veterinarians I can try and suggests talking with animal control as well. I scribble the vet numbers on a napkin with scant hope, and while petting the little dog, proceed to call each one. They echo the same dismal response- call Animal Control. Asherel and I look at the dog and each other.

"I can't call animal control," I say, looking away.

"No," snaps Asherel, "You can't."

We sit petting the little dog. Mosquitoes buzz around our heads and the sun lays an oppressive hot blanket on us.

"Let's get her in the van," I say finally, "Com'on, Dog." (Please don't come.... let us walk away. The next carload of compassionate strangers will surely stop with pockets full of money to help you.)

Alas, she struggles to her feet and then follows us. She limps to the van. I tell her, "Hop in," not daring to pick her up. Remarkably, she obeys, and lies down, wagging her tail weakly. *Note: fumigate the car later.* We blast the AC and start to drive.

I pray for the dog as we drive. Unfortunately, there are no neon arrows in the clouds flashing and pointing me to the answer. This is not expected, but still disappointing. Honestly, if God cared about the little dog and her plight in the midst of a cesspool of canine castaways, she wouldn't be discarded and dying this pitiful death in the first place. I don't feel confident prayer will remove the ticks, restore the pups, and find her a fat lady in a gingham apron to stuff her with milkbones. As usual, my confidence is rewarded. Asherel is silent, sitting in the back, petting the little dog. I know what she is thinking.

"We cannot keep the dog," I say in the accusing silence.

The exit to our local low cost pet store looms ahead. They have a vet in the store, and it must be cheap. Maybe I can talk them into taking this dog. Then, once back home, all my friends must be notified about my good deed. Should the newspapers be alerted as well? Not of course for my own glory. It could spur others on to good deeds. Pay it forward, and all. Feeling very good about myself, I hope Asherel is taking notes, because generosity of spirit is in sore demand in these trying times. I glance at myself in the mirror. The sun plays tricks on my eyes, and a faint halo is shimmering around my shining face.

This particular pet store hosts animal rescue drives once a month, parading pathetically cute, homeless animals up and down the aisles. In lieu of any other brainstorms, this is my destination. Leaving Asherel with the little dog, I hurry inside intending to explain the whole situation to the receptionist with a detailed account of my heroic efforts to rescue this creature. Of course, my role will be downplayed as I abhor conceit. Then I can remind her of her duty as an animal care provider to fix this dog and provide her with the home of loving owners that every dog deserves. Bringing myself to tears with my eloquence, I approach the desk. The receptionist has a ring through her nose. She is, of course, moved greatly by my heart-felt plea and follows me to the van.

"I think she looks ok," she pronounces, "We can check her over for free. I can give you an office visit coupon."

As she signs us in, she asks, "Dog's name?"

I look at Asherel.

"Honeybun," she declares, "She looks like a honey bun." She is indeed the caramel color of a honey bun.

"Dog's age?" the receptionist asks, looking up when we don't answer.

"Oh," she realizes, "I guess you don't know that...So you probably don't know history or breed?" The pen scratches across the form.

I look at Honeybun. She is a quiet little dog. She hasn't made a sound.

"She looks a little like a Basenji," I decide, "And I haven't heard her bark. Basenjis don't bark."

"But they yodel," instructs Asherel, "And we haven't heard her yodel either."

The receptionist writes "mixed breed" on the form.

The vet will examine Honeybun and then call us in a couple of hours. After putting a leash on her, the receptionist tugs her towards a back room. Honeybun looks at us as she is led away. She barely knows us, but hesitates as the leash pulls her. After a long look back, she limps after the receptionist, head down, tail low.

We go home, cautiously hopeful. I have rescued a dog, found medical care, and the connections to save the dog. And it has not cost me a single penny. This is the best kind of sacrifice. Self-congratulatory praise fills my heart.

When the phone rings shortly thereafter, the news is bleak. The dog has obviously had pups recently, and there is some genitourinary system discharge that probably is not good tidings. She is covered with ticks, at least fifty, which, by the way, cost $2 each to remove. She is certainly malnourished, has a heart murmur, and likely heart worm disease. I am already horrified by the first item of this parade of problems. They recommend we call Animal Control, who will humanely euthanize her in all likelihood. She just has too many strikes against her. We can pick her up anytime and bring her to Animal Control. My, that *does* sound entertaining! Maybe afterwards we can head over to the Holocaust museum and fill out our evening watching some movies from Auschwitz.

"Can you possibly call them?" I beg, "I don't think we could pick her up just to send her to be killed." This certainly is putting a damper on my happy ending.

The receptionist says they will, and tells me I have done all I can do. Try not to despair.

It is a sleepless night filled with visions of the little dog's trusting eyes as she lay in my van, knowing she was being rescued. Where are her puppies – and how did she get those cuts and broken ear? How long must she have been on her own to be so emaciated, and to have a stainless steel collar rusted? In bed, flipping about like a beached fish, I convince myself we have done the only thing we could have done. Fitful sleep eventually claims me, while I am chanting to myself, "I am a good person."

Waking up while it is still dark and silent, I then settle down to my morning routine. Despite my resolve the night before to just forget this hopeless case, I call Animal Control, knowing the dog is probably already disposed of. How is the little dog doing, and is there any chance they will fix her up for adoption?

"We never picked that dog up," the receptionist tells me. Dogs are barking in the background and chaotic voices shout and clamor.

"Yes, you did," I argue, "The Petsmart vet called around 4:00 yesterday."

"M'am, I checked our records and our cages. No little dog has been picked up from Petsmart."

Confused, I call the vet. The receptionist tells me they had indeed called Animal Control yesterday. Animal Control had said they would come, but never showed up. The dog is still there.

"Can I speak with the vet?" I ask.

I promise myself I will not cry, I will not cry. Having done all anyone could be expected to do, it is clear I am a good and caring person. Just as I prepare to smack down the phone, the vet says "Hello?" I start to cry, choking out the story of our lean year and how we really cannot afford much, but what will it cost to get the dog fixed?

"Listen we could remove the ticks, get her shots, and do necessary care for just over $100…. However, heart worm disease will cost around $1500 to cure, and the cure rate is about 80%.... maybe less for such a struggling dog."

While we are talking, Animal Control arrives at the vet office.

"Hold on," the vet tells me. Muffled voices rise and fall.

"I am talking with someone interested in the dog. Can you give us a day?" There are some mumbled deeper voices and then the vet returns to our discussion.

"How about if I split the cost with you for a heartworm test?" she suggests, her voice soft, soothing, "If it is positive, which is almost a certainty, you will feel better about sending her to Animal Control."

Promising to do the test immediately, she will call me back in ten minutes. Asherel and Arvo still sleep. Pacing outside, phone in hand, I wonder what I am doing. What to pray for- heart worms that will mercifully finish the dog off quickly, or a miracle that means I have some hard choices to make? The phone finally rings. Well, actually since it is my cell phone, it plays, "God Bless America."

"Vicky?" says the vet, "It is a miracle. The dog tests negative for heartworm. If you want her, we will fix her up, get her de-wormed, remove the ticks, and give her all her shots for $120."

What a deal! The tick removal alone should have been $100. This is almost as much fun as holding open my wallet in a tornado. Asking for time to consult with my husband, I hurry inside. Asherel has just awoken, and turns bleary eyes to me, saying, "I kept seeing Honeybun in my head. I didn't sleep very well."

She lies in bed, dark circles under her eyes, her hair scattered across the pillow. After telling her about what has transpired that morning, she springs out of bed. She knows there is no time to waste in accosting her father. Arvo is still in his pajamas, sitting with his cup of coffee at the computer, happily reading online news, little suspecting the ambush that stalks in the dawning day as we approach him.

"You know that dog I told you about?" I begin, blinking and swallowing. Asherel stands at my side, her hands clutched together. Her tangled hair sticks to her cheek.

"Yes," he says, looking worried.

The story spills out, a torrent of words flooding his peace. Arvo looks at us with a touch of resigned despair on his face. He loves his daughter, and he loves the compassionate hearts that motivate his wife and girl to be continually bringing home hopeless, rejected creatures. This is sadly not a new pattern for either of us.

"We can't afford another dog," he laments, "We can't afford the one we have. How will we pay for it?"

Asherel cries out, "I will pay for it! I have enough in my savings account." This is the sad state of our current finances. College savings, or a dying dog? He looks at her, and then back at me, and then at the floor.

“We don’t even know if this dog is house trained,” counters Arvo.

“No, we don’t," I admit, “But if she is any trouble we will get rid of her. We will find her a home.”

He looks at us, and then again at the captivating floor. I really hate putting him in this position.

“Animal Control will pick her up, but she will just be euthanized if they do,” I add. Do I want the dog? No, but somehow, I don’t want her to face certain death either.

Arvo looks up. He covers his face with his hand, heaves a deep sigh, and moans, "I know I am going to regret this. Go get the dog."

We spring into action. I call the vet immediately, and tell her to get those awful ticks off our poor dog, inoculate her, get the worms out of her, salve her cuts, and can she be ready soon?

An hour later, we are standing at the vet counter, new leash and collar in hand. Asherel's hair is still unbrushed. She has not had breakfast. The vet walks Honeybun out to us. She rushes to us, full body waggling. You would have thought we were old friends. It almost seems like she knew we would be back. The nose-ringed receptionist has tears in her eyes as I pay with quarters and dollars from Asherel's piggy bank. Though a penny short, the receptionist blows her nose and waves us away. Asherel sits on the floor, holding little Honeybun's face against hers. It will all be okay now, if she lives.

Dear Lord,

I thank you for the blessing of my compassion and goodness. I know you reward us for how well we please you with smooth and effortless lives, which bask in your glory. I have done a good work this day and now am very tired. Goodnight, precious Redeemer.

Amen.

CHAPTER 2

Irredeemable, Impossible, Illusions

With imminent death in abeyance, the next hurdle is intercanine relations. As we pull into the driveway, Lucky, our other dog, stands eagerly at the door to greet us. His tongue drips with saliva of joy as he rams his tail violently from side to side. Oh happy, happy day- the beloved faithful owners have returned and he can now shower us with obeisance and dog spit. I feel like a two-timing husband, smiling with a blonde babe on my arm and cheerfully shouting, "Hey hon, I'm home with my new wife! You are just gonna *love* her!"

Lucky is friendly, but neurotic. He is a fifty pound terrier mix, with long wild hair that sproings out in every direction- the Big Bang of Dogs. He has a beard that is invariably covered with mud as he loves to dig. Terrier literally means "of the earth". Terriers are bred to dig out vermin, and so their digging genes are highly developed. We are fighting thousands of years of selective breeding in our futile attempts to make this earth dog keep his claws out of the dirt. As if his digging fetish isn't enough to make me want to live on a gas planet, his other quirks assure my temper is rarely untested. Strange habits and screw-ball fears propagate in him like weeds. He is constantly plotting escapes from the yard, thus we have been forced to turn our backyard into a tacky, impregnable fortress. We urge the neighbors to think of the varying barricades as "nouveau landscaping." (Not every homeowner can convincingly pull off ten foot chicken wire stapled to the top of a three rail fence, with large boulders and spikes along the bottom edge.) The neighbors get the benefit of modern art without having to go to a museum. Like my dog, my creative solutions do not always evoke the warm, fuzzy feelings one might expect when true genius is revealed.

When not scheming new getaways, he is a lazy slug, feigning eagerness for walks, but then minutes from starting out, collapses on a soft green lawn. He is like a bad actor in a B movie. He creeps forward, slowing while I look on in horror; certain he is having a heart attack. Slowly he tumbles to the lush lawn, and then heaves a large sigh and lies his head down. We blink at each other. When this first happened, I dropped to my knees and cried out, "Oh my poor dog!!!" As tears sprinkled his face, he bounded to his feet, dragging me along behind him, beauty nap concluded.

He loves other dogs, but plays with them by growling, and then slamming his chin down on them, and mock fighting. He never uses his teeth, and is dumbfounded when his aggressive play taunts other dogs, who then turn on him.

When attacked, he tries to escape, totally oblivious as to how his social idiocy is provoking attacks. I, like all conscientious owners, recognize that it is always the *other* dog's fault. *My* dog is an obedient and amazing dog, with a touch of canine genius that confuses other dogs. I have trained him impeccably, and while his obedience is not guaranteed, or even likely, he usually *intends* to obey. He is an independent, quirky, creative dog….. much like me, except for the dog part. The rest of the canine world just doesn't understand him. They are jealous, for good reason. Not every dog can be so amazingly unique in his escapades. He has an unquenchable spirit, and these creative types must be treated carefully so as not to destroy their zest for life. I forgive Lucky's behavior and wish that my own talents so often misconstrued would be similarly forgiven. Belatedly recognizing it now, we were ignorant and thought this was a good dog, an obedient dog, a *normal* dog. It is to this dog we bring the starving, recently homeless, and unstable Honeybun.

The initial greeting is encouraging. We put both dogs on leash and escort them out back. Lucky wags his tail and sniffs Honeybun's bottom, the dog equivalent of a handshake. Honeybun stiffens, ears flattened and tail erect, but then largely ignores him. I had read that it is wise to keep new dogs leashed for a few days before trusting them free together.

However, anyone can immediately see they are becoming fast friends. Oh true, some folks may have been more cautious and listened to the experts. This is exactly why I accomplish so much, with my goals quickly determined, and swiftly reached. Occasionally, this involves skipping a few steps. I unerringly discern which are the crucial steps to skip, particularly in areas like this, where I have not the slightest bit of experience or knowledge to hamper me. Then the little sticky notes of my mental to-do list are tossed away, and tomorrow's list beckons. I had not won "most likely to turn in a paper early award" in college for nothing.

The dogs are fine together. The little bit of stiffening of Honeybun's tail and the subtle raising of the fur along her back is perfectly understandable. We can skip over the "get acquainted for two days on leash" phase.

We take off their leashes and let them explore the back yard unfettered. I smile, congratulating myself on my uncanny innate knowledge of the workings of a dog's mind. Lucky persists in shoving his nose in Honeybun's nether region, and she remarkably continues to ignore him. I would have slapped his face, but dogs have different parameters of decency.

She walks with a limp, as though the grass hurts her paws. The vet said the many tick bites on her pads would bother her for a few days, but with time, the pain would subside. There did not appear to be any permanent injuries. She seems to walk on tiptoe, as though there is glass instead of soft grass beneath her pads. It lends her the air of a princess, a dainty and refined creature, gracing our yard.

When she comes inside, she collapses on the new bed Asherel had bought her. She has learned to use the dog door immediately. Her thin sides heave up and down rapidly.

“Is that ok?” asks Asherel, watching her rapid, fevered breathing.

“Yes,” I say, not at all sure it is indeed ok, “She has been through a rough time and now she needs to rest and heal.”

I watch her labored, double time breathing, and hope she doesn’t die. Lucky comes in and sniffs her. He doesn't seem to regard her as a rival, though she does not act eager to ingratiate herself with him. Given her near death experience, she likely feels weary, and she looks depressed. She doesn't welcome his attention, but as far as I can tell, doesn't terribly mind it either.

In the middle of the night, I creep out to the sunroom, where she still lays. Her breathing looks more normal, and she feels a little cooler. Her silky ears twitch with my stroking, but she barely opens her eyes.

For the first couple of days, Honeybun sleeps. She awakens for meals, and eats like a wild animal. She sucks the food down in great gulps, sides heaving, with one eye looking around at all times. She fixates on Lucky, with a piercing stare when the dinner bowls clatter to the floor. Within seconds, her food is gone, and then she continues watching us, licking the bowl for several minutes until it shines. It is heartbreaking to watch. Life in the wild had been lean pickings, it is clear, and she likely had to fight for every scrap she managed to uncover.

I feed the dogs in separate corners of the house. Lucky has never cared much about food, until Honeybun arrives, at which point his nonchalance vanishes. Curiously, he becomes very interested in what she is eating, certain it is better than what he is eating.

Did she just growl at Lucky when he ventured near? I am not certain, and ignore it. I am willing to cut the poor creature some slack, feeling horribly sorry for her. Later the lesson that pity is not always the best response will come to haunt me. For now, misgivings are squelched as I am walking on a cloud of naïve confidence that softens the footfalls of ineptitude.

On the third night, as the food bowls clang on the floor like gongs announcing the highlight of existence, I am smugly satisfied with the harmonious blending of our dog pack. Of course, I have been highly trained to deal with animal rescue, having taken a 4-H class at age twelve. Technically, it was not a class in actual rescue. It was more a class in how to properly brush your dog, but many of the same principles apply. Clearly the challenge before me is within my advanced skill set. Why has the media not gotten drift of my heroics yet?

Interrupting my pleasant thoughts, Honeybun's eyes turn red and flames shoot out of her mouth. This may seem like an exaggeration, but you are not there. With a Banshee call of fury, her head spins around four times, and fangs click into place. The guttural sounds that roll out of her cause dents in the floor. With a whirl of fur, before my heart can be stuffed back in my chest, she snarls and lunges at Lucky. As far as I can tell, Lucky has done nothing to provoke this maniacal attack other than to sniff at the wafting scent of her food bowl. Honeybun pounces onto his neck and begins ripping at his throat. She snaps her head back and forth, spitting out huge mouthfuls of fur. Lucky yelps and rolls, and twists, trying to evade the persistent charges. She is lightning fast, her tenuous health apparently not as tenuous as either I or Lucky had assumed. Her blitzkrieg is furious, and in my humble opinion, far exceeds the crime. She ignores my screaming to stop. My trumpeting commands never penetrate her fury. I wildly, ineffectually swipe at her but she has lost all contact with the outer world. Her brain is set on "detonate" and she continues to storm at him with a barrage of teeth. Asherel stands frozen, eyes wide, mouth agape. Matt, my middle son home from college, races out of his bedroom and swats at the torrent of fur balls rolling together. Asherel joins me in shrieking, and then Arvo catapults into the room. It has been a long time since our family has enjoyed so much quality time together.

Clearly, Honeybun does not intend to stop until Lucky is dead. Lucky tries to run away but she relentlessly snaps at his long hair. She can not quite reach his skin and this seems to aggravate her even more. Arvo reaches bravely in to the maelstrom of growling, rolling, snapping terror, and pulls them apart. We bellow incriminations at Honeybun, who gradually morphs from wild animal to soft, pitiful, thin dog. She seems to awaken from hypnosis, and hangs her head. My voice cracks from having screamed so loudly. Lucky hightails it out of the house, and disappears into the yard. Arvo holds tightly to Honeybun's collar. Bits of Lucky's hair still hang from her mouth as the poisonous swelling of fury deflates.

"No big deal," says the optimistic Arvo, "This is what dogs do. They will figure it out."

We gape at him. I applaud a sunny outlook. However, the only result that I can envision from this type of "working things out" is a dog pushing up daisies in a shallow grave. I am not at all convinced that this is normal dog behavior, nor that it will be worked out, and am terrified by the wild animal just revealed. Could she turn on us just as quickly? She had been completely berserk, and our voices had meant nothing. All my prodigious dog brushing skills had been ineffectual.

My hasty online research about aggression in dogs does not cheer me. In fact, the authorities say, dogs will kill each other, aggression cannot ever go unchecked, and never *ever* break up a dog fight. Optimistic as my husband is, on this point, it is not tempered with reality. The pictures on the internet of damage done to humans who try to break up dog fights could singlehandedly cure obesity if sold as dining room wallpaper. The dog, in the heat of fighting, does not distinguish good owner from the object of his attack. His aggressive switch is on, and anything in the way of his attack is in danger. Some of the pictures show skin ripped open to the bone. Furthermore, the experts warn that serious aggression should never be ignored, and is beyond the scope of most pet owners to handle on their own. Site after site recommends the use of a trained professional to deal with dog aggression.

What have I done? My family and my dog are in danger. Trained professional! That sounds like something people with good jobs that dress in tuxedos for dinner and drink champagne hire. Not people who drink boxed wine on sale and have just come out of a yearlong income slump. And where does one even begin to find a "Trained Professional"? Our current dog is nutty, but he is not mean. We have never had cause to seek outside help. It is like being told our son needs a lobotomy.

Shaking with fear and impotence, I tell Asherel it is impossible for us to keep this dog. All my resolve and competence of a mere half hour ago evaporates. Honeybun would have killed Lucky and maybe one of us in attempting to break up future fights. Asherel's eyes shimmer with tears, but she knows she is powerless in this situation. Lucky still hovers on the far edge of the backyard, shaking. He has miraculously survived without a scratch but I doubt that will happen again. And if we hadn't been there, we would surely have returned to white bones in a pile on the floor. It is true that when the devil flees from her heaving sides, she appears as surprised as we are about her sudden switch to Beelzebub. I may even detect some repentance, a morsel of understanding that killing the dog of the hand that feeds you is hardly the proper way to say thank you. But the fact remains that I am out of my comfort zone by several decibels.

A call to the Humane Society reveals that if a dog shows aggression to another dog, they cannot take her. Brief considerations of lying mar the purity of my character. When I ask them what would happen to an aggressive dog if Animal Control is summoned, they tell me she will undoubtedly be euthanized. Just as in the human world, the deck is stacked against those with "issues". What am I going to do? We put the dogs in separate rooms, and go to bed, with leaden spirits. The good news is she appears to be house trained....

Dear Lord,

I am confused, bewildered, upset.....I did a good deed and this is my reward? This is not what I bargained for. You know our situation, since you know everything even before it happens. If Honeybun was going to hate Lucky, couldn't you have found a way to bring some other stranger along to rescue her?

You know how willing I always am to follow your plan. I think you may have been distracted by some of the pressing world events, but I trust that you will find the perfect solution to this. I know that "all things work together for good for those who love God," and you know I love you. I know you love me too and I look for a miraculous solution in the morning.

Amen.

PS- In case you are stumped, I will research the internet for ideas tomorrow and save you some time.

CHAPTER 3

Irrevocable, Inconsolable

Lucky, never the strongest dog psychologically to begin with, now slinks around the house, with a wary eye always on the lookout for the next attack. After a night of wrestling with my sheets, I stare at myself in the mirror, asking myself over and over again why God created me without a brain. From the heights of self-adulation, I now plummet to the depths of self contempt, sticking my tongue out at the dark circles under my eyes, and berating myself out loud. You idiot, you inflated fool. What mind numbing ignorance makes you think you can save that dog? Look at your motives.... Is it any wonder this endeavor has not ended in gold medals and endorsements? You conceited jerk. With these happy thoughts, the computer is again enlisted to help me determine if there is any hope of healing the food aggression. In painful acceptance of my role in the continuing disintegration of normalcy for my dog or my family, I am very careful to keep the dogs apart and safe. Honeybun lowers her ears when I look at her. She and I both feel our inadequacy glaring at us and we do not like it, not one bit. Even when she lowers her head, and lays back her ears, one is off–kilter. What is up with that? After pulling the sideways ear upright and letting go, it flops back to a perpendicular slant. Her ear is broken. My heart is broken. What a pair. As I stroke the silky golden ear, she ducks her head but looks mournfully up at me.

The internet experts suggest that the easiest solution for food aggression is to always separate the dogs when food is present. Since we have not seen any aggression except in this situation, it is probable that if they are fed in distant opposite corners of the house, the issue will be instantly resolved. Problem solved quickly and easily, in time for dinner the way all troublesome issues should be neatly resolved. My defeat quickly turns to victory. Patience in my book is not a virtue; it is the last resort of incompetents. Perseverance is only necessary to procrastinators. A second coming was only hoisted on Jesus because of the inefficient, ignorant people who didn't get it right the first time. With self congratulation, this simple cure is implemented.

For a day or two, an uneasy peace reigns. The dogs are never allowed to roam loose without me nearby, though what I hope to accomplish with such vigilance is unclear. It isn’t as though my scrutiny had been able to stop the last fight from escalating. Honeybun occasionally emits a very soft, low growl for no apparent reason as Lucky walks by, to my consternation. Otherwise, they seem largely indifferent to each other. We become more relaxed allowing the dogs together. The term 'relaxed' is used loosely. The 'relaxed' posture at this stage of Honeybun's rehabilitation involves me sitting on the edge of my chair, one hand hovering near her collar, the other nervously plucking my eyebrows out.

No further episodes of obvious aggression return, and my confidence increases. Good deeds are rewarded and I am past ready to collect my richly deserved accolades. Nearly two entire weeks of diligence, and my long suffering solicitude will now reap if not fame and fortune, at least tranquility in our home again. While wisely deciding to hold off news conferences, it is no secret that if we continue on this track, Cesar Milan, the Dog Whisperer could well be challenged for top honors in dog training. I of course, am not bragging, but simply stating facts everyone can see.

Returning from a party, we open the door as the exuberant dogs come galloping to greet us. We have progressed to the point where we feel safe leaving them alone together as long as no food is in sight. They both come hurtling at us like fuzzy missiles. Wagging and prancing one moment, suddenly there is an explosion of fur and teeth and the dogs are again locked in mortal combat. Once more, it blasts out of nowhere, and we stand there in the midst of gnashing teeth, and growling, murderous demons. Again, the placid, seemingly submissive little dog becomes a cannon, shooting venomous snarls and flashing teeth like artillery into poor Lucky.

Matt, hearing our screeches, bounds from his room. We are all yelling and whacking at the blur of fur. I slam a chair between the dogs and when they are momentarily on opposite sides of the chair, Matt grabs Honeybun. Poor Matt has recently returned from college expecting a restful summer and discovers he has stepped into "The Wild Kingdom". Not only is he not getting Chicken Wellington with tender asparagus tips; he is being handed manuals on Rehabilitation of Severe Canine Basket Cases, and warned not to leave his room without full body armor.

Lucky is hiding in one room, and we throw Honeybun in the sunroom, slamming the door shut. This fight has erupted without a morsel of food in sight. It appears that Honeybun is not going to tolerate Lucky sharing the smell of her food *or* our attention. Lucky, nutty as he is, was there first, and is patiently suffering his displacement with relative equanimity. To reward him for his tolerance, he is getting the snuff beat out of him. He doesn't deserve it. Despair leaks into heavy pools of despondency. I am out of my league in dealing with this wild dog. The captain of my soul is currently ship wrecked. I have been raised to chart my own course and navigate with aplomb. So much for self-reliance. The aggression explodes out of nowhere, completely unprovoked and unexpected. I haven't the slightest clue how to deal with it. All that is left to do is count my fingers and thank God I can still wear gloves with all five fingers.

As bombastically inflated as my ego had been before the attack, it now shrivels to dejection. This is beyond my meager capacity to cope with. I love animals but without training in anything beyond the normal mischievous family pet, have not the strength, fortitude, knowledge, or ability to endure the pain and hardship (not to mention potential stitches and puncture wounds) that this untamed beast requires. Sometimes, it is best to fold.

"We can't keep her," I tell Asherel, who tearfully and silently agrees. If she would just rant and rave and argue like a normal spoiled brat, I would feel much better.

Our neighbors have recently lost a dog to old age, and they might possibly be vulnerable enough to shift this rather inconvenient problem to. The issues with Honeybun seem to be completely rival-dog related. If we can find a home for a family without a dog, all will be well, at least in our four walls, which is all that matters. I call the neighbors, Pam and Jim, asking if they would consider taking this sweet, but non-dog-loving creature for their very own. They agree to look at her. I don't remember to pray. Good thing God knows what we need before we ask for it.

When the doorbell rings, Honeybun erupts into a cacophony of growls and barks. She stands at the door, hackles raised, teeth bared.

"Way to impress your potential owners!" I congratulate her.

This is new behavior. She has seemed submissive and gentle to all human beings up to this point, even when the vet poked and prodded her. What new uninvited demon is occupying her soul? I let the neighbors in, pushing Honeybun back. She snarls, and tries to get around my jabbing foot. Jim has a cane, and I rationalize the door aggression as a response to the unfamiliar cane. I clutch her collar and usher my inexplicably reluctant guests inside.

Pam smiles and asks which dictionary I am using to define "sweet"?

As we settle in the sunroom, she becomes gentle and docile, letting Pam scritch her belly. She barks at Jim and his cane for a while, but eventually calms and lets him pet her. I sit on the edge of my chair while watching her, my muscles tense and ready to leap up at the first sign of demonic possession. I'm not certain she will not attack. My heart plummets like recent DOW averages. I hope our homeowner insurance covers dismemberment. The neighbors leave; assuring us they will consult and decide by tomorrow.

Once again, that night, overwhelming sadness invades my sleepless hours. Why has God seemingly planted this dog in our midst if only to sabotage our good intentions? Perhaps He wants us to fix her up, spend money we don't have, and then break all our hearts for a wonderful reason we just can't yet see. Asherel has stoically assented to the need to give "her" dog up, but she creeps into her room with wet eyes. My bribe, telling her the vet bill she had covered will be repaid by buying her a new horse statue, evokes a weak smile as the tears gather.

I want to give up. I want to have the doorbell ring and not worry about handing our visitor a stun gun. I want to be able to put food down for our dog and not have trained snipers ready to intercept incoming fangs. I want my life to be simple again. But I can not quite shake the feeling that having put the pot on the flame, it is my fault it has boiled over. I curl up around my copy of "When Bad Things Happen to Good People" and sob. In the morning, I call the neighbors and ask them to give us a month before taking Honeybun, if they would. It is academic, as they had decided not to take her. What a surprise.

So we are stuck until Plan B materializes. Since Plan A has not yet been developed, I am in a pinch. We know we have to separate them when we feed them, and separate them when we are gone so upon our return they will not eat each other. After considering my toes dejectedly for an hour, tears occasionally dribbling down my nose, I decide I have little choice but to do my best, bloom where planted, and all that kind of thing that motivates and inspires people. First, look on the bright side since this is what people feigning optimism do. She is housebroken. At least I am not dodging piles of poop while helping Lucky evade her onslaughts. She is also somewhat trained in basic obedience. She knows sit, come, brief stay, and mooch. Not that we have to command her, "Ok, now mooch Honeybun!" She just does that naturally. As soon as we sit down to eat, she sits next to me, alert and poised ready to snap up any tidbit that might fall, one ear straight up, one ear straight sideways. Then, ignored in hopes of discouraging this begging, she lays her silky head on my lap. She looks up at me with slightly moist eyes, gently wagging her tail. It is so endearing that it is very difficult not to give her scraps, particularly given what living hell she must have gone through for the past year.

During my bouts of depression and remorse, I reminisce about the good old days of relaxing with just one dog and his benign issue of digging through concrete. Sometimes I smack myself in the face, and remind myself again to focus on the bright spots. Honeybun and I share a love of walking. Unlike Lucky who finds walks to be a convenient way to find new napping spots, Honeybun loves going on walks. She obviously has never learned to heel obediently on a leash but learns very quickly.

Cesar Milan- the Dog Whisperer, which I check out of the library, teaches me that an exhausted dog is a placid dog, and less likely to be aggressive. We go on "power walks", three to five miles twice a day, with only brief potty breaks. We are a pack, migrating like in the good old evolutionary past when cavemen and dogs hunted together. We have purpose, and I am establishing myself as pack leader, alpha dog, the sun around which their canine world revolves. They respect me and there will be no more fights. And for a period of time, that is the case.

Considering our complete lack of competence, things are proceeding well. I begin to crawl out of bed with less of a sense of dread, and a small flutter of something that feels like hope. Of course, constantly on high alert, every time Honeybun fixes a riveting stare towards Lucky, I bellow a reprimand. This redirects her briefly, and Lucky skitters away. The lovely doggie friendship between the two that I envisioned is not happening, but my goals have readjusted. I just want them to both survive. Knee and heel pain is developing from our power walks, but permanent disability seems a small price to pay for intact flesh on humans and dogs. Arvo never mentions that this is not fun, that his stressful life is not being made any easier, and it is my fault. While brushing my teeth words like "idiot" and "ill conceived plans" stumble out of the froth.

Lucky never seems to blame me, though it is his life most in jeopardy. He seems to hold out some hope that even this obstacle can somehow be dug out of. He still sniffs Honeybun, his wiry face beseeching. She does not welcome his interest, and similarly does not seem comfortable with us petting her. She likes to be near us, but edges away if we try to stroke her. This is a sad and troubled little dog who evidently does not regard humans or other dogs as sources of comfort, but at some level, longs for it. We sit in silence, she and I, mutually longing for connection, for joy; settling for now with proximity to it.

I begin to lose weight, and sleep, rising early enough to get the dogs out quickly to exhaust them before they start plotting how to kill each other. Old friends call, asking to walk with me like in the pre-Honeybun days. I decline as the "dog whisperer" suggests power walking migration with dogs is not at all what most of my friends do with their dogs. Their walks are more leisurely, dog–directed pee and poop fests. According to the experts, my dogs cannot direct *anything*, or they will see through my fragile alpha status, and they will be using flush toilets while we humans pee on the bushes. My world is closing into managing the two dogs. Despite growing exhaustion, there is no choice but to continue what I have started.

Meanwhile, Asherel, who is enamored with dog agility contests, begins jumping Honeybun over piles of sticks. Dog Agility is a canine performance sport where the dog navigates a series of jumps and obstacles off leash in timed conditions. We have been watching these contests for years, traveling to see any near enough for us to attend. Asherel wants very much to train Lucky to do agility, but he seems totally uninterested. She finds that the little dog, however, is immensely agile, probably honed from her brief life of fighting to survive. Asherel begins training her, and building an agility course in our back yard. She researches the various types of agility equipment, and then creatively replicates them with what she can find in our yard. She uses logs and stick piles for jumps. To create the "dog walk", she suspends a board across two overturned chairs. She designs an "A-frame" by turning an old Adirondack chair upside down, and has Honeybun march up the seat, and down the back. She makes "weave poles" by sticking twigs in the ground. Both Asherel and Honeybun seem to be having fun, and I am certainly in favor with all the sunshine, fresh air, and exercise involved. Lucky watches woefully from the sidelines, but honestly, lazy Lucky has never been very interested in jumping anything. Rousing from my bouts of self flagellation over the mess I have created, I glance out the window to see Honeybun sprinting across the yard, and flashing over the twig pile jumps. It is the first real spark of excitement she has summoned thus far.

While a jumping dynamo, Honeybun does not seem to otherwise have a shred of playfulness in her. Starvation has a way of dampening the playful spirit. When we throw the Frisbee, she watches it land, without moving to intercept it. The balls we toss bounce off her nose. She looks at us, somewhat confusedly, and walks in her dainty tiptoe manner in the opposite direction. During one such attempted play session, she suddenly starts growling at us. As we climb down off the table, we realize she is assuming the dog "play position". She isn't quite sure how to initiate play, but it looks as though a fog is lifting from some primeval swamp of knowledge. Lucky, who loves to play, sees that at long last, she is acting like a dog and he races outside with her. *Hooray*, he barks, his tail wagging, ears perked. Briefly, they rocket across the yard. Honeybun almost transforms to happy at that moment.

Inexplicably, as quickly as the exuberant play springs up, she suddenly lunges at him. Playful barks turn to vicious, ear ripping snarls and the worst fight to date spews forth like sun tan lotion in a nudist colony. Honeybun leaps for Lucky's throat, as he tries to escape. She is oblivious to our cries to stop. She rips huge chunks of long hair from him. It is his hair that is saving him. She seems unable to find his skin. Then she plunges for his underbelly, where the hair is short. Watching from the sunroom window, I race outside, followed by Asherel and Matt on my heels. Her teeth are snapping, and her upper lip curls back like a shark just before it snaps a victim in half. Mindful of the advice I had read never to reach in to stop a dogfight with my hand; I grab a ladder from against the house and slam it between them. It separates them, but then Honeybun skirts around it to go after Lucky yet again. Oblivious to our shrieks, she repeatedly charges at him. I bash the ladder between them once more, giving Lucky enough time to spurt back inside through the dog door, and Matt leaps in front of it, blocking Honeybun from following with his foot. She is demented, and ignores us, throwing herself at the door, with fierce, venomous snarling. He kicks at her. She doesn't attack him, though I fear she might, but continues to try to get around his foot and go after Lucky. No doubt *he* is shuddering in the bathtub reading a manual on self–defense in one easy lesson.

Screeching at her, I thrash the ladder again to get her away from the house. She is so crazed and wild that I am sure if I try to grab her, she will be attacking me next. The ladder clanging in front of her with Lucky out of sight finally seems to register through her insanity, and she stops. She stands looking at me as the glazed, wild look begins to melt away, sides heaving. I pant for breath too, doubled over from fear and exertion. Asherel and Matt stand on the deck silently watching us. We are all shaking. Matt is the first to break the silence.

"When's dinner?"

If a dog has remorse, she looks remorseful. Her breath comes rapidly, as she hangs her head and looks at me. She would have killed him; there is no doubt of that. When going for his jugular had not worked, she had gone for his belly. This was a primal attack. Asherel is on the deck, crying.

"I am calling animal control now," I croak, "We can't let her hurt Lucky."

Matt looks woebegone, but I suspect it is because he knows this means there are going to be delayed dinner plans. Asherel agrees through her tears. This is becoming a common pattern for her usually cheerful character, and I am to blame for thinking my talents could rescue this dog. Worse yet, what kind of arrogance made me believe God had *directed* me to bring this wretched creature into our home? Honeybun tries to follow me up the stairs.

"No!" I screech, "Go!"

She slinks back down, and sits in the yard, watching us as we all traipse inside. Lucky greets us, whining. There is a small bite on his leg, but miraculously he is otherwise unscathed. His long wild hair has saved him.

"Please don't call Animal Control," begs Asherel, "I know we have to get rid of her, but they will kill her."

I look out in the backyard where the little dog waits, still panting, outside the door. Oh Lord, I will try not to ask *why*, but if you could send a heavenly checklist on *how*, I promise I won't tell anyone where I got it from. It can be our little secret.

I have never navigated the "get rid of dog" world before, having always been the one who goes to the pound, anxious to save a dog and make it our pet. Animal rescue is an excruciating world. First of all, there are many small rescue organizations but all busting out of the seams. I call or email all of them within a fifty mile radius. They are without exception filled to capacity, overflowing with discarded dogs. The Humane Society has a waiting list a month long, and they will not take a dog that is aggressive with other dogs anyway. Animal Control will take her, but will euthanize her within twenty-four hours. The outlook is bleak.

Honeybun is banned to the sunroom with closed doors, blocking her from the rest of the house. She sits at the glass door watching us all day long; an eager, hopeful, expectant look on her face. Lucky without access to his beloved sunroom and dog door into the backyard, is despondent.

I spend hours on the internet that morning, emailing rescue organizations and honestly admitting that the dog seems loyal to our family, but hates other dogs, and is wary with strangers. (Ok, "wary" is a bit of a stretch.... but it has a better ring than "blood sucking tyrant"). I call several facilities and leave messages. No one picks up. No one returns my calls. The emails that are responded to all have the same monotonous death toll- no room at the inn.

Whenever I glance at Honeybun through the sunroom door, she wags her tail and cocks her head. Being a confident, persistent soul, I lie my head down and cry. The computer begins to type as my forehead presses against the keyboard. From the primordial ooze of keystrokes, it clacks, "All applicants for Messiah, please review skill in miracles *before* submitting form."

The sunroom where Honeybun is serving her sentence in solitary confinement is not air-conditioned. She will be cooked if left there for long with the doors closed. While that will solve our problems, that cannot be on my conscience as well. She pants as she looks at me. Finding a long rope, I tie it to the pool table leg and secure Honeybun to the other end. Now the sunroom doors can be opened and she can roam about ten feet in all directions. Lucky will have to go by her to get outside, but she will not be able to follow him, and if he is quick he might make it unscathed. However, while she watches him with her steely gaze, she remains still and subdued. She seems to understand that she has blown it big time.

The phone rings. Praying it is the hoped for salvation, I snatch it. Please please *please* be a home for Honeybun. The caller, Peggy, is indeed one of the rescue people, but she quickly tells me she only takes in pit bulls (*are you NUTS!?*)

and like the other rescues, she is full. However, she has the name of a small rescue group in South Carolina that is experienced in working with dog aggression. She also says she will post our information on Petfinder, a web page devoted to matching homeless pets with prospective owners.

Peggy urges me to send her a picture and biography of Honeybun with all the enticing tidbits we know about her. The bio is composed in my mind as she talks: *Seeking home for unstable, aggressive dog that seemed normal until her strength returned, at which point she became dangerous to people and other pets. Only serious inquiries considered.*

"It may take some time," the Pit Bull rescuer cautions, "So you need to find a way to keep your dogs safe and apart. Meanwhile, I can give you the name of some people trained to help."

I take the names, but gloomily. How can we afford a dog trainer? And living the way we are now living for more than the next ten minutes seems impossible. How am I going to survive? How are the dogs going to survive? And what about that promise to my husband that if she was *ANY* trouble, we would find her a home? *ANY* trouble? She is *ALL* trouble, through and through. She thumps her tail as I glance at her. Well ok, maybe not through and through. Sending Peggy the bio, and one of the pictures of Honeybun, I walk the fine line between accentuating Honeybun's good traits, and not lying.

Peggy forwards my Petfinder ad to the trainer who specializes in dog aggression issues. Shortly after that, I receive an angry email from that trainer.

This dog needs to be helped or euthanized, she rants. *It is criminal to just pass these problems on to someone else. Get the dog off the Petfinder list until the issues are resolved or put the dog down. If you want help, call me.*

The trainer, Malta, has a small animal rescue organization called Last Chance Rescue. At first, my gut feels like it has been punched. I haven't *caused* the problems. I am the nice lady who pulled the dog from the brink of death, paid to have her patched up, and now am just trying to do the right thing for my family and the dog. After screaming in my mind at the gall of this blunt, insulting email, I write her back. *OK, if I want to help this dog, what would I do, and what do you charge?*

She emails me back. *$250 for a week with my "pack" but for people who rescue dogs.... Free.*

Rereading that line, certain I cannot be reading it right, incredulity is morphing to hope.

"I want to be sure I understand. You will come help us with Honeybun for free?"

"Yes, free. People who have the heart to rescue a dying dog deserve a break."

Stunned, knowing this can't possibly be true; I ask her how far she is from us in the next email. There must be a catch. No one helps strangers for free. Her response comes immediately: *An hour and a half away*. Oh great. For a moment I had thought another miracle was developing before my eyes. But Malta is just too far away to be of any use. I thank her for taking the time to email me, but I don't know how we can work it out as she is so far away.

"*Oh,*" she tells me, "*We are in Charlotte right near you every day. We install sound systems and there isn't any business for us here in the country where we live. I am working down the street from you next week. How is Wednesday for you?"*

How is Wednesday for me!? How is lobster dripping with butter, hot fudge brownie sundaes drowned in whipped cream, fifty year old faces without wrinkles, and thighs that don't jiggle?!! Wednesday is fine! After calling to arrange the time, Malta listens as I describe the situation we face. She gives me some simple advice. *Don't allow the aggression. It is your home and your dog. Claim it.*

Yeah, right. She makes it sound ridiculously easy, and also vaguely as though it is indeed all my fault. Not daring to say anything however that might keep the Dog Messiah from coming, promises pour forth about how hard I will work at claiming my home and my dog. Can she be more specific, perhaps? She cannot. *Just do it. The dog is responding to you. If you let her be aggressive, she will be aggressive. Don't let her be.* And, she assures me, she will solve the dog aggression in five minutes. Just hang on until Wednesday. I find her claims preposterous, but am desperate, and the price is right.

Wednesday is light years away. How to survive until Wednesday? First, after making sure Honeybun is securely attached to the pool table, I make another trip to the library and accumulate another stack of books on dog training. Upon returning home, I make a cup of tea, and settle down in the sunroom. Honeybun comes and lies at my feet. Her fur is starting to grow in the patchy areas, and her limp is less pronounced. She still has a small discharge that is likely from the recent birthing of her pups. I have never had a female unspayed dog, and wonder how one deals with them when they come in heat. The images that flit through my head are disturbing.

She needs to be spayed. Just in case we still have her, the last thing I want to go through is a dog in heat, with whatever gruesome things that entails. Time to call the vet at Petsmart that has been so helpful to us.

A spay will be $300. Good grief! Perhaps you didn't hear me right... I don't want to *buy* a uterus, I want one *removed.* No wonder there is a glut of unwanted dogs! Further research divulges a $65 spay in a Cabarrus county clinic, a half hour away. *That* I can deal with and immediately call and schedule the earliest available slot- a month hence. She will be long gone, but better safe than sorry.

The books, especially those by Cesar Milan, the "dog whisperer", blast me into an uncharted universe. I have seen his shows on television, but not paid much attention as while Lucky is clearly kooky, no one is in danger of dying from his aberrations. While entertaining, Cesar had never been crucial to my life. With the advent of Honeybun, that all changes. Unlike Lucky with his relatively benign issues, Honeybun's issues could result in extensive hospital bills.

Cesar's training tips mirror the little advice Malta has given. An aggressive dog has to know who the alpha dog is, and it better be every human in the household. Without a clear leader in the home, the dog feels it needs to take charge. It may not even want that role, but in a vacuum of leadership, will respond by trying to take over. Cesar says the human must seize control, exude positive, assertive energy, and communicate with every molecule of his being that he is in charge. The dog is then free to enjoy being a happy follower.

Hope lifts a cautious beak to nibble at the worm of worry. I try to think like Cesar. For the next few days, waiting for Malta to come and change our lives, I chant empowering verses to my family about positive energy. Think like a dog, like an alpha dog.

Contrary to what most well-meaning pet owners believe, love is not the most important thing a dog needs. He needs exercise, discipline, food, and then affection- in that order. A dog needs to know not only his place in the pack, but also that he can trust and count on the alpha dog to keep order in the pack. If the alpha dog does his job, the other dogs are secure and content. Ready or not, I must be the alpha dog. Some are born to greatness and some are thrust tail first into it. I am being shoved into an office I have not campaigned for, and would decline if nominated. Only I have no choice. Having rescued the dog, my impulsive nature is reaping what it has sown. Later there will be time to reflect upon the verse, "Count the costs...." I don't know all that alpha status entails, but hope it doesn't mean chewing and regurgitating food like birds, or being the head goose flapping my wings to exhaustion so everyone else can fly in my draft. This much is clear- lead confidently, and if unable to muster confidence, be a convincing fake. Dogs sense weakness faster than a lemming lurches off a cliff, so under no circumstances give in to my quivering insecurities.

The exercise part of transforming dogs in ten easy steps is child's play in comparison. I faithfully run Honeybun twice a day. Asherel and I begin regimented obedience training. We keep the dogs separated most of the time. The days amble slowly by with the dogs surviving and no further incidents. It is Tuesday night, and we still are breathing with all our body parts attached in the correct order. Malta, the dog whisperette, will be here tomorrow. I can hardly wait, and huddle under my sheets with one eye peeking out as the first ray of dawn breaks.

Dear Lord,

Thank you for helping me persevere for so long. Two weeks of trials are all I can bear and you have told me in your Word that you will never give me more than I can bear. Thank you for sending me Malta, and bringing our trials to an end and finally showing me that victory is within the grasp of all those who diligently seek you. I have learned the lessons you so graciously deigned to teach me, and now rest in the knowledge that you are blessing me for my hard won patience and persistence.

Amen.

CHAPTER 4

Impudent, Impetuous, and Other I Words

I am nervous all day, waiting for Malta. It has been a rough two weeks. I am a prison guard who knows the moment the rifle is lowered, there will be carrion. Honeybun still stares at Lucky whenever he comes near, with a piercing stillness. Her concentration is complete, like a stalking lion. At these times, maniacal shrieks divert her and she glances away, but the constant need to watch her every move is definitely cramping the peaceful calm of our former life. I pore over every available book related to dog aggression, well past my 8:00 bedtime each night. Every suggestion is implemented, and still Honeybun glares with that intimidating stare, and growls when Lucky comes near. Not every time, but enough times. It is apparent if they are left alone together, someone will be missing a tail when I return. My diligence and steadfast spirit has its limits. Malta will not arrive a minute too soon. Lucky slinks about the house with darting glances. Honeybun remains tied to the pool table.

The interminable hours tick by and I watch the animals that are refusing to be cured. I begin to be nervous less for what Malta will think of Honeybun, whose issues we had innocently inherited, and more concerned about what she will think of Lucky whose issues we will have to take full blame for. While waiting, my objective eye turns to the so-called "good dog". Some disturbing thoughts develop. Is it really considered good when you only come if you are called one out of ten times? Is it well-behaved if you bark all night, even when we have dragged you inside twenty times and the neighbors are throwing rocks at you and at us? Is it really obedient if you dig under the fence and when that is blocked, climb it like a cat, and then saunter off down the street? An uncomfortable conviction grows that we have not been as persistent with Lucky's training as we should have been.

Technically we had rescued Lucky too, but he was only six weeks old. His character had not been permanently marred by horrendous living yet. Lucky's addition to our family was another example of my impulsive leaping with no regard for where I might land. Suffice it to say that we found him in the sewer pipes beneath our street, and we were not looking for a dog, but the dog was looking for us. The puppy needed a home, and I was there. Thank God he wasn't a homeless elephant when I walked by.

Lucky had issues from the start. First, he had mange, which can be awful, but in his case, the vet was able to treat it and in a short time his coat was shiny and healthy. We should've known that his escapist overly curious nature that landed him in the sewer system was the same nature that would cost us thousands of dollars in fences that could not contain him. Little did we know that this terrier (same root as "terra firma"), this earth dog, would be able to dig his way out of any enclosure. Could it be possible that I should have spent more time and effort with Lucky?

I realize, while waiting for Malta that Lucky is not a good dog. And it is our fault. We have let him rule our lives because he is nice about it. The few minutes left before Malta arrives will probably not be time enough to reform him. But I give it my best shot.

"Sit," I call out, hoping a crash course might yield a miracle. Lucky laughs at me.

Malta rings the doorbell. Both dogs charge the door, barking loudly enough to destroy what multiple ear infections have left unimpaired of my hearing. Malta peers in while I try to corral the two dogs, leashing Honeybun and kicking at Lucky. Finally I open the door while shooing Lucky away with my foot. He easily moves around me and races up to Malta and her husband, Will. Honeybun strains at the leash, barking and snarling. Lucky stuffs his face in our visitors' crotches, and then licks and slurps their legs, tail wagging. Honeybun continues to yank at the leash.

Malta must have extensive experience with people with jellyfish brains. She does not seem at all put off, or fearful. She walks backwards, back to Honeybun, who looks ready to pounce. Malta keeps her eyes on me and instructs Will to ignore the dogs. This is not an easy demand, as Lucky is trying to discern Will's gender in a most impolite manner. After about five minutes, both dogs are quiet and Malta is reaching out the back of her hand to Honeybun. Lucky meanwhile keeps nosing against Malta, winding his way between her and Honeybun. Why had I ever thought he was endearing? She asks me to put Lucky in a back room.

"Your first problem," Malta snaps, "Is Lucky." (I have a sinking feeling this is not going to be an ego building visit.) "He is actually the more unstable of the two."

"How do you see that?" I query, keeping the sudden flood of disbelief out of my voice.

"Do you see how when I reach out to Honeybun, he keeps getting in the way? He is demanding my attention and in a very annoying way."

So what is wrong with wanting attention? And besides, sometimes you have to demand because sometimes people don't know your needs. Personally, I see no problem with desiring attention, do you? This does not necessarily indicate deep seated neuroses or even shallow neuroses, does it? Who doesn't want attention, after all?

"He's trying to manipulate you and I suspect some of the behavior you have seen in Honeybun is in response to him instigating it."

I almost wish Honeybun would bite Malta now. I mean Lucky may have a few sponges instead of grey matter, but he hardly can be blamed for Honeybun trying to kill him. A surprising flashback from my childhood poofs to mind. I was insanely jealous of my talented older sister and used to scratch her with my fingernails, at which point she would attack and pummel me. Of course I would cry, and Mom would race in and punish Wendy. Wendy proclaimed she was unjustly provoked and urged my mom to just look under my fingernails where the bloody evidence lay.

Malta's voice snaps me back to the present instigator and instigatee.

"If Honeybun were a bite threat, she would have bitten me now, a total stranger walking in your home. She is sketchy, no doubt about that. And she is fearful. But I don't think she is aggressive."

This is a surprising assessment as Honeybun still has her hackles raised and her eyes are sharpened like lasers on the intruders.

"That stare doesn't scare you?" I ask.

"That's what herding dogs do," explains Malta.

"She did that every time before growling at Lucky," I persist.

I feel this talk is going on long enough, and don't want her side-tracked on peripherals like how much we have screwed up with Lucky. Just tell me how to fix *this* dangerous dog, stop insulting me, and leave before the sun sets.

"I am not trying to be argumentative," I add, (despite the distinct appearance otherwise), "But I really don't think Lucky was doing anything to provoke the attacks."

I think Malta is trying hard not to punch me. She sighs and takes the leash from me. She walks around pulling Honeybun after her. Honeybun looks concerned, her loose skinned brow furrowed, but she prances beside Malta. Lucky is scratching at the bedroom door.

"I think she is insecure and frightened. She doesn't know who is in control and she feels the need to take control. I suspect she had a hard time scrapping for food and life and doesn't know who to trust. I am not saying she doesn't have issues. I just don't think Lucky is stable, so she doesn't feel safe."

I am feeling more and more certain that we are going to be required to make some deeper adjustments in our lives than initially hoped for.

"Are you afraid of her?" asks Malta, interrupting my fearful thoughts.

OK, now this is going a bit far. We are not here to psychoanalyze *me*. *I* didn't go try to take a chunk out of someone's major artery. Warning bells are dinging in my ears.... I think I am about to be blamed next. First Lucky, now me. Whatever happened to the criminal getting blamed for her own actions? However, Malta raises a good question.

"Well, yes, when she flips I am. She is completely wild. She doesn't listen to us and clearly wants to kill him."

"She knows you are afraid," says Malta, "Dogs sense instantly when someone is unbalanced."

Was I just insulted? No wonder Malta is doing this for free. Who *pays* for this kind of abuse?

"Is it hard for you to be in control?" she asks.

No! The issues with Lucky are because he is such a headstrong dog. No one could follow through on stopping his barking or his escaping. You would have to be vigilant twenty-six hours a day! And dear God, you are not trying to insinuate that I am not in control because I don't want that crazy dog to sink her canines in me?

"Dogs are pack animals," Malta continues, "And they need a clear hierarchy with a clear pack leader. If they sense fear or hesitation in the human, they will not follow you. You have to be the alpha dog. In fact, every human needs to be the alpha dog in their eyes or they will be a danger."

I swallow my burgeoning pride and anger. Some of what she is saying begins to make sense. Lucky loves us, but it is clear he doesn't respect us. Or at least now it is clear. He whines from the bedroom where he has been banned.

"How do I become the alpha dog?" I ask sadly.

I think that sparks the first glimmer of Malta believing she could work with me. She softens a little.

"First, you need to take away Honeybun's job. She doesn't need to be in control if you are. She needs to know that you will protect her from Lucky, and that you are in charge."

Protect her from Lucky? Skin from my sister under my nails……

"But *she* attacked *him*."

"Because she feels threatened. She has a short trigger, and her response is overblown, but she feels the need to protect herself. She doesn't know that you will. So the first thing I will do is give you a magic tool. It will solve the dog aggression problem in five minutes."

Now why did she wait this long to tell me that? This is the kind of 'dog whispering' I like. I suppose I am more like a 'dog shouter'. Whispering is too subtle and slow-acting. She had mentioned this "magic tool" earlier in the week when she called me. I cannot wait to see this miracle tool. She scurries to the car and returns with a horse whip. I blanch. While wanting to save our dogs, I do not condone animal cruelty. I suspect Honeybun has had enough of that already.

"You don't hit the dog with this," she assures me, though not until she has a moment of satisfaction that I thought she was Hitler, "Unless of course you are attacked or your other dog is in danger. Everyone has the right to self defense."

She has me review the episodes that triggered the aggression.

"The food issue for a dog that was starving takes time to work through. For now, the food issue will be dealt with by separating the dogs. Always feed them in their crates."

A worried frown crosses my normally happy face. Time? How much time? You mean past 3:00?

"You do have crates, don't you?"

Of course we have a crate.... We had borrowed it two days before. Time, I don't have... I have a life I want to return to and I would like to return to it ASAP.

"Put Honeybun in the crate every time you feed her. Put her in now and do you have a biscuit? Get that, and then let Lucky out."

I follow her instructions, glancing at my watch. Honeybun settles down happily to her biscuit, and Lucky comes rushing over to sniff at the crate. True to form, Honeybun leaps up and growls. There is a terrifying crash of metal crunching, causing me to lose my balance as I jump back. Malta has slammed the whip down on the crate creating a deafening fright in all of us. Except Will. He smiles placidly. I have not heard him speak at all yet. With Attila the Hun as a wife, one probably learns to still the tongue. Honeybun too yelps and cringes. But she doesn't growl again.

"Do that every time you hear a growl. Stop the small signs of aggression and you will be more likely to keep them from escalating. It is much harder to break up a fight than to prevent it."

Similarly, she commands that when the dogs rush the door, we are to slam the whip on the ground with a resounding crack and force them back. We are to get between them and the door, and "claim" the door, "own the visitors", and show the dogs we are in control. We decide who they can or cannot kill.

Then she demonstrates. She has Will sneak outside and ring the doorbell. As expected, the dogs perform a reenactment of Armageddon. Malta cracks the whip as they warn us of hell breaking open, and they realize with a yip that life as they know it has ended. All sound ceases as they scatter. The echoes of the whip melt to silence. The dogs stand like statues in the far corners of the room, de-barked. I am speechless as well.

"Problem solved," says Malta. My kind of solution! I love instant fixes!

She teaches us numerous strategies in becoming the alpha dog that afternoon. With whip in hand, I know no dog will ever mess with me again. She instructs Will to ring the door bell again, and lets me crack the whip this time. The dogs scramble to hide as before, peering at me from a safe distance, their barks sucked right out of their throats.

"Learn to read her signs," advises Malta. She warns us that rehabilitating and gaining trust is a long process. I am not to expect results overnight and there will be setbacks, and more fights. My pasted smile does not reveal the distress such words inspire in my fast-food soul.

As she leaves, she pauses to stroke the little dog's soft fur. "I suspect this dog will teach you things about yourself you never knew," she says gently. *I* suspect they are things I would rather *not* know.

From that moment on, the whip is with me wherever I go, even to the bathroom. The whip is my talisman, my amulet, my shield against a sea of troubles. Whenever Honeybun growls at Lucky, I smack the whip on the floor and tell her to desist or be destroyed. When I feed them, Honeybun is always crated, but if Lucky comes near, she growls. The whip thunders disapproval and no more growls at least for that meal. Within a day of the whip treatment, I feel courageous enough to untie Honeybun from the pool table. We still separate them at night, but during the day, they roam freely in the house together. The whip is with me, and I am in charge, alpha wolf, top dog, Pluribus Unum, numero uno. No more sweating at the teeth of the wild dog. I have claimed the door and life is good and worth living again. We tell my parents of our hopeful progress, and my dad sends money to have both our dogs microchipped. He cannot bear the thought of this little dog facing the despair she had faced on her own ever again. Confidence glistens like a firefighter in Hell, and we bring Honeybun to the vet to be microchipped. We will keep her...and the whip.

Whenever the AKC (American Kennel Club) National dog show comes on TV, Asherel and I make a lapful of goodies, and camp out before the television. We always laugh at the hairless Chinese Crested, or the bull terrier with his egghead, or the Pekingese that looks just like a furry caterpillar. We cheer for the terriers, out of loyalty to our own nutty terrier. However, my unquestioning approval of the AKC is challenged with Honeybun's entrance into our life. Unexpectedly, this occurs with the discovery we might *almost* have a pedigree dog.

The kind Pit Bull rescuer, Peggy, who had first responded to our pleas for help and led us to Malta, is delighted to hear that we will be keeping Honeybun. After examining our dog's picture on Petfinder, Peggy writes and excitedly informs us she feels certain she has found Honeybun's breed. We *know* her breed- all American mutt. She has a spotted purple tongue which we think signifies she is part chow. The little I know about chows is enough to insure I never wanted one. Some insurance companies raise home insurance rates for chow owners and some campgrounds don't allow chows. It is considered an aggressive breed. While Honeybun looks nothing like a chow, the vet assumed the purple tongue signified chow and it was indelibly put on Honeybun's record. They may as well have branded her with a swastika. I sadly write Peggy back, and tell her the vet claimed Honeybun was part chow, a breed I had vowed never to own.

Peggy replies, "No, she looks nothing like a Chow. This dog looks exactly like a Carolina Dog- maybe even purebred."

Purebred? Our dog could be of the caliber of those dogs we watch on television? Outed as a closet canine snob, it is with mounting excitement that I read Peggy's email. She sends me the websites with information on Carolina Dogs as well as photos. It could've been our Honeybun in every picture. Perusing the photos and descriptions, I feel there is no doubt. She is clearly a Carolina Dog. Her size is correct, her coloration, her ruff, her tail, her dainty paws. Everything matches the website details. I tingle with the first bit of real excitement this dog has engendered. Not only are chows *not* the only dog with purple tongues, Peggy informs me, but Honeybun looks nothing like a chow, and she looks exactly like a dog that is so fascinating, even National Geographic has written about them.

Carolina Dogs are a primitive breed, descended perhaps from Dingos (and are also called American Dingos or Carolina Swamp dogs). They are still found in feral packs in the remote swamps of South Carolina. They are considered among the oldest domesticated breeds in America, and yet, the AKC does not recognize them as a breed.

“Well why not????” I shout at the computer, "We are turning our lives upside down for this exotic and mildly dangerous Carolina Dog, and you are telling me it is not recognized as a breed?”

Initially angry with them, I later learn it is not the fault of the AKC, but of the Carolina Dog Association(CDA). Entrance into AKC would require closing the gene pool on the breed, and the CDA is concerned that would lead to genetic problems with such a small pool of registered Carolina Dogs. Malta on the other hand dislikes the AKC and any other group that promotes breeding of any animal.

"Just what we need," she smirks, "More dogs for me to save."

We now look at Honeybun with new respect. She is a noble non-breed, maybe even a purebred non-breed, descended from some of the oldest and most noble dogs to ever roam the earth. Her behavior matches what the websites describe, including some very bizarre behavior. These dogs are known for a curious habit of digging little "snout pits" in the dirt, and seemingly eating the dirt. Honeybun makes "snout pits" in her bed. She nibbles on the blanket, never ripping or tearing a hole, but nibbling as though to kill vermin lurking inside the material. I have never seen a dog do this, but Honeybun does it every single time she settles down for the night. We have already noticed that Honeybun, like all Carolina Dogs is a "den builder". Almost immediately upon exploring the back yard that first day, Honeybun vigorously went to work noodling her way into the dense thicket of bush out back, and then digging a pit. We also read that they make excellent pets, after the initial adjustment period. Ah. What we have been going through is an adjustment period. They go into heat more often, and younger than other breeds….What!!!! I check the calendar. The spay operation is in 2 weeks. Whew! Agile and fast, they make great Agility Trial dogs. Asherel's eyes light up when we read that.

Asherel has been trying to convince Lucky to become an agility dog for months. He will good-naturedly lumber over jumps and collect his treat, but you can tell his heart is not in it. Lucky is plodding, and grudgingly compliant. He does not particularly enjoy exerting himself, and sees no reason to go over jumps at all, unless we tell him not to. Asherel runs full speed at fallen logs, leaping over them with Lucky in tow, and he plants his feet like anchors, refusing to move. She pulls, cajoles, and bribes.... but he is decidedly disinterested.

Honeybun is a different story. Asherel turns a log on its side and runs toward it, Honeybun in tow. She sails over it, tail behind her like a rudder, ears lopsidedly perked. Asherel sets up a series of logs. Our little Carolina Dog scampers over the jumps, clearing them joyfully, easily. Her life work is sealed, and Asherel has found her agility dog at last.

Asherel begins researching how to make agility courses. No longer content with her ersatz jumps, logs and overturned chairs, she wants to make real equipment. After all, she now has a dog of a breed especially suited for Agility work. The easiest kind of jump to make, she discovers is with PVC pipes plunked on a long nail in the ground. Arvo makes two jumps that way, but they are unstable, and difficult to move around. Asherel finds a slightly more complicated design that makes the jumps portable and more stable on a PVC base. However, working many hours with his new job, Arvo balks at making the more sophisticated jumps. If Asherel wants agility jumps, she is going to have to make them herself. I am busy cracking the whip, and Asherel is busy building a dream. Both of us hope to achieve it by Tuesday.

We hurry to Lowes building supplies, and get sixty feet of PVC pipes, and a pipe cutter, then lay the supplies out on the ping pong table. Arvo teaches her how to use the pipe cutter, and donning her safety glasses, my determined eleven year old sets to work measuring, designing, and cutting. Arvo demonstrates proper drill use, and she drills holes for the screws that will hold varying heights of poles. She works tirelessly. In three days she has made seven jumps. She further honors her dog with the new found pedigree status, by her careful detail and beauty in wrapping red tape in a candy cane swirl around each jump bar.

Next, she researches other agility equipment. In beginner agility trials, the dog must also go through a small tunnel and zigzag through a series of upright poles called weave poles. Asherel notifies me we could find a tunnel at a toy store. She is satisfied for now with the weave poles made from sticks stuck in the ground. Later, she promises me, she will tackle some more permanent design of weaves. In more advanced agility contests, dogs also must go up and down an A-frame, sit on a "pause table", and go up and down a seesaw-like thing called a Teeter. Asherel uses objects she finds around the house to finish her construction of a complete course. The overturned plastic chair will do for now to mimic the A- frame. She places a board over a log for the "teeter". A sawed off stump becomes the "pause table". With her course complete, she begins training Honeybun eagerly.

Every moment she is soaring over jumps is a moment I am not on constant alert for growls or raised hackles. I pry my fingers off the whip, and collapse in a chair and close my eyes. Meanwhile, Asherel grows flushed and sweaty, and comes in covered with mosquito bites, but glowing with joy.

"She is doing great!" she enthusiastically reports, "She loves it Mom! Look, she is smiling." I open one eye and look at the little dog. I don't see a smile. I see a savings account wiped out, an exhausting burden, and a never-ending project that may not end well.

Now Asherel sets her sights on greater goals.

"I want to enter her in agility trials, so we need to do a class," she proclaims.

Malta feels this is a great idea, that if Honeybun has a job, and an obedience class, it will help with the aggression issues as well. I do some research and find the oldest kennel club in Charlotte has both obedience and agility classes. I write to them filled with my daughter's infectious excitement, but am deflated upon examining their web site more carefully. NO dogs with aggression are allowed, and the handler has to be at least thirteen years old. While we have not seen aggression outside of the home, Honeybun is certainly not yet trustworthy with a classful of other dogs. We find another training facility which doesn't mention age or aggression restrictions, and quickly enroll. They don't have agility classes, but they have beginner obedience classes. I am not certain Honeybun belongs in a beginner class. Asherel has been working hard with her, and she does all the basic commands fairly consistently. However, she may not respond optimally in a class filled with consumable distractions like other dogs or small children, so beginner class seems best.

She starts classes in a little over a month and will be spayed in a few days. All remains quiet in our demilitarized zone. I never venture to any room without the whip. Our peace is really just a truce, brokered by the presence of the whip. And there is a looming problem. We are scheduled to go to a family reunion for a week in Pennsylvania. I investigate boarding costs, lamentably discovering the fee for one dog is not equal to the national budget, but close. If Honeybun could stay in Lucky's crate, it would not require a second mortgage, but we will obviously need to board them separately. Unwilling to declare bankruptcy in order to pay boarding fees,

I mention the problem to Malta. Our normal vacation plans in the past either included the dog, or we had a neighbor come in and feed Lucky. Since we have the dog door, he has always had access to come and go as he pleases, and the expense is minimal. What will we do now? Honeybun is far from ready to let a stranger come in our house without us there. Nor would I trust her alone with Lucky yet. This is a cost not considered while deciding whether to help the dying dog on the side of the road. Cost number one million and three not considered.....

"Well *we* board dogs," proclaims Malta.

"But you are an hour and a half away," I bemoan.

"We can pick them up," she decrees, "After work... and return them to you the morning after you get back. And we will work with them with our dog pack."

Trembling with hope, I ask, “What do you charge?"

"For rescued dogs, $10 a day. Oh and bring your own food."

Malta will work with both of them during that week, and they will be returned to us healed and perfect. She of course didn't promise that but I know while our reward has been delayed a month, it is now Payday. My good deed is finally registering with whatever heavenly department is in charge of Samaritan Awards. I would not have been surprised to see a halo suddenly glow over Malta's head, or wings sprout from her back. Convinced that no physical place Last Chance Rescue really even exists, I envision Lucky and Honeybun spending the week somewhere in the clouds, with the sound of harps lulling them to sleep. If Honeybun doesn't attack the angel, it might all work out after all.

Dear Lord,

You have provided the perfect solution and I am grateful. I know you wanted me to learn to "be still and know that you are God". Stillness is not generally my forte and I have noticed a disturbing trend in our relationship for you to notice those few things I don't excel in and then pick at them like a scab. Since you don't really specify how long I am to be still, I am struggling to know at what point I can stop being still and finish my checklist.

Also, I am a little concerned that while the situation is improving, it has a long way to go. You might consider that the severe shortage of Good Samaritans willing to risk all on your behalf might be due to the lack of tangible or forthcoming rewards. I am not sure I see the blessing in all this. I thought the Bible says that those who trust in the Lord will rise on wings of eagles? I am trusting you, Lord, and flapping like a hummingbird, but my feet are still firmly planted in my trials....Amen.

CHAPTER 5

Irresolute, Intolerant, and Impoverished

In a state of perpetual alert to squelch any sign of aggression. I move like a prison guard through the house, whip in hand. If the whip is raised, the dogs usually stand at attention and salute. Honestly though, I am edgy, knowing our cease-fire is tenuous.

Furthermore, new wrinkles are furrowing my brow over concerns about taking the newly trusting dog to be spayed. While it will only be a few hours she will spend away from us, it will not be a pleasant few hours for her. Her trust in humans is fragile and could be easily shattered. But we have no choice. She has to be spayed.

Since Arvo works near the spay clinic, he takes her with him early in the morning as he heads off to work. We kiss her goodbye, and then go about our day. It is almost like she is still here, as the vacuum picks up a full dog's worth of hair. I have never known a dog to shed so much. Every time we pet her, the air fills with a mist of golden hair and we have to put filters over our mouth to breathe.

We go a couple of hours early to the town where the clinic is, so that the moment she is done we can whisk her back home. It is surprising how anxious I am to see her considering how hard she has made my life. When I ask the receptionist if Honey will be able to walk, she laughs. Then Honeybun comes prancing out, happy though a little groggy. She greets us, wagging her tail, and acting like she has just gone out for a quick cup of coffee rather than having her full set of motherhood apparatus put on a table, and whacked off.

We buy an Elizabethan collar (E-collar), designed to keep the dog's snout out of reach of stitches. Unexpectedly, she never once tries to rip them out. Since everything that can go wrong according to the dog rescue manual *has* up to this point, it is comforting to have a small stroke of good fortune.

The E-collar is amusing if one has a sadistic nature. It is a big plastic cone that fits over the dog's head, a bull's-eye in the plastic target. Since she doesn't bother the stitches, we put the E collar away, hoping never to need it again. Famous last words.....

We are given a list of instructions. They encourage us to keep her on leash and quiet for a week, no climbing or running or jumping. At the end of two weeks she can resume her activities slowly. This of course, means two full weeks of no agility training, to Ashcrel's chagrin. I ask the receptionist how she has been, with all those strangers handling her this morning. She had been fine, friendly and sweet they tell us. “What definition of ‘sweet’ are you using?” I ask.

Ten days after she is spayed, she is finally allowed outside off leash. As she comes trotting inside, fresh blood drips in her wake. Panicking, I conclude her guts are on the verge of spilling onto my kitchen floor but upon inspection, see that she has ripped open one of the non-weight bearing pads on her leg. Note- the alarm is less for the severity of the wound and more for the quick calculation of the impending vet bill. In case you are keeping track, this is now unexpected expense number three looming for this dog that I promised would be *no* trouble. We have already decimated Asherel’s piggy bank savings, so now we have no choice but to consider liquidating IRAs or robbing a bank.

I clean the cut, a little tenuously at first since I have never handled her when she was injured before and don’t know how she will respond. She is completely submissive, allowing me to look at the deep cut, clean it, and wrap an antiseptic pad on it. Not sure if it is deep enough for stitches, I bring her to the vet, hoping they will examine the cut while checking her spay stitches, and perhaps give her the go ahead for normal activity. Asherel can’t wait for her to get the "all clear" so she can continue her agility practice again. So we traipse off, once more, to our home away from home, the animal hospital. While the spay wound is healed enough that she can resume jumping, the pad needs stitches now. The good news is that since the stitched area is not in her paw but on the back of her lower leg, she will be able to walk or jump without any trouble.

Unlike our experience with the spaying, the moment we get home and take off her bandage per vet instructions, she promptly removes a stitch before I can say, "watch our money go flooding out the door like the Nile." I figure the three remaining stitches will be adequate, re-tape her foot, and hope all will be fine. It is not. Within an hour she has removed the tape and is working on stitch number two. We have no choice but to try the Elizabethan collar till the vet reopens in the morning.

Honeybun is a smart dog, but the E collar apparently sucks her brain out and pushes it into her rear end, decreasing effective cognition. She walks into walls, and then stands there, stuck, because she doesn't realize she can walk backwards. Or she walks into the chair, and remains stoically disconsolate, head lowered, for hours if we leave her. Eventually, we take pity and pull her back and set her on her way again. She goes to drink, and dumps the bowl countless times as the E collar smashes into its edge, toppling it. I am wondering if it would've been easier just to amputate her foot.

The vet glues the wound back together and warns me to never remove the E collar.... for ten days. We begin counting seconds, stretching into interminable minutes as Honeybun pathetically looks at us, her woebegone eyes framed in the white plastic cone. Ten days? We can't leave the house because we know if we do she will spend the whole time stuck on a piece of furniture. She tries to go out the dog door, and her head goes through, but not the collar. She stands there, head in the great outdoors, and bottom still inside, unable to figure out what to do. This may be why it is human beings that drive cars and develop computers. Dogs, while highly intelligent, don't adapt to technology.

I construct a temporary booty to cover the stitches, knowing none of us will survive ten days with the E collar. An old backpack is called into service for a plastic outer coating which will hopefully keep the booty dry when she goes out, and keep her teeth from ripping it when we aren't watching her every nanosecond. A sock taped around her leg a few inches above and then below the wound is added to our makeshift armor. I only slip the plastic part of the booty on when she goes outside or when we are not right there guarding her. As long as we watch unceasingly, she leaves it alone. Impressed with my ingenuity, I wonder if I can market the booty to cover the vet bills.

Several field trips and fun outings must be cancelled while we are on dog watch. These long dreary hours afford me uninterrupted periods of deep thought, and I pull out my diary to write the same sentence one hundred times: "Drive by dying dogs *no matter what*."

Oodles of time stretch before me to ponder what my impetuosity has gained us. We are several hundred dollars poorer, living in a state of constant tension, with Lucky lurking in the shadows avoiding possible confrontations. Our house has a fine layer of red-gold fur accumulating at an alarming speed. My homeschool days are frequently interrupted with visits to the vet, power walks twice a day with the dogs, and ongoing instruction and training as I pour over a constant stream of dog obedience books. American History and Algebra take a back seat to "Basic Wild Dingo Control". We have been forced to come to the uncomfortable realization that we are horrid dog owners, and the one dog we thought was good is an underhanded, disobedient instigator, and as much a problem as the dog we rescued.

Honeybun, oblivious to the turmoil she is stirring in my soul, follows me wherever I settle in the house, curls at my feet with her little booty tucked beneath her, nibbles a snout pit, and lies down. Her languid eyes gaze rapturously at me, until they slowly drift closed, and within seconds she is snoring. I am still commiserating. Lucky lies down nearby, and I realize that he has not been barking so continually, incessantly, annoyingly to both us and the neighborhood. Nor has he attempted an escape in a month.

The ten days somehow pass and finally with the walking money pit now whole and stitch free, it is time for obedience class to start. We have been filled with excitement and trepidation over this next hurdle in Honeybun's rehabilitation. I do not want to share too much information on the class application regarding our concern that Honeybun might kill every animal and person in the class, as they may have reservations regarding our participation. However, it is prudent to give them some insight into our 'issues' so I can possibly squirm out of any lawsuits.

We arrive an hour early so we can chat with the instructor about Honeybun's little deficiencies. It is readily apparent that the instructor's philosophy is totally different from Malta's. This instructor is the equivalent of some people who believe if we just were nicer to terrorists, they wouldn't fly airplanes into our buildings. She is very sweet, and assures me that the answer to Honeybun wanting to rip the intestines out of visitors is not whips or discipline, but more treats! She proposes that Honeybun sees visitors as a bad thing, and my response of restraining her and screaming at her as she tries to remove their fingers from their hands is just exacerbating the situation. She needs to know visitors are good, and so I should have them give her lots of treats. While all for positive reinforcement, this trainer's approach is so different from Malta's that I immediately suspect the quality of the class we have signed up for. I trust Malta, who has saved our lives, in my opinion. Honeybun while far from healed, is certainly better than when we first found her. It did tickle the back of my mind, however, that what this trainer is saying makes some sense. Are we doing the right thing? Yes, Honeybun is better, but far from perfect. Is Malta's tactic the best one?

This philosophy of "ignore bad behavior and reward good behavior" is how the trainer approaches the obedience class as well. The pitfalls of this approach are manifested immediately. When the class arrives, one dog barks like a metronome. None of us can hear a word the trainer is saying because no one tries to quiet the dog since we are ignoring bad behavior. The fact that this particular bad behavior is impossible to ignore does not dissuade our brave leader. A little dachshund on a retractable leash ziplines into Honeybun's face. Oblivious, the owner misses the looks Asherel shoots him as well as Honeybun's menacing stillness. I glance at the trainer, who has been clearly forewarned that if a dog gets in Honeybun's face, all bets are off as to whether we leave the floor slippery with blood or not. Asherel quietly moves a few seats away from the dog. The trainer is so busy ignoring bad behavior that she doesn't seem to notice the impending disaster. The little hot-dog continues to pull over to torment Honeybun. Finally, I can stand it no longer. Not anxious to undermine the person supposedly in charge, I feel I have no choice if the trainer is not going to prevent the inevitable carnage that this little dog is about to cause.

"Please sir, if you like your dog, I would advise you keep him away from my dog."

I am not sure he hears me since he is ignoring his own bad behavior. The barking dog keeps barking, the retractable dog keeps walking up to Honeybun and tempting death by decapitation, and a young Bull Terrier keeps wagging its tail and bounding about with typical puppy exuberance.

Asherel's friend, Lucy, is in the class at our suggestion. Her dog Max is well behaved and under control. I am feeling increasingly embarrassed over my recommendation of the class to Lucy. Sitting nearby, her father and I exchange quick glances. The other completely uncontrolled dogs remain apparently unnoticed by the trainer. The din continues unabated, while the bad dogs remain bad and the trainer smiles complacently. We sit there for twenty minutes, trying to listen to the instructor above the noise, wondering when class will start. She is talking, but it is difficult to hear, and as far as I can tell, we are not yet doing anything but ignoring bad behavior. Since this is the focus, it is good there is so much bad behavior to ignore. Honeybun is a model student. Despite all our voiced concerns to the instructor, Honeybun is the calmest and most attentive dog in the class. After a short time, the man with the retractable dog asks if he can trade his dog in for Honeybun. Not on your life, I think, though I smile sweetly.

The trainer is very personable. Twenty minutes pass while I wait for class to start. She suddenly informs us that class is over. The only thing the dogs have learned is "look at me" with a treat by our eyes, and "touch" with a treat in our hand. Honeybun's obsession with food holds her in good stead for this difficult maneuver and she is a star with her riveting attention on the treat. This is all we are to learn tonight? Something every dog knows instinctively- when food is swung in front of his face, to keep his eye on it? I am very disappointed, though we all smile like we have just had a college physics class, revealing wonders of the universe. We all sit there, waiting. Surely she is kidding. Even the bad dogs look incredulous. Then the instructor chirps, "Ok, so we will see you next week."

We decide that must be the cue that indeed class is over. Had I unknowingly had an epileptic fit and checked out of consciousness for most of the class? As we file out, still a bit puzzled that class is over when we were never quite sure it had exactly begun, the puppy jumps on Honeybun. Honeybun, with infinite patience and dignity, gives a low warning growl, causing Asherel to quickly jerk the leash. With disdain, Honeybun trots quietly on, disengaging from the exuberant puppy. That was the most instructive moment of the class for me. Honeybun will conduct herself with reserved dignity and control around other dogs, even other dogs with comatose owners. However, I am determined to un-enroll her from the class. A phone call the next day expressing our concern gets us our money back, and praise from the trainer that our dog really belongs in an advanced class, and Asherel has a future in dog handling.

The next day, I call the oldest dog training club in Charlotte hoping to convince them to suspend the minimum handler age requirement. Explaining our situation, I promise to stay the whole class time, and convince them my eleven year old handler has more control of her dog than all the adults in the class we have just attended. They agree to let Asherel in the "rally novice" class. While elated, I know we are taking a bit of a leap of faith. "Novice Rally" assumes a basic level of obedience classes have been mastered. Honeybun has had no classes, but she obeys at home with no distractions. Still, when she is surrounded by dogs and people, it might be a whole different story. I explain that the trainer at her last obedience class told us that our dog was beyond a beginner level. They seem to accept this, and are willing to give Asherel a chance. The Rally class is not full, so there will be less dogs and people around than in other classes. We all hope this will be a good testing ground for the unpredictable Honeybun. Fortunately, the class doesn't start for a month, so we have some time to prepare Honeybun and soften those rough edges. Maybe file her teeth……

Truthfully, with Honeybun's dog wariness and door charging aggression, I am not at all sure we are doing the right thing. The rally class takes us one step closer to Asherel's dream of agility contests, but are we skipping too many steps to get there? True, she has about a month to whip Honeybun into shape for the rally class, but is that enough time to overcome the many issues of aggression?

Her jumping program on the backyard homemade course assumes a greater intensity. Several times a day Asherel takes Honeybun over the jumps, raising them so that Honeybun is sailing over two foot jumps with ease. Asherel improves the log stump "pause table" by switching to an old plastic kiddy table she has. Honeybun hops onto the rickety table wagging her tail, and Asherel tells her to sit. Next, she goes up and down the "A frame", the plastic chair Asherel has turned upside down.

Meanwhile, lazy dog Lucky watches from the top step of the deck. He is lying flat out in the sun, but when he hears Asherel praising Honeybun, he shifts his head and opens one eye. There is an ever so slight flicker of interest before he crashes his head back down and resumes sunning himself. But it seems that he is pondering the state of affairs. While being lazy has distinct perks, that demon dog is getting goodies for jumping those jumps.

"Your turn!" cries Asherel, putting the leash on him.

Inexplicably, he races at the jumps, sailing over them. He clears all but one. Later.Asherel comes inside with the happy, scruffy Lucky, both ushering in a whoosh of fresh air and sunshine. Lucky glances at me, winking. Is Honeybun sparking latent enthusiasm in our somnolent dog?

Now with stitches out, and dogs recovered, it is finally time for our vacation, the family reunion. We know the dogs will be in competent hands boarded with our doggy expert and her pack of twenty free roaming dogs, seven billy goats, three fat cats, two crazy cows, two soft deer, a one legged duck, and a partridge in a pear tree! (You knew that was coming….) I do not feel the usual angst I feel when dropping our dog to be boarded somewhere.

We are doing well, better than expected with Honeybun, but I am exhausted, never able to relax, constantly on the alert for any hint of aggression. Growls are of course easily interpreted and quashed, but the more subtle forms of canine aggression and dominance are harder to spot. Like Honeybun's riveting, frightening gaze. Is it aggression, as I suspect, or is it "herding instinct" as Malta claims? Honeybun has large eyes on a small head, and she rarely blinks. She stares with an unnerving stillness and is very aware of movement. If Lucky moves nearby, she jerks her head around, points her ears up as best she can with the funny broken one, and bores her eyes into him. I do not quite trust Malta's assessment that Honeybun is a herding dog, bred to respond to movement with a stare-down designed to paralyze a herd into submission. Malta does not believe "the look" is aggression. However, every act of minor aggression like growling is always preceded by "the look." So I reprimand "the look" if it goes on more than a few seconds. Peace has been maintained, but at a cost. I am badly in need of a few days away from the dogs.

I have no fear for their well being in Malta's care, nor for Malta's well being. She is an animal lover, but when it comes to her rights vs. animal rights, she wins.

"Until the dog is paying the rent and cleaning the toilet, he is not in charge," she retorts.

If Malta walks in the room in a bad mood, the dogs scatter and run into their crates and bury their heads. I have seen Malta interact with our dogs and she can exude love and kindness, but DO NOT cross her. Malta is alpha dog personified.

When we travel with the two dogs in the car, we always place one in the far back, where he is unable to jump over the back seat. The other one we belt in the middle seat. The dogs cannot reach each other, thus there is no way aggression can ever lead to blood and gore or inadvertent tonsillectomies. But when Malta comes to pick them up to take them to doggy rehab, she opens the door of her truck, and steers them towards the little cramped seat behind the front seats. They have never been that close together except when attempting to spill each others' guts out. She tells them to "load up". They are squished just close enough to reach each other's jugular. Lucky hops in first, and looks a little worried as Honeybun pounces in, shoving and jostling him a bit so they both fit. They sit looking at us. Lucky's look could not have been more eloquent. “Do you think this is wise? Have you lost your mind?”

Asherel and I glance at each other and gulp. Lucky and Honeybun glance at each other, glance at Herr Malta, and cower. I don't know what kind of scent Malta gives off, but it is one that dogs understand and heed. They sit in their little back seat like two choir children, paws neatly to themselves. It is an hour and half drive to Malta's farm. I wonder if the truce will last. We watch them drive away, both dogs looking straight ahead as they head to doggy therapy. Before they go, I ask Malta to email me if she could while we are gone, and let me know how the dogs are doing and am excited to receive an email from her a few days later.

"Nothing much to report," she writes, "Pretty boring actually. They just eat and sleep and go out. I will send pictures but not much excitement."

When they return, they both have bright eyed, happy expressions, and look shockingly normal. They are also amazingly fluffy. Malta has bathed them to nearly unrecognizable softness and sweet smellingness. We have not bathed Honeybun ever, as we really didn't want to impose any extra stress on her yet. We bathe Lucky rarely since his hair is so thick and long he takes forever to dry and his wet dog smell is strong enough to remain in the air for weeks. Visitors to our home have enough to bear without wet dog smell accosting them. I have never seen Lucky as fluffy as he was after his bath at Malta's.

She tells us the week has been largely dull. No fights, and no aggression, except towards cats. I had not known cats would be loose and available for consumption as well. Lucky despises cats. Malta tells me the cats are excellent therapists for dogs who hate cats. Neither of her cats fears dogs and most dogs learn very quickly these cats are not worth messing with. Lucky did indeed go after a cat, once. As a result, he got the "dreaded roll," a special alpha wolf maneuver that Malta employs to secure a dog's attention such that they fear they will die. She doesn't hurt them, she assures me, but they are quite sure that they are seconds from annihilation. I remember Cesar Milan writing about the roll he uses to make an aggressive dog submit. It does not look like something an untrained professional could pull off and retain all their limbs.

In the "dreaded roll", she single-handedly manages to trip the dog, hold its head to the ground, and grip its throat with a hand mimicking a claw. She holds the victim down until its eyes stop rolling and it submits. This is even harder than it sounds. She claims she usually only has to roll a dog once, and then issue solved. Lucky never went after the cat again.

I wonder if the "Dreaded Roll" works on children.

And husbands.

Laughing, she recounts Honeybun behaved well with all the farm creatures, and with all the volunteer victims that entered her home except for one that even Malta wants to bite. Other than that, she saw no evidence of aggression. She found them to be perfectly normal, happy, well-adjusted dogs. She admits Lucky was a grump at times with other dogs, but we know about his grumpy nature. One puppy apparently kept annoying Lucky and she finally had to separate them. Of course, the unspoken conclusion is the dogs are normal except when I am in control. I squelch this defeatist thought, but it lurks with a persistent tickle. I would hardly have described them as *normal*. Why am I struggling so much? What am I doing wrong? While glad they were good for Malta, I am pounding myself for my ineptitude. If I am the problem, how will it be solved? I am doing my best.....aren't I?

With her encouraging pronouncements, Malta drives away, and we are left with our clean, happy dogs, hoping the peace of normal dog ownership now awaits us. However, it is not to be. Every time the doorbell rings or someone walks by, the dogs still become lunatics, Honeybun more so than Lucky. She charges the door when my friends enter, her back bristling, throat snarling. When my braver friends hold out their hands, she licks them, but the initial greeting is hardly good etiquette.

Many friends have taken to ringing the doorbell and then backing off twenty feet, peering warily around a tree. I convince my good friend, Andi, to be a guinea pig. I cajole her to march into our house after Honeybun is safely muzzled. Honeybun charges at Andi, jumping on her and growling.... even though she has appeared to like Andi in prior meetings. The muzzle falls off in her frenzy and she lunges at Andi. I grab her in time to prevent damage to Andi and our friendship. For the first time in my many prior attempts, I successfully employ the "dreaded roll", holding her down for several minutes. When she is allowed to stand up, and leashed, she greets Andi politely. However, there is no doubt she would've bitten Andi, had I not grabbed her when the muzzle slipped off. Having grown cocky with our prior success, I find this set back even more disheartening than the ones before it. Aggression towards dogs is one thing, but to threaten people clearly diminishes our chances of winning *Neighbor of the Year* Award. I don't mind if she does this to solicitors at the door, but she cannot do it to my dwindling supply of buddies. And it is puzzling, this initial response of fearful attack followed by humbled gentleness.

The phone rings and I grab it, knowing with the garbled butchering of my last name that it is a telemarketer.

"No," I screech, "Take me off your list!!!"

"Mrs. Kaseorg? This is just the Financial Aid dept notifying you that all your son's loans are approved…." I hang my head and apologize for biting their heads off. Honeybun blinks at me.

Disconsolately, I email Malta. Remembering the advice of the obedience class trainer, I ask if pairing the strangers with treats is a better tactic than using the whip and the roll. After all, the other trainer had suggested just that. Is Honeybun indeed learning strangers only mean bad things, loud whips, dreaded rolls, angry owners....?

Malta is having a bad day. She has just rescued a pit bull used as a fighter dog. It is wounded in body and spirit, and she is furious at humanity and their stupidity with dogs. This is a dog scheduled to be euthanized, and someone called Malta in a last ditch effort to save the dog. She storms in her house with the scarred and traumatized dog in tow and her pack scatters. It is not the day to email Malta whining.

She bullets back an email, *"If treats would've solved the aggression, why has it not worked when you tried it before? Does the trainer who suggested you use treats have a pack of twenty rescued dogs living in her house loose under near perfect control? Does she have twenty years of dealing exclusively with aggression issues? Treats work with a normal dog. Treats don't work with a dog that has had to scrap for its life and food for a year or so. You are too nice and too worried. Bring Honeybun to me, and I will keep her, and trade you one of my nice dogs whose worst trait is licking you to death. Call me tomorrow. I have a wounded, hurting, aggressive dog I need to start healing right now."*

I slump, stunned at the computer. First of all, I cannot recall ever being called "too nice" before....rarely even "nice". Worried, yes. Secondly, trading up for a trophy dog sounds like a good deal. This will solve everything! Lucky can have a real playmate that he isn't afraid of. We will not have to cringe whenever strangers or even friends are coming to the door. We will not have to live on high alert anymore.

I joyfully begin to type my response realizing salvation has been offered. *Who are my choices? Can they visit with Lucky first to see how they get along? Do you have a dog that will be good at Agility?* Inexplicably, I feel a growing unease as I picture the wonderful dog that will soon replace the trouble maker at my feet. Honeybun diffidently looks up at me, and lowers her head, hoping I might pet her. This is new. She didn't use to want me to touch her, but now she occasionally nuzzles my hand, and shyly asks me to stroke her silky ears. I hate the treacherous thoughts that strangle my escape.

It is *this* little dog we had wrested from the jaws of death. *This* dog came to us flea bitten, tick encrusted, weak, dehydrated, emaciated, and dying, teats still dripping from puppies newly born and gone. Through our care and love, she is now sleek and soft and smooth with a glorious rich golden coat, her ribs no longer visible, her attitude towards us and even Lucky now sweet and submissive, following us peacefully wherever we go and lying at our feet, demanding nothing more than our presence. However misguided, she is charging the door because she loves us and wants to protect us. How can I throw her out now? And what will this little dog think, who has been so misused, and finally come to trust us, if we abandon her to a new home? Whatever her faults, it is clear she now considers us her "pack". I am not brave, and hate stress. Patience is not my virtue and I don't like goals that take too long to reach. These are all clearly character requirements for redeeming troubled dogs. However, sadly, I love *this* dog, and it is *this* dog sent to almost die in front of me.

No, I write instead to Malta, *we don't want a normal dog. We want this dog. Tell me what I need to do, and I will do it.* Oh how the "delete" button tempts me, but instead, gritting my teeth, I tap "send".

Malta writes back the next day, in a better mood. I am to begin the "dreaded roll" therapy. Every time strangers walk by and Honeybun barks, roll her. Every time she growls at a dog, roll her. Every act that is even a hint of aggression, roll her.

I reread my Cesar Milan books with pictures of the roll and the "wolf claw grip" that accompanies it. Fortunately, we begin the rolling therapy on a day when I teach my homeschool art classes. Many opportunities will be marching into our rehab center. Ten students come in one by one. Honeybun barks and lunges each time a new student enters. She is tied where she can't quite reach them, but each time she tries, she gets rolled - ten times in ten minutes. I don't seem to be making a huge impression on her.

"Look Mom," says Asherel, "She is smiling."

Panting for breath with all this exertion, I gape at Asherel and then Honeybun. I don't see a smile. I see wasted effort, ambiguous progress, broken dreams and disrupted plans.

After the tenth student and tenth roll, she puffs out her cheeks with a final bark, and then she curls up to sleep. She is blissfully quiet till the end of class. As the students rise to leave, she stands and wags her tail. The braver students each throw her a biscuit to reward her not biting them, and the suicidal ones who know dogs, pet her as I hold on to her collar. She licks them and wags her tail.

This is progress and I am ecstatic, but Malta warns me this is not a problem solved in a day. It will take months and hard work - be consistent and firm and do not let up. But Honeybun will be cured she assures me. Though weary of all the work involved with this dog, I have invested so much in her by now that I have to see it through to the finish. Lucky watches all the rolling with a smirk under his terrier beard, but when we finish, he goes to her and licks her ear, the broken one. She touches noses with him.

I buy a "coupler" leash for the two dogs, so both can be walked with just one leash. The coupler connects them with about two feet of slack between them, and then snaps onto a single leash. When I first start using it, they are newly arrived at their peace treaty, and détente could give way to all out war at any moment. I carry the whip with me whenever I walk anywhere with them. At first, they tangle in the coupler, and glare at each other. I wave the whip and sort out legs from leash, and then we walk a few more steps before some paw ends up in someone else's ear. Amazingly, neither dog ever seems overly upset with the tangle of tail and limb. They stand quietly while I weave the leash out of whatever knot they have managed to tie, and then trot on. As we all march forward, our ears and eyes on the road before us, eager to see what lies beyond the next hill, we are remarkably in sync. Our legs move in tandem; our heads turn to the same sound as though choreographed. The tantalizing smells overcome their fledgling obedience as they careen in unison towards them. Within a short time, Lucky settles into the right position, next to me, and Honeybun takes the outer edge of the coupler. Our walks become purposeful and peaceful.

When we pass people, Lucky wildly wags his tail, and begs me to let them pet him. Honeybun stiffens, her tail jutting ramrod straight in warning, ears back. When we pass dogs, Honeybun cowers warily, and Lucky growls and lunges in his cockeyed manner of asking them to play. The best way to keep control is without exception, every single time we pass dogs or people; make the dogs sit. They invariably remain calm and controlled. Neighbors begin to talk about that lady with the whip that makes her dogs sit when they pass by. Other people with wild, lunging dogs begin to demand that their dogs sit too. Sometimes it is a contest to see who will have their dog sit FIRST upon seeing me in the distance. Then it is a stalemate, and someone has to pass the other dog or we will all sit there until the stars twinkle on. I appear to have sparked a movement, a movement of stillness in the neighborhood. Dogs everywhere are calmer, more controlled. Harried people are pausing with slack leashes and sitting dogs, watching the fireflies.

On those walks, we are bonding, just like Cesar had written. We are becoming a pack with a common purpose. When we are all moving forward in unity, I feel a rush of love for these creatures that are exhausting me. These brief interludes of peace give me hope that all our struggles are leading to someplace worthy of this effort. I can't wait to get there and take a nap.

Dear Lord,

I know I probably am missing some things. I probably should have been nicer on the phone. I hate telemarketers, and of course you know that is who I thought it was. How was I to know it was someone worth talking to? Well, forgive that little slip of the tongue, Lord. I know in your eyes, all have worth, but you are God and have to like everyone. I guess you are waiting for me to notice that I snapped on the phone at a perceived intruder in a shockingly similar parallel to Honeybun's aggressive defensive stance toward strangers. You probably have not noticed how often these interruptions disrupt my good works- homeschool, training the dog YOU put in my path.....

And by the way, did you notice that I could have thrown off the yoke of this crazy dog, but I didn't? That deserves some credit, doesn't it? I am trying to trust you, Lord Jesus, really I am. But you might have confused me with someone with competence and patience. I am not qualified for what you are asking me to do, but I am developing at least a modicum of success.

I think now that I have learned with a humble spirit all that you set forth to teach me with this little dog, we can move forward to glorifying your name with final and complete healing. I thank you in advance for that blessing.

Amen.

CHAPTER 6

Inconstancy, Infidelity, Ineptitude

Email Letter to Malta 8-31-08

ok, so the friend came to pick up her painting, the one HB knows and likes, and she rang the doorbell. HB went ballistic, I tackled and held her down (btw, I have been completely unsuccessful in rolling her, I can just get her down and then claw my hand to hold her head to the ground, but she is not belly up). She continued to make low growls for about a minute, then must've realized it was my friend, and wagged her tail. So I let her up and she was fine.

The cable man was a different story. When he knocked, she went nuts. I rolled her and held her down, and she continued to growl for about 5 minutes. He walked back in and out about 10 times and every time he went by she would growl, hackles raised, lunge and bark, (I had her on leash) and I would push her back into the ground and hold her there. It was exhausting and I am not sure I accomplished anything. When my husband would come by and shout DOWN, she would lay down, but the barking and growling continued every single time the man walked through (he was here about 20 minutes).

Our summer has been fairly visitor free, but the school year is when I teach art and soon start another weekly science group I teach. People are in and out all the time. I hope you have some advice because it is overwhelming at the moment to think of doing this every time someone walks in. nor is it feasible to crate or tie her every time someone walks in, unless that is just for the short term. I am disheartened wondering if this dog will ever be safe for Asherel to have friends over, running in and out, without fear of being attacked. I don't want to give up, but I do feel like right now, it is beyond my skill.

I think it would help most for me to see you handle it the way it should be handled with the same circumstances- strangers walking in, who don't know dogs, are likely small and fearful. Not positive I have any willing victims for you.... one neighbor might comply if she is around when you come (if I can guarantee she won't get bit). Another thought is to leave HB with you for a long time, as I know you can help her.... but will what you do then translate to our home? We have a free afternoon, and I would be willing to drive her over and watch you work with her if you have time today- we get back from church around 12:30 (where I will be praying up a storm for wisdom and guidance here.....)

I know I sound down and I am so sorry for whining.

Lucky , btw, barked and stormed the door, but then backed off when told, and when the guy entered (while I was strangling HB) Lucky wagged his tail and licked him. I have not used the whip to back them off in a long time (since that seemed to have been losing effect) but maybe I need to do more of that.

Please don't scream at me. If I am on the right track even though it doesn't feel like it, I will stick with the program.

Blessings,

Vicky

Email from Malta:

She continues because she knows it is allowed. I know that sounds wrong. But it is not. Lucky is also still raising the excitement level when guests arrive. (Alert- HB goes up a notch) Lets look at it this way..... Lucky is allowed to do this but HB is not.

There is no barking allowed - no going to the door. *You have a doorbell.... let the doorbell tell you when someone is there. Your door, not the dogs. Easiest thing to do would be to send HB to the crate when people arrive at this point. I am going to make this clear to you - NOBODY wants HB in her current state. I don't want her as I have 20+ great non aggressive dogs. It would not be fair to pass her to any family* *in this current state. This is either fixed or HB needs to be disposed of. Sounds harsh..... But HB is not the only dog in need and other dogs simply are in a better position to actually find a home.*

So time to poo or get off the pot with this dog. Or you can accept that every time someone comes she must go in the crate. End of story. We can try the air horn - electric collar..... But neither will change her aggressive nature. They will control it but not change it. Pretty much instant fixes. But for a real change, it takes months and even years of reconditioning. She is still doing her job of boss and protector..... Take the job away.

When I arrive, I am sending Will into the house first.... if he is bit he will not tolerate it. This is a warning to you. You may want to ask Asherel to wait in her room. A human has the right to defend themselves. If she does bite him, he will not hurt her but there will be a physical confrontation. Just let her run loose with a leash on when we come. I don't believe she will bite him. I have a theory that the physical restraint of the leash is causing some of this behavior.

We need a fresh victim as well while we are there. Can this be arranged? Or I need a video of what happens to witness the behavior with a person besides Will or myself as a victim.

I haven't felt this low since watching Bambi when I was five. No one wants Honeybun, and we are stuck with her. If we don't get her behavior under control, she walks the long green mile to execution. Death penalty. No passing Go and collecting two-hundred dog biscuits. We now have no choice. The safety net has been yanked. Malta had falsely raised my hopes that I could bail out when engulfed by the waves of total failure. Tucked for emergencies in the back of my mind was her email that I could trade Honeybun in for a newer model, one that wouldn't run over us all. But now, Malta seems to have had second thoughts. Malta, the last hope for hopeless dogs is sending me a clear message. This one really *is* hopeless. It is up to me – *me,* with exactly one month of experience in dealing with dog aggression. Any way about it, I need to find a strength and depth of courage in myself that I don't have or break my little girl's heart, not to mention my own. I of course am not able to do this, having no idea where to locate this reservoir of courage. Oh, I know what you are thinking.... What about God? Yes, He has the strength, but He is very busy right now with the mess caused by Al Qaeda, not to mention the plight of the penguins and melting polar ice caps which are needed to film Coca Cola commercials.

I am grateful for Honeybun's acceptance of Lucky, and she is certainly trustworthy with all of us. However, it is intolerable that every time a friend or salesperson comes to the door, we will all have to scramble into action for the rest of our lives. Friends will peer in, wondering what could be important enough for them to even think of entering this house. They will drift away one by one, and I will die a lonely death with no one daring to attend my funeral, unless of course Honeybun dies first. These happy thoughts drown me for the next hour, but then the doorbell rings and the explosion of dog rams me back to the present.

It is time to call in the reserves. This is war, and I am determined to win. I will show that Malta, with her snippy little email telling me to poo or get off the pot. I can poo with the best of them. Calling my friend Debbie, and explaining our need of a videotape of Honeybun being vicious at the door, I ask if she would agree to ring the doorbell and enter our dog infested home. With my promises to prevent serious wounds, Debbie is amenable.

I am increasingly struck by the devotion and kindness of my friends. Some watch the dog saga unfold, and tell me I am crazy to continue. They urge me to send her to Animal Control before something awful happens. I waver with their advice, because success is so distant and uncertain. Praying for wisdom and discernment, all I hear is silence, and barking….and growling.

However most are very encouraging, cheering me on, and telling me how lucky Honeybun is to have been found by me. (Because no one else in their right mind would have gone near her, they don't add, but their sympathetic looks convey the message loud and clear.) Debbie is not one of those doubting Thomases. She repeatedly pronounces, "I know you will be able to cure that sweet little dog," long before the dog is sweet, and I am grateful for her confidence in us, especially as mine is so shaky right now. I of course don't believe her, but am eager for praise.

I receive an email asking for donations for homeless victims still struggling after Hurricane Katrina. Not now, I mutter, I am too busy building faith, resilience, and care for hopeless, discarded creatures critical to helping this dog. Busy with the Lord's work, I delete the email.

Asherel is excited about the prospect of chronicling our adventure by videotape. She spends several minutes setting up her camera where she can capture the whole drama as it unfolds. She stakes her position right behind the couch where she can film unobtrusively, but has a clear view of the likely attack zone. She asks me to pose with Honeybun near the door so she can check lighting and distance. I am not certain she is approaching this with the proper respect for the gravity of the situation.

Debbie calls us when she is five minutes away so we can get in position. She and her daughter Lucy both get out of the car. The dogs are already on high alert, obviously aware something is up. We put Lucky in a back room so he will not add to the bedlam. When the doorbell rings, Honeybun performs her usual rabid dog routine. She jumps on the door, barking and growling, hackles raised, a thin brown line of aggression prominently displayed. Her tail sticks straight up, like a machete, ready to cut down the harvest. When the door opens, she predictably lunges, and I roll her. She struggles only briefly, "woofs" feebly and then lies subdued on the ground. Asherel is gleefully filming.

“Hello Debbie,” I say crouching over Honeybun, who wags her tail. Yes folks - *wags her tail.* She lies peacefully under my claw alpha wolf grip, grinning and wagging at her friend Debbie. This is not exactly the man-eating behavior I have told Malta about. Hopping upright, she sniffs Debbie and continues wagging. Honeybun has met Debbie before and apparently knows she is a friend. She could not have looked more like a normal dog greeting a person at the door.

We catch it all on tape. While I am glad that she has not mauled my friend, I know this will only solidify Malta’s belief that the perceived aggression is in my head. It is likely that this very smart dog just remembers Debbie, and she certainly knows and loves Lucy. This is not her typical response to strangers walking in our door. There is no doubt in my mind that had I let her off leash while the cable man was here she would have removed his ankle bones without the aid of anesthesia. But where can I find a total stranger willing to walk in our house to obtain a more accurate video of what Honeybun is like when her normal dog spirit is replaced by the spirit of darkness and spooks?

Perhaps we have not provoked her enough, so I urge Debbie to run around a little. We have noticed in the past that Honeybun can seem relaxed and accepting of someone in the house until they begin to move away from her. Many times she will then lunge and nibble at their backside. She has never bitten, but she seems to be warning them not to take another step if they value the ability to sit down without pain. Malta may believe this is just "herding" dog behavior, not aggression; however, I am pretty sure that nibbling someone's behind would qualify in most of our guests' minds as undesirable dog behavior, at the very least.

Debbie complies with our request to run past Honeybun. Honeybun watches, wagging her tail while Debbie jogs back and forth.

"Start waving your arms and making noise!" I command.

This game with the humans is strange, but fun, thinks Honeybun. She stands up happily still wagging, and looks expectantly at Debbie. Debbie continues jogging, waving her arms and shouting threatening remarks, egging on our vicious dog. Glancing at me, Honeybun cocks her head, wondering if Debbie is having a psychotic breakdown.

I ask Debbie to pretend to fight with her daughter, Lucy. Debbie begins shoving Lucy, pushing her into the wall, even wrapping her arms around her neck and pretending to choke her. Since Honeybun knows and loves Lucy who is often at our house, I am sure this will elicit the desired undesired behavior. Nope. Honeybun sits down, wagging and entertained by all the humans cavorting cheerfully about.

"CUT THE TAPE!!!!" I cry, "Malta will never believe me now. Destroy that videotape. What can we do to make Honeybun vicious again?"

"You could invite a neighbor she doesn't know," advises Debbie, "Ask them if they would like to come over for a bite."

We all laugh, but I am not comforted. There is a demon inside this dog that I cannot control and have no hope of controlling if my dog expert doesn't know it is there. I know it is not "I think, therefore she bites". It is not all in my head, or only emerging because my fears create it. What will my life be like if we cannot control the aggression? I will be chained to the front door waving a whip with bloodshot eyes and tangled hair. If Malta doesn't help me, who will? I have children traipsing in and out of my house all the time, between my art classes, Destination Imagination team, and Asherel's friends. I can't trust Honeybun, and am fairly certain that if children are sent home with chewed off arms, parents will be hesitant to let them return.

At the last art class, a boy who was comfortable around dogs had pet Honeybun and she had seemed very loving and sweet. She nuzzled against him, lifting her lovely brown eyes to him. But as he stood up to walk away, she had lunged. I had my hand on her collar, just in case, and jerked her back, and then she began barking and growling. I suppose it is possible I was communicating fear and that intensified the response... but was not aware of feeling fearful while he was petting her.

Her response has caused my fear, not the other way around. How can I show that to Malta? Her vast experience with dog problems has led her to conclude that most human beings are idiots with dogs. Largely, I am sure she is right, and clearly, as our failures with Lucky demonstrate, we are not the brightest examples to sway her opinion otherwise. But I also know that I am not causing the responses we are seeing in Honeybun….am I? She "flips", for no apparent reason. And *most* people would respond with fear to her aggressive demeanor. If fear is accelerating her actions, then the result is still the same - she cannot be trusted with people.

Malta and Will are installing a sound system a few minutes from our house, and will come tomorrow when they finish. I am amazed at her patience and perseverance with me, at this point, with all my questioning her every suggestion. I know she doesn't believe I have what it will take to rehabilitate Honeybun. In fact, she feels that I am largely responsible for the problems Honeybun is currently exhibiting. Confused by Malta's assertion that I am causing not just responding to the aggression, I find myself alternately wanting to coronate or kick her. Of course I would never dare kick her. Like the dogs, I have a healthy respect for her.

But in fact, I *am* a little ticked off that she insists on blaming me. Doesn't she realize what a wonderful person I am by trying to help Honeybun? It is annoying to be forced to resort to self promotion so the full extent of my selflessness is revealed.

When Honeybun curls up near my feet as I school Asherel or settle down with a book, I feel a rush of sympathy and love for her. This little discarded dog wants to be part of our family or at least wants to be *fed* by our family. If I am part of the problem, how can I solve it? And if Malta is correct, this poor little dog's survival depends on me. I see two faces in the mirror, depending on the day. Sometimes I see a face that is shining with optimism and very few wrinkles. The next morning, there is a hag who is old and tired and wonders why God created dogs in the first place. My faithful execution of a cogent plan has room for improvement.

I find myself hoping Honeybun will be as rotten as I know she can be when Malta shows up. This is not going very well. Being a Good Samaritan is certainly not all it is cracked up to be. The easy stroll to sainthood is not unfolding as I planned. By now I should have been on television with Honeybun in the chair beside me while Katy Couric interviews me and little children pull on Honeybun's ears as the camera pans over her. Instead, I spend a sleepless night, thinking how Honeybun has never met my oldest son, Anders. Anders will be coming home at Christmas, my beloved son who lives in Boston and I am lucky to see twice a year. Since going to college, he has grown increasingly enmeshed and content in his intellectual world at MIT. As the years go by, he comes home less and less frequently, answers the phone fewer and fewer times, and even ignores emails more and more. I grieve tremendously over his distancing from us. He has found a circle of friends who understand and relate to him, something that has been a sad failure for him in Charlotte. I understand his attraction to fellow egg heads, but I miss my son.

Anders is a quiet genius; his mind engaged in places not only most people cannot begin to understand, but most don't even know exist. He is not arrogant about his intellect, but he long ago learned that most of what he cares about is totally incomprehensible to all but an elite few. He comes home to see us because I am an expert at the fine art of guilt. I think he loves us in theory. We are harder to stomach in practice. I know it is lonely and difficult for him, under the best circumstances. My suspicion is that he would not consider Honeybun to be one of those "best" circumstances.

One of the many failures of my life is my inability to connect to him. I tried to read *Technology Today* and *Computing* magazines so that I could toss words like kernel source code, Debian packages, megabytes and gigahertz with wild abandon. It didn't work. Like dog training, computer programming is not conquered in ten minutes. I long for the days when he was younger and we were inseparable. Back when I could still teach him things he didn't know, before he was two, he clung to me. He is beloved to me in a way I know is as incomprehensible to him as Linux is to me. You have to be a genius to program computers and you have to be a mother to fully comprehend the depth of a mother's love. Or God. I suspect God understands both, though I doubt He needs a computer.

Maybe that is why He sent Honeybun my way. I am so busy clutching after children who are leaping left and right away from me that maybe it is all part of some heavenly help to untie some apron strings. Malta warned me I would learn things about myself through the dog.... Is it possible I could learn things about others too? It is true that much of my energy that was channeled into obsessing about what I could have done differently as a parent is now being channeled into how I can unscrew this screwed up dog. And I am spending a good bit of psychic energy trying to see inside the brain of an alien, uncommunicative, and troubling creature. I am learning however grudgingly to patiently read and understand behavior that seems incomprehensible.

Could understanding Honeybun help me understand Anders, or at least how to better relate to him? There *are* some remarkable similarities between them. Neither talks very often.... And when they do it is difficult to exactly understand what they are saying - one speaking in a different language and the other who might as well be for all I can comprehend. Both have big brown eyes that seem to reflect a deep soul hidden by fur. Anders' fur is now shoulder length and when he washes it, he never brushes it, so it hangs in long dreadlocks, obscuring his face. Both spend a lot of time watching the world with what looks like frightening perception. Both seem wounded but they don't seem to want to discuss it. Honeybun attacks. Anders withdraws. He has told me that most words are a waste of time. For someone like me who needs words to order my thoughts, it is almost impossible to know how to relate to another who finds words useless and annoying. I get the same blank look from Honeybun that I get from Anders when I wax eloquently about how they should best be civilized. Of course, he might well just say he is busy reconstructing Einstein's theories and that is more interesting than interacting with or smiling at Mom.

But smiling or not, Anders will be home for Christmas, and I am counting the days when I will see him again. Not just because I look forward to that day, though of course I do. I also am calculating the odds of Honeybun having some sort of miraculous conversion by then. If Anders walks in the door right now, I have little doubt that Honeybun will go straight for his throat, if she can find it through his dreadlocks. That will certainly make him think long and hard before coming home again, which I am not sure is on his list of top ten vacation spots as it is. What an unintended mess I have created.

Malta's call interrupts my pleasant thoughts when she is ten minutes away.

"OK," she tells me, "Have Honeybun on leash. I want you to close the screen and the wood door, but don't lock them, so that we can come in. Then here is what we need. Are you taking notes?"

"Hang on," I say, fumbling with a pen and paper.

"OK," I pronounce, "I am ready," feeling a flood of relief. If she is giving me detailed instructions, then she is taking the issue seriously. If she is taking it seriously, then that means there is still hope.

"Now," explains Malta, "Take your cleanest towel and roll it into a rope."

"You mean a bath towel?" I ask, wanting to have everything exact.

"No," she says, "A regular kitchen towel will do. Be sure it is a clean one."

"Lengthwise or widthwise?"

"Either is fine. Then put your daughter in a back room."

"She will want to see this," I counter. In fact, Asherel can hardly wait. This is great fun. She has her videotape set to go. She does not seem to be approaching this whole situation with all the gravity and concern I feel it deserves. In fact, she is distinctively flippant, and enjoying all my whipping and rolling and angst-ing.

"It will not be pretty," warns Malta.

"She is tough," I insist. Asherel stands near, grinning and nodding. If she had been born in the Middle Ages, she would have been a knight fighting dragons and using them to roast marshmallows after taming them.

"Well then," continues Malta, "Get two of your cleanest kitchen towels. Roll them into two ropes."

I carefully write this down, assuming it is some sort of tool to help control Honeybun should she go into a feeding frenzy. Cognizant that Malta specified clean towels in case there are wounds, I am feeling scared.

"Next," demands Malta, "Stuff them in your mouth and your daughter's mouth. No matter what you see, do not speak. If you must, bite down on the towel."

It takes me a moment, but I have the sense to laugh.

Malta rambles on, “I am sending Will in after he rings the doorbell twice. Leave the leash on Honeybun, but leave her loose. He will walk right in. If Honeybun bites, Will intends to defend himself. He is a skinny guy, but he packs a punch. Warn Asherel that no matter what he does, she cannot talk or scream.”

I am back to feeling pretty nervous again, but get off the phone and pace while preparing the two towels. The dogs sense something is up. Asherel can’t wait. She claims she wants all Honeybun’s door charging aggression gone, but I think she gleefully is anticipating high drama.

The doorbell rings. Asherel stuffs the towel in her mouth, giggling. The dogs explode as usual. Will walks in. Honeybun runs up to him, wagging and sniffing. He stalks her, arms akimbo, but she keeps wagging and trying to lick him. Then Malta enters and Honeybun joyfully greets her. I am crestfallen. She will never believe me now. May as well resign and see if I can collect unemployment for retired vicious dog rehabilitators.

“This is normal,” says Malta, "and acceptable."

No kidding. To Malta's credit, she assures me she doesn’t think I am lying about my dog’s reception to strangers. She recognizes that Honeybun had stayed with them for a week and thus knows them. The only way she can assess what I am experiencing when strangers come to the door is if strangers are produced. I call the two neighbors that I know would not be terrified and would trust Malta, if not me. Neither of them is home. The only neighbor available is Comer, who turns ninety next year. I don't want to jeopardize his chances of reaching that milestone. Where are all the strangers when you need them?

Fortunately, Honeybun has enough delinquent traits that door charging is only one of many issues Malta can work on with us, so her visit is not wasted. She notices that when we tell Honeybun to sit, she wags her tail, looks at us, and maybe, twenty seconds and three or four repeated commands later, slowly complies.

"You are teaching her to ignore you," says the ever observant Malta.

I have often told Asherel that delayed or partial obedience is not obedience. It is subtle defiance. So happy that Honeybun is doing something other than biting or growling, I count it a victory if no one is bleeding in her presence. Malta would have been a remarkable mother in that she understood that as soon as you relax your standards you are dead meat. But she wants no part in animal procreation, she reminds me, not of dogs, nor of humans.

"So you tell her to sit once, and only once," she instructs Asherel.

We look at Honeybun. We tell her to sit once and only once, and she remains standing.

Malta squeezes gently on Asherel's shoulder, thumb and forefinger on either side, the same way Spock used to do on *Star Trek* when he wanted to make someone instantly collapse.

"What do you feel?" she asks.

"Strong pressure," answers Asherel.

"Do you know why I did that?" asks Malta, "Besides that I like to hurt little girls?"

Asherel laughs, "No."

"Well dogs have pressure points too, and you can use them to make her sit, on command every time. You push your two fingers on either side of the base of her tail and you don't need to even push too hard."

She demonstrates. Honeybun sits instantly.

"Next time," promises Malta, "You won't have to push barely at all."

She commands Lucky to sit, the sweetly obstinate Lucky. He of course ignores her, but with a scruffy, happy look on his face. She does the Vulcan grip gently near his tail, and he sinks instantly to a sit with just a gentle touch.

"Do this for a week," Malta teaches, "Every time. She will never disobey sitting on command again."

Every time? Malta clearly is not aware of all the responsibilities a home school parent juggles. I must learn and teach every subject in every grade, as well as care for the home, the dogs, the bird, the yard, teach my art class, manage the Destination Imagination team, transport Asherel to dog classes, speech club, Spanish class, horseback riding….. and then spend countless hours wallowing in guilt for how poorly I am doing it all. Who has time to follow through on telling a dog to sit?

Then she plops down on the floor with Honeybun who is calm, and content. Malta scratches behind the little dog's ears, and under her chin. Honeybun rests her head on her front legs, her eyes glazed a little with peacefulness. As she pets Honeybun, Malta informs me that for a Christmas gift to herself, she is sending hand grenades to the organization that confronts Japanese whaling ships. I am speechless. I love whales and definitely believe no one should be hunting those placid, intelligent creatures. However, I cannot condone killing the people who are so ignorantly and sinfully even doing so.

She watches my face, which probably conveys some degree of horror.

"Best Christmas gift I ever got," she says, grinning.

"Hand grenades?" I squeak. Who *is* this maniac in my home?

"Stink bombs," she laughs, "Makes the whale meat unusable. Really smells bad! Not real hand grenades...."

"Oh," I sputter, relieved.

“Your job,” she pontificates, as she pets the euphoric Honeybun, “Is to relax. I am not saying this dog doesn’t have issues. She does, and it is not your fault that she is territorial. But it will take time, and if you can learn to relax, you will be able to help her.”

So Malta does not believe I have ruined this dog! It is also true that relaxing is not easy for me, the prototypical type A personality. When I start a project, I work feverishly at it till it is done. I have often stayed up all night completing a piece of artwork, unable to tolerate unfinished projects. This dog, requiring sustained patience and diligence is taxing my entire genetic predisposition. Staying the course is excellent advice if the course is no more than five minutes long. In that case, I can stay with the best of them. On the sixth minute, I implode.

"You become what you want to become," she adds, "Like I have ten horses we rescued at home, and I don't know how we will have the money to feed them.... But somehow, we always do."

We as yet have little surplus money ourselves. Arvo left his entrepreneurial foray into the mortgage industry, and has been in a new finance position with a telecommunication company for about a month now. The past year of lean income has drained our bank accounts and we have already raided what we can in good conscience from Asherel. Honeybun's propensity for injury has further depleted funds. However, before Malta and Will had come that day, I had written a small check for their rescue farm. We can't give much, and I am a little ashamed of that. This is becoming a mantra of our life, I muse, while handing her the donation check.

"See," she proclaims happily, rising to go and petting Honeybun goodbye, "Money to feed the horses. Let's go Will."

Malta is not satisfied with Honeybun's door greeting performance since she and Will are not total strangers and likely not eliciting her full arsenal of viciousness. She seems to believe me that Honeybun is a different dog with people she has never met. Malta wants fresh meat, victims who don't know Honeybun so Malta can assess more accurately. She wants me to find people willing to risk dog attack when she returns in two days.

I scour the neighborhood for willing victims. I don't like asking others for help, preferring to handle things on my own and give an aura of self-reliant competence. Letting others know you need help can lead to many undesirable consequences. For example, sometimes then, they expect you to help *them* later on. Who has time for that? And additionally, if they notice chinks in my armor, they may also notice rust on my sword, and holes in my heart. This can lead to uncomfortable questions and scrutiny. It is not good to show one's weakness. I glance at Honeybun, who is barking again as a stranger walks by. That's right, I tell her, a good offense is sometimes the best defense.

Nonetheless, I email my neighbor Carolyn who has her own dog that I recently cared for while she was away. I have amassed enough good deeds with her that maybe a bite or two would be considered payback. The sweet Christian couple on the corner might agree to be victims since they are very assured that when they die they are going to heaven. Carolyn's son is co-opted to be sacrificed for the cause. That is a total of four bodies of varying sex, age and skin toughness. Surely if

Honeybun is inclined to eat someone, this is a smorgasbord of what is typically available at a hominid buffet. I call Malta and report that we have four willing victims. She is beside herself with glee and preps me by phone. I am to have all the victims ready to gather when she arrives. She and Will plan to enter the house first, alone, and with intent of riling our vicious dog. Since she cannot heal what she hasn't observed, she is pulling out all the stops in this endeavor.

A short time later, Will and Malta ring the doorbell. Without speaking, Will is first to enter the house. He is in disguise, with large dark sunglasses. He is greeted by a happy, tail wagging Honeybun. Will grabs her leash and walks around like a gangster as Honeybun prances joyfully beside him.

“She’s on to you, Will,” I say as she licks him.

Malta had wanted him to wear a poncho and sombrero to further test Honeybun’s paranoia, but all he had in the truck were the sunglasses.

Next Malta rings the doorbell and enters. Honeybun is delirious with joy to greet her old friends. Malta approaches her rapidly, and snatches the leash from Will.

"Sit!" she commands gruffly. Honeybun complies quickly, probably remembering the Vulcan pressure point grip.

As before, Asherel has her video camera ready. She crouches behind the couch and smiles at me, giving me a thumbs up. I am very happy everyone is having so much fun but *HELLOOOO*, I would like a little more seriousness in tackling this rampaging dog issue, here.

I receive final orders from Malta. The four victims have been anxiously waiting for the call, and are over in a flash. They seem eager. This is perplexing to me. Perhaps they are hoping for big pay-offs from the law suit. At any rate, I make a mental note to send them Christmas cards this year.

I give them their instructions. We decide Walt, having lived a good, long life should go before the women and kids. The victims are gathered in the front yard, milling nervously like cattle before the slaughter. Honeybun knows something is up. The elderly neighbor from next door ambles over slowly, his cane tapping like a heartbeat, to see if everything is okay at the Kaseorg's. His concern touches me, and I add him to the Christmas list.

The crowd assures him this is all part of the vicious dingo training, and Comer shuffles away. I peer out, and announce to Walt it is his time. He gulps, kissing his wife goodbye. The door closes with an ominous click as I settle into position with Asherel.

The door bell rings and both dogs spring into action. Malta instructs me to watch and learn at the hand of the master while the dogs bark to warn us all of the end of the world. Malta nods to me silently, and I open the door as she holds Honeybun's leash. Honeybun is the picture of a dog owner nightmare - hackles hackling as she growls, barks and lunges with snapping teeth. Finally, I think to myself, opening the door to sweet Walt, my dog is misbehaving beautifully!

Malta snaps Honeybun back so that her eyeballs bulge, while dragging her twenty feet back, roaring, "Enough!!!" Honeybun is certain Malta does not understand what a menace Walt is, the man who travels several months a year to help build churches and homes for struggling people. She snarls again as he moves, which gives Malta the opportunity we have all been waiting for. Malta grabs her ruff and tumbles her down into the "dreaded roll". Honeybun lays there, tail between her legs, silent. Vindicating me further, once she is allowed up again, she sees Walt move and erupts into Volcano Dog, spewing venom. The dreaded roll descends upon her a second time.

For several minutes, Walt wanders around my living room as Malta repeats commanding and rolling Honeybun. It takes her an eternity to understand. Walt cringes a little each time the leash is jerked, and I can't say I like watching it either.

I am pretty sure Honeybun likes it even less. However, in her current state, we cannot handle Honeybun. We have to know she will not kill the little Girl Scouts who came to our door selling cookies.

When Honeybun is finally sitting calmly, and looking at me wondering if it really is ok if she lets Walt live, Malta declares it is time now for victim number two. Walt is allowed to leave in one piece. His wife Marge will run the gauntlet next.

She rings the door bell. Honeybun again barks and lunges, but with a little less gusto. Malta does her alpha dog thing, and Marge plays the victim role. Honeybun is clearly not as anxious to defend my home from the wily and dangerous Marge as she had been with Walt, because frankly, what Malta is doing to her is not too much fun. Malta only has to jerk the leash four or five times, commanding Honeybun, "Enough!" Honeybun's aggression is now reduced to a quick growl, a half hearted lunge, and then she sits looking quietly at Malta. Marge walks back and forth and Honeybun glances back and forth from Marge to Malta. She stays seated however; having figured out that this is the only assurance that she will remain upright.

It is time for victim number three, Malta announces. Marge rejoins her husband and nods to Carolyn.

Carolyn now dings the doorbell and marches in. Honeybun grunts some feeble attempts at viciousness, but mostly watches Malta, with one or two half-hearted barks, and glances at me. She begs me to throw these people out and please feed her dinner, which in case I have forgotten has not been served yet.

Having watched Malta handle our dog with three victims, I am proclaimed sufficiently trained to attempt this myself. With a long history of performance anxiety, I am not thrilled to try this in front of an audience, particularly one that might die by my incompetence.

"Will you jump in if it looks like she is going to go after Mark?" I implore, "I mean, he is young and has a lot to live for still."

Malta laughs, assuring me I will do fine; just open the door to Victim #4. Taking a deep breath as she hands me the leash, I am ready. I snap Honeybun back while opening the door. She barks briefly, but clearly, her heart is no longer in it. Malta, the taskmaster, insists I should have dragged her twenty feet back even with mild barking because we need to absolutely squelch all barking or lunging. But Mark is not bitten and I am feeling confident that I can indeed prevent the annihilation of little children entering our home.

Malta is enjoying herself and as total victory is within her grasp now, she decides to push for a full assault on normalizing this little dog. Carolyn, who is happy to have the free tutorial should she ever acquire a half crazed wild dog is eager to help. Malta orders a group march now so we walk out, towing the subdued Honeybun with us. Marge and Walt have already sneaked home.

Prompting me to start off with Honeybun heeling beside me, Malta commands us to walk together, and then pass the leash to each other, taking turns walking Honeybun down the street. Her goal is to help Honeybun learn that *all* humans are alpha dogs, and must be respected. Meanwhile, I glance at my neighbors while passing the leash, hearing their cheers and their joy for me, and feel a little teary. They have given up the better half of a lovely afternoon to help me. They seem genuinely joyful for our communal success. Honeybun glances at them too. Maybe we both have spent a little too long in the solitary wild. It surprises me, this selfless good will. I have lived here for fifteen years, but this is the most time I have spent with my neighbors… ever.

"She is responding out of fear," Malta tells me as we walk, and the leash is passed to Mark.

"That is really the hardest aggression to heal, but it can be done. You will need to practice this often. Get your friends to come and ask them to ring the doorbell. She will learn, but it will take time."

Funny, I have thought of them as neighbors, but not really friends. Carolyn is raising her hand and bobbing her head. “We’ll do that!” she exults.

And while I am waxing poetic about friends, that nasty old message of perseverance clangs into my consciousness. I am getting mightily tired of Malta’s message that anything worth having with this dog, is worth working for. And even worse, this work will be arduous and time consuming. Goals will not be reached in time for dinner. I think perseverance is highly overrated.

Honeybun trots complacently beside each of us, seemingly unconcerned about who is at the helm. Despite my reservations, my anxiety is draining away. Burgeoning enthusiasm and hope is tapping at my heart. The village has turned out to help me and my poor nutty dog. My little dog, less impressed, emphatically asks, “Can I have dinner *now*?”

Malta calls the next day. She informs me she has just left the house of someone with a dog that makes Honeybun look like a choir member.

"I had a great idea," she cries, "This dog lives just

down the street from you. He needs victims to help him train his dog, and you need victims. I was thinking I could get all you people with bad dogs together, and you could be victims for each other."

I pause and consider her idea, "We could call it the Bad Dog Club."

"Do you know of any other bad dogs?' she asks.

"Oh we have lots of bad dogs in the neighborhood," I admit, "The problem is most of them don't know their dogs are bad. It could be sticky inviting them into the club."

"Well I think we have a movement going," she chuckles, "The guy I just left says he has seen people suddenly all over the place walking their dogs while carrying a whip."

We are changing the world, one whip at a time.

Dear Lord,

Now I see why you had me wait so long for victory. Perhaps I had not trusted enough in what I could not see. I know faith is being certain of what we do not see. When I started this project, I sure didn't see how much struggle would ensue. I didn't envision months of perseverance, nor the financial drain, nor the need to trust others. I didn't expect saving the dog to teach me about friendship…Or community. I am pretty astounded at how you worked that message in. I hope you are almost done now, because I am getting weary.

I have learned that good works don't necessarily mean life will be easy or stress-free. In fact, I think it means sometimes following you involves hardship and duress. I have learned that I am not able to do everything on my own, and sometimes relying on others is a good thing. I also am not very nice to others sometimes… and I do feel a little conviction on that point. And of course, most of all I have learned to be still and trust that you will empower me to accomplish your purposes. Personally, I am thinking those are plenty enough lessons from such a small dog.

Amen.

CHAPTER 7

Introverted, Immodest, Isolated

I have tried to teach all my rather shy, introverted children that they should reach beyond their natural isolationist temperament to try to talk to everyone they meet as everyone has value. I try to teach them while avoiding social intercourse myself, because I am shy and not certain I really like people. I prefer to hide in the bushes and shove them forward, and then yell at them for being an introvert. From the vantage point of the sidelines, I expostulate that every person can either teach them something, or perhaps they can be a blessing in some way to that person. Every encounter is a divine appointment, and an opportunity waiting to happen.

I want desperately for them to learn this, knowing how hard it is to overcome shyness, that inclination to withdraw within oneself. As a creative, introspective person myself, with an introverted nature, I understand firsthand how talking with people can be a chore. Honeybun is becoming a conduit for opening those floodgates from shyness for both Asherel and me, but I have a long way to travel on the path to social grace.

I probably need to get past my pervasive belief that most people are dumbkofs, thick headed morons. Jesus would likely take issue with this but He may not be paying close attention to the "*sans cerebrums*" in my milieu. Naturally, I do not tell my children this is how I view others, because that might defeat my goal of teaching godly tolerance and love.

One snappy crisp day in the orange of autumn, Asherel and I are sauntering home from our power migration with the dogs. Out of nowhere, a little ball of bulldog muscle comes racing at us, snarling and in full attack mode. A retractable leash trails ineffectually behind him. (How I have come to despise retractable leashes!) The owner is calling the unneutered and rather overly testosteroned bulldog, but he could not have cared less. He blasts like a torpedo for Honeybun and Asherel. Asherel is an enormously cool kid under fire. It was she that had calmed me down a few months ago when I had almost stepped on a Copperhead snake in our hallway. Now, she calmly tugs on Honeybun's leash so that Honeybun will not attack, and figuring they are fast enough to outrun a bulldog, she sprints away. Honeybun snarls briefly in warning, and then quietly trots off with Asherel. The owner steps on the leash, in a desperate lunge, and the bulldog screeches to a stop, his teeth snapping in the space between him and my child. Asherel stops, completely unflustered, ordering Honeybun to sit. Lucky sits calmly beside me; Honeybun sits calmly beside Asherel, and the bulldog is barking, snarling, and lunging. My normal response of smug superiority is dampened by the fact that I recognize up until a month ago, our own sweet dog behaved just like that bulldog. Instead, I sympathize with the mortified owner.

"I am so sorry!" she yelps, nearly in tears.

"That's okay," comforts Asherel sweetly. Honeybun lies down, the poster dog of obedience.

"You have done us a service," I console, "Don't apologize. We have been training our dog for three months not to be aggressive, and this was a really good test."

The poor lady is still struggling with the bulldog.

"But if I could offer some advice," I continue, feeling I have earned the right to speak, "Your dog is just what my dog was like three months ago."

Surprisingly, the lady pours out her heart in response, rather than tell me to mind my own business. She laments about how hard it is, how sweet the dog really is, but how walks have become a nightmare. Her husband refuses to be consistent in disciplining and controlling the dog, and it is growing increasingly difficult for them to handle him. Their marriage is suffering.

"But I have seen you and your daughter," she states, "I

noticed how you always make your dogs sit when we go by. I remember how that one used to bark and pull.... and look at her now."

"You can do it too," I encourage her, "And the first thing you should do is get rid of that retractable leash. They are dangerous, and you have no control of your dog. And worse, he is going to use the whip like effect of that long lead and injure your arm."

"Next," I suggest, "Our trainer showed us a magical way to make your dog sit. When dogs go by, you make your dog sit, and be calm. And don't move on until he is. "

Her dog is still straining at the leash and growling.

"Put one finger on either side of the base of his tail and push while saying sit."

The bulldog sinks into sit, disgruntled but overcome by the pressure point. He doesn't stay there, but I implore her to keep doing it, and not stop until he gets the idea. He finally sits still, and is blessedly silent.

"See?" I congratulate, "It will not be easy, but I promise you, if you do that consistently, every time, and don't let up, he will be calm when you pass other dogs."

After recommending the great books I have read, we talk a long time about how dogs must know they are not the ones in control. I feel good about spreading my infinite, hard won wisdom. As we walk on, I praise Asherel for her cool, calm response and the amazing good our little dog is slowly spreading. Unfortunately, altruism and arrogance are kissing cousins in shallow souls. My deep reservoir of canine knowledge and expertise and the showers of wisdom cascading from my every word can now be collected by bucketfuls. I begin to calculate how soon I should be writing Cesar Milan, the reigning dog expert with my advice. However, I do chuckle at my conceit. Based on past experience, I am probably in for some soul popping deflation within the hour.

A few weeks later I see the bulldog and owner again. As we pass, her dog sits calmly. She tells me that her husband, seeing the difference in the dog, is now doing the same training method as she, and the whole family is growing closer as a result. I pet the furry marriage counselor at my side. As is clearly evident, I don't like to brag unless my efforts go unnoticed, but I will not be surprised if the Nobel Peace prize committee is soon knocking at my door. I wonder if I should get my hair cut with the expensive stylist. Again, as these thoughts bump up with the honest joy for the bulldog and his happy owners, I laugh at myself. Will I ever get past these irrepressible spats of self-adulation? Honeybun, on the other hand, ducks away from my congratulatory pats and murmurs of "Good dog!" She is satisfied to be who she is without notice as long as we notice if many hours have elapsed without dog biscuits forthcoming.

The following day, I am on a run with the dogs, and pass by a garage sale. There are kids everywhere, all under ten years old. They are swarming around like ants, carrying piles of things out to the garage sale tables. Of course, they all come racing toward us as soon as they see the dogs. I stop, and the dogs sit. The children swarm over us.

"Stop. You can pet the big one, but not the little one."

Several pairs of large, dark eyes peer at us. Honeybun sits, wagging her tail. The very large dad approaches, reaching out his hand to Honeybun.

"You can pet her if you insist," I warn, "But I don't guarantee she won't bite." This is an example of my endearing gentle nature in social situations.

He kneels down, and holds out his hand. She wags her tail as he scruffs her neck. I am flummoxed. I thought I knew this dog. Where was all this sweetness hiding? Well the kids will have none of that, Dad petting the forbidden dog, but not them?

"Can we!!!???" they shout.

"If your dad lets you," I concede, "But one at a time, and let me put my hand over yours cause she won't bite me." (Probably)

And my vicious rescue dog lets ten small children, jumping, running, and chattering, pet her without a single snarl, growl, bark or aggressive look. She glances at me often, as if to say, “Is this okay with you? Personally, I could do without it, but if this is part of the program for getting those bones and cushy bed at home, I am ok with it."

Under normal circumstances, I would never interrupt a run. However, Honeybun seems genuinely to enjoy the attention so I click off my stopwatch. Normally I would not bother chatting with strangers either, but as long as I am stuck at the end of a leash of a happy dog.....

I learn the mob of children is from two huge families, all homeschoolers. A rather frazzled, weary looking woman, mother to five of the urchins emerges and shakes my hand and pets the dog. The man is married to another woman there, who waves but is busily putting garage sale items out. The frazzled woman asks if I live in the neighborhood.

"One over," I answer, "I homeschool too."

"Are you the art teacher!?" she exclaims.

"Yes," I declare, surprised, “How did you know that?"

"We lived with some friends- and they have a child you teach. We shared their house for about a month."

I know about this story! My friends are the family that rescued her! This mother of five children had been tragically and suddenly widowed. She was living in an RV, with all those bereaved kids and little money, when a local Messianic church found out about her. The church told our friends of this sad situation, and despite having five kids of their own, they took the family into their home until the poor widow could find a place to live. I don't know exactly what miraculous circumstances put her in the house where she lives now, but she is settling in, homeschooling her kids, and apparently surviving.

"I need to talk to you about art classes," she remarks.

My classes are full already, I think in dismay looking at the five children. Knowing she has little money. I don’t dare tell her my prices anyway.

"For how many?" I question.

The little boy who is petting Honeybun looks up brightly.

"For me!" he proclaims.

"Are you an artist?" I ask.

"Yes," he asserts, cuddling his face in Honeybun's luxurious ruff.

I calculate the number of chairs that can be squeezed around the art table. He smiles up at me imploringly. He is a thin boy. It will be tight, but doable. I am not sure what comes over me but I offer him a place in my class for free. If nothing else, Honeybun seems to like him. When I continue my run a half hour later, I feel my legs stretching out with unaccustomed lightness.

We wait with mounting excitement for the first class at the Dog Training Club. As the first class is an orientation session, we have been instructed not to bring our dog. As we pull into the parking lot, we are astounded by the number of large vans, and pickup trucks with dog crates in them. Most of the crates have dogs in them. Beautiful dogs. We pass a Bernese Mountain Dog, one of my favorites. Another has a gorgeous tan dog with a wrinkled face.... maybe a mastiff. These are not mutts. Not a half-breed in the bunch. These are champions. Some of the crates have ribbons on them, blue ribbons. We feel instantly intimidated and outclassed.

"I thought we weren't supposed to bring our dog," whispers Asherel.

"We weren't," I croak, "I asked three times. This is just to orient us. The dogs are supposed to come next week."

Nonetheless, everyone else apparently has brought their dog, their dog crates, and their dog ribbons. Additionally, everyone else seems to know each other. Every dog there poses quietly by its owner, ignoring the throngs of other dogs and people. Polite happy faced dogs with wagging tails and winning dispositions.

No one is saying, “Stop, please don't approach or my dog might bite you.” Nor are the dogs suddenly stiffening, straightening their tails, frightening small children. The people look confident; the leashes hang slack. They don't have darting eyes, and are not nervously biting their nails and seeking a quiet spot where the dog will be less likely to eviscerate prey. In short, they look exactly what we do not. We alone are frauds and outcasts.

There are signs everywhere of the many different classes. My heart is a plummeting stone when we notice that the beginner class line has the same sort of confident, miraculously obedient, nice dogs that the advanced class line has. We are imposters, only allowed to enter because no one has as yet seen our dog, I obsess miserably. Asherel looks similarly disheartened. We walk glumly over to the Rally Novice sign. A lady with a Cardigan Welsh corgi stands in line. The dog looks up at us with cheerful, friendly eyes and wags his tail.

"Are you in this class?" the congenial owner asks.

"Yes," I squeak, “My daughter is."

"Where is your dog?" she questions, looking around Asherel's feet, as though maybe a very miniature schnauzer might be hiding.

"They told us not to bring her tonight," I answer,then add, "Didn't they?"

"Oh maybe they did," she replies cheerfully, "But I am a club member. They know me. My dog is a champion, has had all but one class that would win her the CGC award."

At least that is what I think she says.... I don't know what a CGC award or any combination of letters award means in the canine world. I just know that the only award our dog could possibly be given thus far would be the B.A.D. award.

I also notice that not only are there no children under thirteen, there are no people who couldn't do advertisements for Geritol or Ensure. If I am feeling outclassed, I cannot imagine what my eleven year old is feeling. I guess dog training is on par with sports like Shuffleboard and three wheeled bicycle races.

The nice lady is still talking, oblivious to the turmoil in my soul.

"I wanted to get in to that last class, and get him the award, but since it was full, I decided this would not be too bad. I know the other dogs in here have reached at least a basic level of obedience."

Have they, I ponder, pulling the corners of my mouth into a smile, and nodding. Of course they have. The one notable exception does not escape my iron sharp mind.

Out of the corner of my eye, I notice an owner striding around the ring with a dog that is heeling, off leash, sitting when she pauses to talk to others, and then lying down when the owner settles into a long conversation.

The lady is still chattering away as I jerk my attention back to her.

"And what kind of dog is yours?" she asks.

Since Asherel has become completely mute, I answer, "Carolina Dog. At least that's what we think. We found her."

There. It is out. The jig is up. We do not have an AKC recognized breed. In fact, we do not even have a clear idea of *what* we have. All we know is that our dog has no ribbons, no travel crate, and is in fact likely to be booted after she attacks the first little champion she can get her teeth on. This is exactly why I hate society. I never fit in. I am a worm.

The lady smiles, "Really!" she exclaims, with evident and honest enthusiasm, "I know that breed! It is like a dingo, isn't it?"

"It is," I concede, feeling marginally better.

The class trainer arrives now, and signs in the lady with the corgi. Then he looks at us, who are trembling imperceptibly.

"You must be Asherel," he says kindly.

She nods. She has stopped speaking and is not to utter

another word till we are back at the car. The trainer, Lloyd, is a nice man, a large man, just the kind of nice large men that Honeybun most likes to growl at.

Lloyd gives us our orientation papers and explains that there will be a general orientation, and then we will all meet back with him for more specifics. We head off to take a seat among the crowd of well-behaved, AKC champions.

The general orientation is thorough and well run. I learn more just sitting there listening and watching the demonstrations than we had learned in our entire first class at the other place. This is clearly the place where serious dog people come. I fear that if we remain, and our dog is not sent home with a B.A.D. cap on her head, we are in serious danger of crossing the line from dog lover to kook.

"Now some general rules about dog etiquette," pipes the announcer, "Not all dogs are friendly..."

WHAT??? This roomful of champions might admit that not all dogs are AKC perfect????

"Not all dogs like strangers...."

NO! It cannot be! There are other dogs deranged and troubled like ours?

"Please remember that. Keep your dogs on short leads. Do not let them approach other dogs. Do not approach other dogs yourself without asking. This is just common sense for your own safety, here or anywhere."

My tension streams away as I gaze at the announcer with rapturous love. The people around me are smiling, encouraging, kindly. I feel the cocoon of their accepting warmth. They concur that dogs can be unfriendly, not like other dogs, wary of strangers. Our dog is not *evil* because she is cautious with others. It will be ok; it is accepted. Even this roomful of champions is willing to acknowledge this.

The general orientation is over and we head back to Lloyd. There are only three people in our class line. Most of the crowd is in obedience classes. The performance class seems less popular. With only three dogs in the class we have half a shot at keeping Honeybun under control. Lloyd enumerates what to expect and then gives us a comprehensive book on Rally Contests and terms. Asherel still doesn't utter a sound.

The others thank him, as do I and begin to drift away.

"Asherel," he calls to our departing backs, "I only require two things. That you and your dog have fun... and smile."

Then he turns to me, "And the dogs with issues...."

Oh no, and here I am thinking these people understand….

"Usually by the third class, they melt away."

We depart, passing by a beautiful giant schnauzer, an elegant afghan with a blue ribbon that heralds "today is my birthday" around its neck, a miniature greyhound, a butterfly eared Papillion... and waltz into the steamy day which has morphed somehow to night with a hint of fall in the breeze. It feels good, comforting, and gentle. We drive home under a sky full of stars, clustered together in the warm sparkles of each other. I wonder when people started being so accepting and so nice.

The following week, we load our little American Dingo into the van, with a pouch full of goodies that clip to Asherel's waistband. Asherel has read over the Rally rules and the myriad complicated signs. The signs are mostly big yellow arrows with instructions like "270 degree right turn", or "right u turn", or "halt, walk one step, halt walk two steps, halt walk three steps". It is like doggy ballet. Approximately twenty orange cones are set out on the floor, with numbered signs which direct the handler to the maneuver she is to perform with the dog. For novice rally-ers like us, the dog is on leash. However, if the handler tugs on the leash, she receives a one point deduction, and if she tugs on the leash three times, she is booted from the contest, asked to leave the ring, and probably required to commit hara-kiri to preserve any shred of dignity she has left. Now this sport may seem simple to the uninitiated, but Lloyd makes it quite clear that to excel in Rally and achieve Excellent Rally status, fancy footwork and complete concentration is critical. The handlers are warned the week before to bring crates for their dogs, since Lloyd will be reviewing the footwork first, and the complexity necessitates the handler's full attention. Every fiber of the handler's being must be focused on the footwork to correctly obey the signs. Since we don't have a portable crate, I am unanimously voted to be Asherel's "crate". She reminds me that crates always do what they are told.... and that crates do not get cranky or angry. I remind her that very few handlers have mothers for crates, and thus she better watch how she speaks to her crate or her crate will resign.

We arrive a half hour early, so Honeybun can acclimate herself to this new and scary environment. When we arrive, only two or three dogs are there, and the building is nearly empty. We walk Honeybun in the large, adjoining field so she will not humiliate us by defecating in the building, and then we meander inside to let her sniff all the frightening corners. She notices the few people and dogs, but mostly ignores them. As more dogs and people come, Honeybun quietly sits at our side, and looks at us calmly. She doesn't seem interested in mauling anyone, and that is encouraging. She knows Asherel has treats in the bag at her hip, and so her attention is riveted on Asherel.

Lloyd places the signs and pylons, and then directs the class to put their dogs in the crates so the handlers can focus on the footwork. Asherel hands me Honeybun's leash. I admit that I am laughing at the seriousness with which the subject of the footwork is approached. However, I am sitting on the sidelines. It is, like many things, deceptively difficult.

It is even more taxing if you are a shy eleven year old in a sea of senior citizens. Lloyd demonstrates one maneuver a few times, and then urges the handlers to try it. Asherel is frozen to the floor. I nudge her, reminding her that she should do what Lloyd suggests. She moves her feet in a halfhearted shuffle. I glare at her. *This* is the amazing eleven year old that I have bragged about in order to receive special dispensation to allow her in the class, and she is pulling a 'scared out of my gourd' act. Lloyd trots over.

"Did you get it?" he asks.

She nods. (Now she will be in for it, I hope)

"Show me," he implores.

Hooray for Lloyd! Asherel shuffles her feet in a circle.

"It helps the dog if you pick up your feet," he says, not unkindly, "Try again."

This time, Asherel does it with a little more vivacity. He nods and her pink cheeks move ever so imperceptibly as a smile begs to be let loose.

The next thing Lloyd shows us is how to entice a dog to go backwards. If you are like me, you are probably thinking this borders on ridiculous. To most people this may not seem like an important maneuver. However, in Rally, a dog that backs up on command is apparently useful. And everything Lloyd teaches involves giving the dog a treat for every nanosecond of obedience. This insures intense interest in doing things like walking backwards on command. To encourage a dog to go in reverse, a treat is pressed near her chest, and then she is commanded to "back up", with the treat low and just out of reach. The dog, if it is not Honeybun, will then walk backwards until fed the treat (which, by the way, Lloyd keeps calling a "cookie".) Honeybun, however, knows that if she just sits, she has no trouble snatching the treat.

Asherel practices a few times, with the same result - Honeybun sits and gobbles the unearned treat. Lloyd patiently demonstrates eliciting one backward step and then rewarding her instantly. Within a few minutes, she takes two steps backwards. She is definitely eager and attentive. This is the one advantage I see of the poor dog having nearly starved to death. She will work for food. The other class members are quite chatty and seem eager to engage with both Asherel and me. They seem to think I know what they are talking about as they chatter about various classes and proficiency levels and I am too embarrassed to admit that they may as well be speaking Japanese. Smiling and nodding, my temporal mandibular joint in my jaw aching, I am longing for a hot bath all by myself with a good book about loving one another.

Next, Lloyd brings Asherel onto the rally course. Honeybun is highly focused on the treats that Asherel has in her little treat bag, and so sticks to her owner like a remora on a shark. Asherel finishes the course and the class cheers. Despite all the competitions this group seems so conversant in, they are anxious to support this young hopeful contestant. It is not the dog-eat-dog environment one might expect. No one appears to be poisoning kibble to enhance their prospects with their own dog. Honeybun collects yet another "cookie" and wags her gluttonous tail. A classmate reaches out to pet her. I gasp, but Honeybun is gobbling cookies and doesn't mind. And Lloyd, who is an encourager exemplar, comments, "Did anyone notice what Asherel did that no one else did? She talked to her dog the whole time. You have to talk to your dog!"

A smile wavers on Asherel's lips and the class claps. Class ends with no mishaps, no gnawed off limbs, no mangled dogs left in our wake.

In our second class, Honeybun's demeanor begins to change. She perks up when other dogs came near, and wags her tail. She sniffs their bottoms when they aren't looking. She sits attentively when people come near and looks up, bright eyed, wagging. I realize this is not a miraculous change from suspicious scared killer dog, but a keen awareness that in this building, people carry "cookies", and not just regular "cookies" but what they refer to as "high value cookies". A dog may focus on training at home with a low value cookie, even a piece of old dogfood. But in the highly distracting show ring with dogs and people all around and a ceiling forty feet high, a low value cookie becomes a no value cookie. It is a nuclear arms race of goodies. Honeybun scoffs at our "cookies", and pays attention, riveted attention, on the lady who brings a whole grilled chicken breast as her dog's "cookie". The dogs in rally class are being fed better than my daughter.

We have no choice but to up the ante. So to the second class, we bring soft bacon/meat treats, albeit on sale at Petsmart, but definitely a cut above what we brought the first week. Asherel, per my pointed threats, tries everything Lloyd teaches with a big smile on her face. Asherel is not a naturally very smiley kind of person. She is nice and sweet, but tends toward serious and shy. We are paying too much money for her to be serious and shy at Rally class though, however, so I demand she will smile and engage, or she will need to find a new crate. Thus, while Lloyd is telling the class about the new Rally signs, the U-turn, the Sit/Stay, the 270 degree dreaded right turn.....Asherel is smiling like a crocodile. He glances at her, somewhat perplexed by the change in her demeanor. Honeybun, meanwhile, is smiling at the lady with the chicken breast.

Our class is much larger the second week. The pros had apparently stayed home the first class, because there are several new dogs that seem to actually know what they are doing at the second class. One is a very beautiful little poodle, who prances next to his owner, with his attention solidly fixed on whatever cookie she has in her pouch. I suspect it is filet mignon.

When Asherel's turn comes to do the course, Lloyd barks, "Ready?"

That is the signal in actual competition for the handler to get his dog's full attention, and stride confidently off to the course. Since every tug on the leash is a deduction, and three tugs a disqualification, a dog's undivided attention is critical in rally class.

"Ready," murmurs Asherel.

If Honeybun could have spoken, she would have said, "Not on your life, buster, until you get what that poodle owner has in her pouch."

She is gazing rapturously at the poodle owner, whom the little hussy would gladly have walked off with were she not attached to a leash. Asherel tugs the leash, and Honeybun walks grudgingly forward, still watching the poodle owner. She pays intermittent attention to Asherel, when she knows a treat is forthcoming. The rest of the time she looks beseechingly about, sniffing, because everywhere are tantalizing smells - chicken, cheese, and meatballs. When Asherel finishes the course with only about 4,756 leash tugs, thus over 1000 disqualifications, Lloyd asks what treats we have in our pouch.

"Are they *hard* cookies?" he scoffs, taking us for total Neanderthals.

Everyone knows hard treats have zero value, and at the least, one has to have soft chewy morsels.

"No," Asherel replies, "They are soft."

"What are they?" he asks, unconvinced.

Now this is a little embarrassing, but truth be told, not only did we get these particular treats because they were on sale, but also we loved the name. They are called "Dingos". Kismet! Who could pass up a treat with a name like that when your dog is an American Dingo?

I can tell Lloyd has never heard of this particular "cookie".

"Have you ever tried cheese?" he asks.

He explains that while Dingos might work at home (I detect a touch of contempt in his voice), in the show ring we have to have a high value cookie that will suck every ounce of inattention out of our dog, so her "raison d'être" is to watch us closely. The poodle owner explains that she even puts the treats in her mouth, so that the dog keeps her focus on the handler's face.

Yuck, is all I can think to answer, so I keep silent.

"Here," says Lloyd, handing Asherel some string cheese, "Try this, and take her on the course again."

BOING! Honeybun's head swivels around three times as her eyes bore into Asherel's hand. I had not known she liked cheese, but there is no question she would ride the Titanic for a chance at that cheese.

"Ready?" repeats Lloyd.

"AM I EVER!!!!" woofs Honeybun, stuffing her nose in Asherel's hand.

She prances around the ring, and the leash is completely unnecessary. No way is she going to let Asherel move one millimeter away while she has that cheese in her hand. As she finishes the course, Lloyd smiles.

"That got her attention," I laugh.

Asherel is giggling. We both forget to jerk our dangerous dog away as the poodle bumps against her.

Class is over, and since we still have some cheese left, as we walk to the car Honeybun is still prancing, her eyeballs locked on her owner and her owner's cheese. I guess we need to buy some cheese before next class.

Letter from Malta... Oct. 2

Sounds like you are now pack leaders. Now you can relax a bit! Just don't become human food dispensers..... That will not keep the respect. You have to continue to go left when she pulls right.... go slow when she goes fast....... you lead..... Never follow. You want someone to lead that you trust. You respect. That is consistent. Not someone that just gives you cheese. When they run out of cheese ....what is left?

I am so proud of both of you!!! (And don't tell anyone I said that- cuz they wouldn't believe it anyway! - I just don't say that sort of thing) lol

"Stay away from poodle people..... They are all crazy" - Malta Doganisms 16:12-14.

You and Asherel have performed a miracle. Most people would have whined and whined and never stepped up to the plate. You actually did it.

Life is settling into a routine. Every morning, the dogs greet me, Honeybun prancing and licking- the only time of the day she licks, and Lucky whining and curling around my legs. Then Lucky goes back to sleep, but Honeybun sits nearby, alertly poised with one ear skewed, eyes dark and bright, waiting. She doesn't whine, or nudge me, the way Lucky does when he wants something. She just sits there, every muscle tensed, willing me to get up, collect her leash, and say the magic word. When finally I have finished my coffee and breakfast, read my emails and my Bible verses, and moved towards the door, she leaps up and races in her funny, dainty footed prance to the door. There she waits, wagging her tail, and cocking her head. If by some mistake, I move away from the door, she sits, eyes dark and unblinking. When I return, she is still there, waiting.

Then the ritual begins that is meant to teach the dogs calmness, and that I am still the one in control, not the puppet they believe me to be who would not miss the morning walk if my life depended on it. Both dogs are told to sit on the rug in front of the door. Lucky races up to me, and screeches to a sitting halt. He can pretend to be a very obedient dog when he wants to be. Honeybun will usually take a more leisurely approach to the sit command, though in the end, she knows if she doesn't sit, we don't walk, so she eventually acquiesces. Next I snap the coupler leash on them, and they remain seated, in theory, while the accoutrements needed for the walk are gathered. Lastly, the whip is tucked under my arm. I have not used the whip in weeks, except to wave in the air to accentuate points when chatting along the way. However, there is no doubt that if it is left behind, Honeybun will revert to the feral beast she had been and I will be without defense. Finally, the door opens. The dogs quiver with excitement, but they remain sitting.

"Wait," I say, as their entire being is poised like a slinky at the top of a staircase.

"Okay," I then proclaim, and the reason for canine existence is realized as they catapult out the door.

No longer cringing when meeting strangers, I now welcome them. Inch by hard earned inch, Honeybun and I are both recognizing something we didn't know before- people can do something more than just drain and annoy you… they can even be a source of joy, and soft chewy treats. I encourage them to pet my dogs, but hand them a treat first. This invariably leads to chatting and life stories being exchanged and I am learning the fine art of neighborliness. Honeybun is very happy with this new procedure, and now wags anxiously when people stop to chat with us. She occasionally still lunges on the leash towards them, but now with wagging tail and drooling lips, looking for the treat that strangers have come to represent. I even begin letting little children pet her.

Everyone loves to pet her because she has such a luxurious soft coat. Lucky for all his idiosyncrasies, is by far the sweeter creature, and loves people. He even greets the chemical-covered Terminex worker with loving licks and tail thumping ferociously. However, Lucky's coat is a wiry terrier mess. He is very cute and funny to look at, but not so sensual to pet. Honeybun is soft as a cloud, and lowers my blood pressure every time I stroke her. Thus, our walks and our life become almost mundane.

Asherel now begins to pester me about when we can tackle agility classes. I discover some discouraging facts. Honeybun may be purebred, but not in the eyes of AKC. AKC intends to change the rule in 2010, but this is still 2009 and they will not allow mixed breed dogs to enter any of their events. There are other dog organizations that sponsor agility trials, but they are not nearly as numerous or locally available. Lloyd informs me that if Carolina Dogs are "foundation stock" pending acceptance to the AKC, I can then apply for purebred status based not on her lineage, which we don't know, but on her traits as characteristic of the breed. I write to the AKC and discover that Carolina Dogs are not yet accepted as foundation stock. They inform me that the breed association has to apply for foundation stock status, and as of yet, the Carolina Dog Association (CDA) has not done so.

The association is headed by a lady who seems to have singlehandedly saved the breed from near extinction. It is considered a "rare breed" by all the major kennel clubs, except the AKC. All the information to apply as Foundation Stock is collected, she tells me, and ready to file with the AKC when it is beneficial for the CDA to do so. Apparently there is not yet enough breeding stock, in her opinion. She explains to me that one of the problems with rare breeds that apply to AKC is upon acceptance, the breeding stock is "closed". No new blood can then enter the lineage of all future pups. There is then the very real danger of inbreeding, which is exactly what happened with the famous "Laughing Dog" (which I had never heard of, but apparently it is not laughing any more- filled with genetic problems that inbreeding causes.)

Malta is disgusted as I relay all this information to her. As she collects discarded dogs like toasters at a wedding shower, she grows increasingly furious with breeders and organizations that promote breeding. It isn't even the snobbery of the whole purebred designer dog that irks her - it is the idea that several million dogs each year are already being euthanized. What insanity makes anyone think we need *more* dogs, even fancy ones? Dogs do a fine job of overpopulating even without breeder's assistance.

At any rate, once CDA is ready, and Carolina Dogs(CD) are accepted by AKC, I can send photos of Honeybun and if she is accepted as characteristic of the breed (which she is, I claim with my snoot in the air, that pesky sense of pride invading my lovely character again), she will be able to get an AKC number. However, I discover another big problem while perusing the CDA website. Honeybun is in every respect a perfect Carolina Dog - except purebred Carolina Dogs cannot have purple spotted tongues. Honeybun has a purple spotted tongue. In a fury, I do intensive research that takes at least a full ten minutes. My careful research reveals that purple spots are melanin, pigmentation, like freckles, and *any* breed can have them, and many purebreds *do* have them. Thus, it rankles me that our *perfect* Carolina Dog might be denied purebred status because of purple spots on her tongue.

Actually, she has other imperfections as well. Her flopped ear is considered a major flaw, according to the breed standard. Her pink nose is a minor deduction. Black noses are much preferred. Her funny curve in her tail is an anomaly. However the only trait that disqualifies her from the breed is the purple tongue. Can I convince the CDA to let purple spotted tongues be allowed in the breed standard? The more I consider the purple spotted tongue issue, the more I wonder if there is a devious undertone that explains why Honeybun has been abandoned. Not content to own a dog that has likely been dumped because she was discovered to be pregnant and thus more costly to an irresponsible owner, I create a compelling mystery, complete with villainous, money grubbing creeps, similar to the plot of 101 Dalmatians. Soon I am convinced that Honeybun was bred as a prize winning Carolina Dog. At great expense, she is mated with another champion Carolina Dog, with high hopes of beautiful and costly pups to result. But alas, the dastardly breeder has not noticed that Honeybun has a purple tongue, since she certainly never wants to lick him. When the pups are born, they all have purple tongues, and the cruel breeder tosses them into the SC swamps.

A quick internet search reveals how much non-purple tongued Carolina Dogs (CD) sell for. I am quite sure the CD breed was resurrected altruistically, but purebred pups sell for $800 each. None of those pups have purple tongues. Is it possible someone *had* bred Honeybun, hoping to make money on her pups, until they were found to have purple spotted tongues? Had she really been dumped along with her brood because of the color purple? Malta laughs at my theory and insists the whole Carolina Dog breed thing is a joke. They are just brown dogs and can't I just be happy about that?

Undeterred, since I now desperately want an exotic dog worth bragging about, I exchange several emails with the CD organization president and begin to read some of the fascinating articles on her website, with postings from National Geographic and the Smithsonian magazine. I am awestruck. The Carolina Dog is a genetically distinct breed, and considered to be one of the few "primitive" breeds which were with early Americans and maybe even cavemen. Ancient pictures show dogs remarkably similar to the CD. They are nearly identical genetically to the Australian Dingo, and it is surmised, crossed the land bridge that once existed over the Bering Strait. They also have remarkable traits, unique to the breed, which we have already noticed in Honeybun. Not only do they build dens, but unlike domestic dogs which will crawl under a porch to bear young, CDs will only bear their young in the distinctive earth dens. They also dig "snout pits", or small holes, which they then seem to be eating out of. The theory is they are actually eating the dirt for the nutrients it supplies. They enter estrus as often as three times more frequently than other breeds, and the experts theorize this is to allow them to have as many pups as possible before the inevitable onslaught of heart worm disease kills them, a hazard of living in the swamplands of the southeast where they roam in feral packs. They are suspicious of strangers, even if raised from puppies in domesticity. They are very aware of status and pecking order, and will seek to establish pack hierarchy in whatever pack they find themselves (thus perhaps the issue of dominance and aggression early on with Lucky). They are described as "fox like", calm, intelligent, and aloof. Hunting in packs like wolves, their fur and body is uniquely adapted to the southern swamps where feral packs still exist. The numbers are dwindling, and breeding programs costing thousands of dollars have kept this remarkable piece of history from extinction.

After reading all the articles, I am a little ashamed of worrying about the purple tongue thing. The CDA assures me we will be able to show Honeybun in plenty of agility trials, and we could claim her as a CD. The CDA will support our assertion that she is a Carolina Dog, even with her purple tongue. She tells me many other agility trials outside of AKC are available, if I am willing to travel a little to find them. How ironic to discover we have been entertaining "angels unawares", with our little American Dingo! Who would ever have thought that starving miserable creature was royalty waiting for her crown?

Malta is characteristically caustic in her response while listening to my boasts of the magnificence of our canine treasure.

"They want to increase the gene pool of Carolina Dogs? Gimme a break. Just what we need, more dogs. More dogs for me to find discarded on the roadsides. I want to, just for giggles, start a breed registry of 'Four legged Brown Horses'. Do you know that there really is a 'Blue Eyed Horse' breed registry? Do you really want to give money to the AKC, filled with people who work so hard to increase the dog population while people like me mop up the mess they create?"

No, I really don't, when she puts it that way, but I do want my enthusiastic daughter to have opportunities to show her dog in Agility classes, and the best local opportunities are clearly AKC.

While talking with an AKC judge at our next rally class about our dilemma, and the Purple Tongue issue, I discover even she didn't know that breeds other than Chows could have purple tongues. She is also surprised by the "Purple Tongue Standard" on the UKC website regarding CD. As far as she knows, no other breed standard specifies a dog cannot have spots on their tongue. I find that I am enjoying chatting with the class members now. I have confessed to my ignorance regarding dog shows and breeds, and really everything except how to smack a whip. They are surprisingly willing and happy to share their knowledge and don't seem to be laughing behind their hands. I look forward to our classes now almost as much as Honeybun, though would enjoy them even more if it was me scarfing down lobster and filet.

Meanwhile, Lloyd is teaching new confusing Rally signs, and encourages Asherel to go first through the course. Honeybun has been excitedly waiting for this moment. She has the routine down now, with four classes under her tail, and understands that keeping her eye on Asherel means food, lots of good food. We feed her only a small dinner on class night to keep her motivated to work for the "cookies". She is becoming a class star, with less than five hundred leash tugs now, thus down to only about 150 disqualifications. After all our struggles, I am determined we will see this journey through to my daughter's dream ending - competing with this dog in agility trials.

"Look Mom," exclaims Asherel, as they gallop off the rally field, "She's smiling!"

I look but I don't see a smile - I see countless dollars still to be tossed into classes, and travel to distant competitions, with hotel bills, and harried schedules.

On a mission, I call the World's Premier Carolina Dog Agility Trainer (I believe he is also the *only* Carolina Dog Agility Trainer). His wife answers the phone. She is a sweet older woman who currently owns six Carolina Dogs. Her husband is the Agility trainer, and their dogs have won several national titles.

Nearly twenty years ago, her husband had gone to the pound and fallen in love with a feral dog incarcerated there. He took the snarling, anxious dog home. Little did he know that this wild dog was a Carolina Dog. Years of work and training tamed the wild dog, and it became a beloved pet. It had died a few years back, but its picture and triumphs in the Agility ring over the years are all over the Carolina Dog website.

This sweet lady spent an hour on the phone with me, assuring me that there are plenty of agility contests by the various other Kennel Clubs, including USDAA, UKC, ARBA, and a bunch of other initials that stand for things related to dogs. When Honeybun is ready, purple tongue or not, she will find places to strut her stuff. Encouraged greatly, after hanging up, I realize chatting with a total stranger has just brightened my day. Honeybun actually licks a new neighbor that pets her on our walk later that day.

Rally class continues into week five. By now, Honeybun flies into the car on Wednesday night, tail wagging in its upright position, as she knows the treat bag signifies fun and food. She begins to approach strangers while wagging her tail, knowing people represent meatballs and cheese sticks in that place. She even begins to greet other dogs with a wagging tail, and sometimes flops into "play position". Asherel enters the building with a jaunty stride. She approaches the poodle lady, and asks how the poodle's week has been. Then she veers off to the Corgi owner and reaches down to pet his friendly head.

"How is Max?" she asks. Asherel approaching and speaking to people is almost as surprising as Honeybun not attacking all the dogs.

My sister Wendy calls to tell me she will be in town for one night and day. Wendy lives on the West coast, and I rarely see her. While I no longer rake her with my fingernails, we have many differences, not the least of which Wendy is not a dog lover. She is a little afraid of dogs, and finds their shedding, sniffing, and licking disgusting. I am delighted to have her stay with us.... but ask if she remembers about Honeybun? When we were still early in our Honeybun adventure, she had written to me telling me she did not intend to visit.... ever.... while we had that wild dog.

“I won't let her bite you," I promise.

Her friend Joe will be dropping her at our house. It will be an excellent test of how far Honeybun has come.... unless she chews them up, in which case we will need to reassess her progress. I reassure Wendy that Honeybun is reformed, though I do not bore her with all the doubts and caveats that lurk inside my head. She agrees to spend the night and next day with us.

When the doorbell rings heralding their arrival, both dogs careen into the front door, barking and crashing against it. Wendy and her tall friend, Joe, step back. Wendy looks worried. I *am* worried.

"Back!" I command. Lucky backs off, but then as I jerk on Honeybun's leash and demand that she sit, Lucky runs around me back to the door. It is as though Malta and the whip and the “dreaded roll” and the classes had never happened.

"GET BACK!" I yell again, angry now. I have been raving about our progress and these stupid creatures are making me look like a conceited liar. I may indeed *be* one, but am ticked off at their lack of gratitude in exposing me.

Both dogs are straining and barking as the door opens. Without even saying "Hello", I hand both of them a treat.

"Here," I command, "Tell her sit, let her sniff your hand, and then give her the treat."

They both comply, a somewhat terrified look on their faces and the dogs instantly calm as they snatch their treats.

"Pretend they are furniture," I order.

I think Wendy trembles a bit. There is momentary flashback to all those years of torment she brought me by being so darn good at everything. However, I do not have more than a fleeting moment of smug satisfaction. Honeybun is leashed but Lucky is free to stick his snout in both their crotches with his usual rude greeting.

"He is friendly," I assure them, "You don't need to worry about him."(Unless you don't like a cold wet nose in your crotch, in which case, you are in the wrong house.)

We have not had an overnight guest since we have acquired Honeybun. She seems to like Wendy, but I am not certain she will behave if she sees a stranger emerge from a bedroom in the middle of the night. Honeybun is barricaded in Asherel's room for the evening, and Wendy closes her bedroom door - probably locks and bars it as well. Before we all head off to bed, I hear Wendy emerge from the room, and glance up from the book I am reading. Honeybun is standing in front of her, and Wendy is nervously saying, “Good girl....," obviously frightened into immobility.

Honeybun is looking at her with that unnerving, unblinking stare we have come to know and understand but is downright scary to the uninitiated. I assure Wendy it is ok to move. She keeps a wary eye on the silent little dog.

In the morning, Wendy comes out, and when Asherel's bedroom door is opened, Honeybun races out, overjoyed to see me as she is every morning, waggling her whole body and licking me. Then she sees Wendy. She catapults towards her, with the same exuberant full body waggle and licks her.

"She likes you," I cry joyfully, realizing that lately she likes everyone. Perhaps even more miraculously, Wendy likes her. Wendy pets our little dog, and I smile at her. When did Wendy become nice?

Dear Lord,

I didn't realize how much fear has impacted both me and my dog. I mean I knew Honeybun was responding out of fear. I guess I am surprised to learn how much I was…am. I don't seek others out enough, and I have been stingy with my time for others. I am always rushing, and I think maybe it is because then I don't have to bear others' burdens, or give too much of myself. I have never felt very comfortable with people. I think I may have been negligent in loving others as you have loved me. I have been pretty quick to find fault and to pass others by, all the while trying to teach my children otherwise.

I have been snarling as much as Honeybun. I am ashamed Father.

I am not even as wise as our little dog. At least she is completely unequivocal in her love for all of us in her "pack". I think sometimes I am perhaps hardest on those I claim to love the most. I know you have loved me despite my anger, pettiness, arrogance, and failure. I have not been so gentle with others as you have been with me.

Lord, this is a hard lesson. I don't like what I am seeing at all. I hope the lesson includes what I am discovering about Honeybun....that it isn't too late. "He who began a good work in you, will be faithful to complete it."

I'm sorry, Lord Jesus. I want to be better.

Amen.

CHAPTER 8

Impatience

Last Chance Rescue, Malta's animal rescue farm is in the quiet empty countryside of South Carolina. She has paddocks filled with the rejected creatures that no one wants. The horses are from farms that no longer would or could afford to feed them, so left them to starve. The deer were found as fawns, and foolishly taken by a misguided but kind person from the hiding place the mother had probably left them. The pig was a pet that became too much trouble. The duck was tortured and left with just one leg (Malta named him Pogo.) The pit bull was a mangled fight dog, too aggressive and troubled for anyone else to want to help. The list is endless, as are the food bills, vet bills, and poop piles.

Malta met her husband Will when he came to inquire about one of her rescue horses. He fell in love with the horse, and with Malta. For their honeymoon, they traveled to New Orleans after the devastating Hurricane Katrina left thousands of pets homeless and stranded. Malta and Will began collecting some to return with them to the Land of Lost Pets.

Malta hates breeders, because she believes they contribute to the homeless pet problem. She has little tolerance for people who buy pets on a whim, and have not weighed the cost of the responsibility they now have to that animal. When I asked why she does what she does, she told me, "Animals helped me when I needed it. I can't repay those ones specifically, but I can help other ones."

I don't know exactly what help Malta needed and specifically what those animals had done, but can relate nonetheless. I was a wretchedly shy child who didn't understand small talk, and stood speechless in the midst of crowds where everyone else seemed to know what to say. When something worth uttering occurred to me, my heart pounded so violently that I was sure I would die before the words escaped my mouth. It was better to be silent. I had few friends, but didn't mind too much. I loved to be alone, to draw and paint, to climb trees, and to ride my bike and pretend it was a horse. And I gathered strays and brought them home. Animals replaced the need for people who only frightened and confused me. The animals didn't laugh over stumbled words. They didn't judge my poor taste in clothes or disinterest in fashion or makeup. They were silent nonjudgmental companions. They eased the turmoil from child to adult. I know what Malta means when she professes animals helped her when she needed it most.

The vast majority of animals land at Malta's farm because they are considered unadoptable, mostly due to aggression issues. The remaining five percent are there due to injury or disability. Some of the animals, Malta finds herself. Almost anywhere, if you throw a t-bone in the air, twenty homeless dogs will be on it before it touches the ground. The rural south is a dumping ground for animals people don't want to bother with anymore. Not even having the decency to bring them to a pound, these callous owners drive down a deserted road, open the truck door, and boot the poor animals out to fend on their own.

Many of the animals come to Malta from other rescue sites and shelters. The animals Malta inherits are frequently too much for anyone else to handle. Malta is their last hope. Since 2002, Malta has rescued and placed successfully over five hundred horses, a thousand dogs, and countless other myriad creatures. Even more astonishing, Malta requires that potential adopters go through rigorous examination to prove they will care for these animals, not leave them to live outdoors, and promise not to breed them. She will not let her animals go home to just anyone. The animals are afforded a value by Malta that no one else can initially see or understand.

She offers all adopters free follow up training if needed, and long term boarding for only $10 a day.

She has a pack of about twenty five dogs, some of which she owns, and most are up for adoption. Unlike other rescue centers, these dogs incredibly live in her living room. They all have crates, and new dogs are introduced slowly to the pack but Malta's mission is to completely rehabilitate these tortured creatures in the same setting she will eventually place them - a loving owner's living room. She has cats that are masters at training dogs to become cat-accepting. One cat is utterly unafraid of dogs, and by her sheer disinterest, dissuades many dogs to bother with her. Another cat terrorizes any dog stupid enough to mess with him. One well delivered swat, and most dogs are cured.

The core dog pack itself trains newcomers how to behave with other dogs. If the newcomer does not behave, the pack quickly and swiftly reprimands him in the manner a dog understands. And leader of the pack is indisputably Malta. If all else fails, there is Malta with whip in hand, and her no nonsense demeanor. If a dog is aggressive with a human, or any of her creatures, that dog gets rolled. And while she never hurts the dog, the dog is quite certain it is going to die. Malta rarely has to roll a dog more than once. Honeybun is obviously a persistent bad dog, given she has already been rolled a good hundred times, and is still not cured.

Malta's dog stories can break anyone's heart, except of course the scum that abused or abandoned them in the first place. Those people clearly don't have a heart.

Mimi, the pug arrived in 2001 after a news reporter found her roaming the streets. A story was printed about her and nobody came forward to claim her. She had lost her eye and appeared to have had significant damage to her jaw as well. Mimi is at least fourteen years old, losing her hearing and sight, on heart medication, and still, Malta describes her as a dog "we cherish each day".

I remember the day Malta came home with sweet Melissa, the Pit bull used in dogfights, mangled, aggressive, and in most opinions (including my own initially) irredeemable. When Melissa had kidney failure, Malta called on one of her fine volunteer vets, and panned her supporters for money to try to help Melissa. "Sweet Melissa just can't catch a break," lamented Malta.

She sends her email group of which I am now a member - the friends of Last Chance Rescue - a letter, that speaks volumes about her heart:

Well we have done it now!!

We kept getting emails about a dog with no eyes..... (Yes no eyes) in need of a home. So what better place than

LCR for a dog with no eyes!? We have lots of experience with blind dogs so no big deal to us... But we need help getting her to the farm. We are backlogged with work at our real job and at the farm. We can't find the time to get to the grocery store for human food right now. Thankfully, our weekends have been filled meeting adopters (super thankful for that!)Can anyone help get Peepers to us?

Name your price.... this comes out of our paycheck not the farm funds or donations. We are probably the best chance for Peepers at this point.

Thanks, Malta and Peepers

Fortunately, one of the farm friend's writes back and is able to help Peepers.

There is barely enough money for the farm to survive. Malta is always trying new ways to attract donors, and volunteers, and create income. She and Will install television/audio systems for income. Will is a gifted cabinet/furniture craftsman, and they manage to survive with donations and their small business. As the economy tanks, so do donations, and they are constantly scraping. But one rarely feels that Malta despairs, though surely she must. She writes to me frequently with wonderfully creative ideas for raising money. Many do not pan out as she hopes. She organizes an open house to show everyone what a wonderful place she has but unfortunately, it is poorly attended. Even we are out of town that weekend. She wants to make doggie gift packs to sell to the new adoptive dog parents, and asks if I want to add my art to the gift pack. I agree and tell her a percentage of my sales can go to her farm. We are still broke, but we don't have a hundred mouths to feed.

The ideas never seem to gather traction. A national contest awarding $25,000 to the top rescue site as voted by the public is announced, and Malta pours out emails, asking us all to vote for her and to send her name out to everyone we know. I vote every day. She rises to seventeenth in the state, but nationally, has no hope of winning. I want to help her, and we send donations when we can, but we have little extra money ourselves. With two boys in college now, our funds are helping young brilliant minds go to parties and meet nice girls. On the side, I think they are even attending classes.

And a nagging thought keeps itching in my head..... Money sent to Malta is money that might have gone to feed a hungry child. Is saving a dog to be put on the same level as saving a child? If the dogs and cats and horses are not being fed in this economy, what is happening to the poorer people? We give to charities, and there will never be money enough to eradicate poverty. I know that. Jesus himself said, "The poor you will always have with you..." What would Jesus think of so much money going to save animals? He would surely be pleased to help the donkey that carried him into Jerusalem but I don't recall any other instances of Him hanging with creatures. Well, except for the irrefutable fact that if there were no animals there would have been no manger for his sacred cradle, and our Christmas cards would not have been nearly so charming. And if no one had cared about the needs of camels, it is likely the three wise men would have been carrying the gold, frankincense, and myrrh on their own sweaty backs and may have collapsed before they ever found Him. The song would have to be changed to "We three kings of Orient are, wishing our camels could make it this far…."

Whatever the heavenly plan for animal rescue might be, I am not privy to it. I know that for whatever reason, Honeybun and Malta have been placed in my path. All things happen for a purpose. This vast tapestry of life often is turned from me and I am a lobster crawling across the underside snagging its tangled threads with my scuttling claws. Not only does my crustacean brain fail to comprehend the magnificence of the whole heavenly masterpiece, but in my haste I may be ripping threads with clumsy, sticky feet and perhaps altering it beyond repair. One day perhaps the masterpiece will be revealed and I hope my claw doesn't break smacking my exoskeleton and wondering how I have been so off course. I may want to cure world hunger or stop ice caps from melting, or even be so convincing a witness that the whole world will seek God.... But God seems to have sent me a dying dog to heal first. It seems the prudent choice is to scuttle where I am being led through murky waters.

Right now those murky waters are the threat of financial ruin. When we first found Honeybun, she had a weeping eye and a small sty on her lower left eyelid. As this was the least of her worries with the plethora of urgent health and behavioral issues, we ignored it. I had had sties before, and they were annoying, but always went away on their own.

However, entering our sixth month with Honeybun, the sty remains. It occasionally becomes pus-filled, and she claws at her face. Her eyes are then teary, and eventually the sty opens, drains, and grows small again. But like a telemarketer, it keeps coming back. I don't want it to be there, but have discovered that wishing things are not true rarely works. If that were possible, cellulite would have gone the way of the dinosaurs.

Finally, I decide we have to have it examined. We visit the vet, the sweet woman who had paid half of Honeybun's heartworm test a lifetime ago, in the early AD era (After Dog-rescue). The technician comes in first and asks if, while we are there, we have any other health concerns.

"Yes," I remember, "Sometimes she smells fishy."

He sniffs her.

"Not right now," I explain, "But sometimes it is a strong odor."

"Have you ever heard of anal glands?" he asks.

I have, but I am quite certain I don't want to hear what I fear is about to follow.

"Some dogs have trouble expressing those glands, and they fill up. They need to be manually expressed, in that case."

Lovely. Apparently this most basic of functions is not always automatic in some dogs, and if the glands need expressing, the vet charges $18. Of course this is not a once in a lifetime condition. It is like oil changes on a car, needing to be done about every 3,000 poops or so.

"If they are full, it is a strong odor," he continues, "So I will do it in the back room. I'll have the vet look at her eye as well."

He picks Honeybun up, to our amazement. She hangs in his arms like a sack of potatoes, no growls, or snarls. Just hangs there, with a woebegone look on her face. He carries her into the back room, hoisting his load of dog like a football. Asherel and I sit on our little bench silently. Then we hear a loud exclamation from the back room. Honeybun comes trotting back in, obviously perfumed on her butt.

"They were REALLY full!" he exclaims.

"Is this something that will need to be done regularly?" I ask, cringing a bit.

"I have to bring my dog in once a month," he concurs.

I do the quick math. That adds up to over $200 a year to squeeze out foul smelling goop from my dog's bottom.

"And what about her eye?" I ask the vet, when she enters the room.

She begins punching in numbers, lots of *big* numbers into her computer. She hands me the bill, obviously too kind to want to speak that number out loud. $400-$500, and that's if all goes well. My eyes well up... and I don't have a sty. I suspect if I did, it would cost less than $500 to remove.

"I am sorry," I mourn, tears dribbling, "You all are so kind to me.... but $500. I cannot bear to tell my husband."

I sob then unable to hold back the grief over money we don't have disappearing for a dog we don't know will ultimately be safe, who can't even express her own stupid anal glands. Somehow that seems a cosmic joke of particularly cruel proportion.

"Do you need a hug?" she asks.

I nod, overcoming my own stranger anxiety, and she hugs me. I don't feel a whole lot better, but they do remove the cost for the office visit, saving me $40. As I stand at the counter, paying for the anal gland expression with all the joy that such a procedure fills my heart with, the kind secretary notices my dribbling tears and cries, "Oh no! Is Honeybun okay?"

"Yes," I stutter, "But that teeny little sty will be $500 to remove."

Asherel returns from walking around the store, and doesn't even ask why I am crying. In fact, she asks if I can come see the cute little hat she has found for Honeybun. I laugh through my tears.

We drive home and I cannot stop crying. What will I tell Arvo? Christmas is two months away. The financial crisis in America is battering everyone.... and the dog we have pulled from the brink of death is about to cost $500. The vet warns me that if the sty is not removed, it could hurt Honeybun's cornea. It has to come off.

"Something will come up," promises the ever faithful Asherel.

When we get home, we take the dogs on a walk, and pray for a miracle.

After the walk, I research low cost vets, calling one, but the evaluation alone will be $50. The operation is not going to be a bargain there. Asherel sits in the sunroom doing her math work.

"Don't worry," she calls out, hearing me moaning and muttering, "It will all work out."

In misery, I email Malta. Does she have a suggestion?

"You bet I do!" she fires back. Call her vet, she demands, call before 6:00. They will pick up Honeybun the day before surgery and deposit her back the day after. Her wonderful vet will be far cheaper; she guarantees it.

I call her vet, and ask for Melissa, as Malta has instructed. Melissa, with the sweetest voice I have heard in a long time, tells me they will do it for $150 tops, and only that much if there are problems.

“See?” calls Asherel.

She is busy putting the new hat on Honeybun. This is one of the beauties of home schooling. When finished with math, the student can take a quick break humiliating little dogs with silly hats that she has so much free time to construct.

“Look Mom,” she chortles, “She likes it! She’s smiling.”

I glance up. I don’t see a smile. I see tangled plans to work in the operation, reduced money to cope with all the extra expenses of Christmas, and fishy anal glands exploding in my living room. I also see the limits of my patience for healing both behaviorally and fiscally reaching the end of a short tether. Honeybun *does* look cute in the hat, however.

I email Malta and iron out the details. Will plans to pick Honeybun up Monday, take her to the vet Tuesday, and return her Wednesday. I can't do it all myself, with my teaching schedule and how far away the vet is. Fortunately, Malta's farm and her vet are very close to each other and Will works in Charlotte, very near me, every day this week. Malta insists it will be no problem for him to swing by. It is yet another one of God's incredible marvels of cosmic engineering, though I am still wondering why He feels the need to throw in that anal problem. Honestly, would it really disrupt His grand scheme for one more dog to be able to express her own anal glands? I suppose this is a problem for greater theologians than me.

However, the logistics for the sty removal are proving to be a bit problematic. My Destination Imagination team field trip to Parrot University, a bird rescue is scheduled at exactly the time that Will is planning to get Honeybun. I cannot cancel the fieldtrip. While hating to impose on Malta further, I ask if Will can pick up Honeybun even though we won't be there. He can call her to the backyard, through the dog door and the leash can be left on the front porch.

"*OK*," emails Malta, "*But I am afraid Sticky will bite him*!"

She calls our dog Stickybun because when she first met us, she could not remember Honeybun's name, but knew it had to do with some sort of pastry. She often shortens it to Sticky.

I write back, "*Well if she does bite him, could he punch her in the sty and maybe she won't need the operation*?"

I further instruct her to tell Will to just crawl in through the dog door if Honeybun refuses to come out. He is certainly thin enough.

She writes back:

"If Will can punch her sty off we will only charge you $15 for the procedure..... LMAO!! I am getting a dog with no eyes...... top that..... And another rescue is trying to get a stinky Billy goat in some poor unknowing fool's car to bring here.....

Never a dull day in the world of animal rescue..... I am laughing so hard right now I am crying and punching Stickybun in the sty was the topper...... my side hurts..... And I am picturing Will going through the dog door to get her out of the house..... Too much....

At least there is something to get a good laugh out of no matter what. And don't feel bad about a $150 sty. I just paid $150 for a dog with no eyes! Perhaps she would make a good agility *dog..... Frisbee dog? LMAO! And her name is Peepers! Too much..... Oh too much. And the one legged duck........my side hurts! thanks for adding to the tears of laughter.... sty punch."*

My world crumbles over a $500 vet bill. Meanwhile, Malta soldiers on with her assortment of misfit animals, and finds laughter despite having written the previous week that there was no time or money for "human food", but the animals were well fed. I am certainly humbled by her response, but still sick of the stream of mishaps. How much longer am I expected to hang on? What new maladies are yet to appear? There are at least a thousand parts in a dog and any one of them could break. Many of them have, but there are lots more to go. She is still barking like a maniac at the door. She still wants to devour salesmen. She still can't be trusted with other dogs. And she smells like rotten fish. I ask Malta if while she is caring for Honeybun, she can teach her how to express her anal glands.

I dream that night about being in college again, but unable to find my classroom, or my schedule.... It is right before Finals, and I have not even read the books. Completely unprepared for what awaits me, I am never going to pass on my own power. The meaning is obvious. If I go away to college, someone else can save this stupid dog.

At the sixth rally class, Lloyd watches Honeybun sail through the course with confidence, prancing attentively next to Asherel. It is his "Halloween course", designed to flummox all the unsuspecting novices, but Asherel does well. And Honeybun, focused on the cheese, is flawless. As she finishes the course, Lloyd reminds me, "Be sure to go online to our website this week. The applications come out for Performance sports, and that class fills fast."

"Performance sports?!" I snap, “But we want to do Agility next."

"There is some talk about requiring Performance before Agility class."

Oh brother. My plan to sashay to an accomplished agility dog for less than $1000 is crumbling faster than our roof, which needed to be replaced at least a year ago. Each class is $100, and I had hoped we could get away with just one more. Vicci, Lloyd's wife will be teaching the Agility class. She overhears my reasoned, patient response.

"Performance is a good class," she admonishes gently, “It will help you."

So will a face transplant but you don’t see me racing off to get one of those do you? I am sorely disappointed. We cannot afford endless classes. Vicci had spoken with me during the last lesson about the agility class she was starting. It would be outdoors, at night, under the frigid winter stars, but I was willing to stand there in the cold for my girl. After one more class, we can apply for membership at the Dog Club, which hosts the classes, and future classes will be half price. That will allow us to take the final (I hope) class called Foundations 2, after which we will have a fully trained agile dog. We will then start traveling around the country with Honeybun in her gold plated crate, collecting ribbons like flies. Asherel will become rich and famous, and Arvo and I will retire and watch reruns of Star Trek while sipping expensive wine.

Now yet another hurdle is being thrown in our path. Not only is there the added expense of yet another intermediary class, but Performance Sports class fills up within nanoseconds of being posted. If we don't get in, that means we have to wait another several months for it to be offered again.... and then a good half year before agility. Dogs' lives are short. Honeybun is in her prime now. I have to find a way to get her in agility classes. While contemplating how large a bribe to offer, I watch our dog distractedly. Honeybun is oblivious to the high drama swirling around her. Asherel parades her through Lloyd's "evil" course with slack leash. Honeybun's attention is fully on Asherel (or to be more exact, on the food Asherel holds tantalizingly close to her nose), and she prances like she is an AKC dog. Her tail is fully erect, flashing its gold and mocha blend like a sail in the sun. She is a gloriously pretty little dog. As she scampers off the course, Asherel praises her and she bows her head, and flattens her ears, the way she always does in her humble acceptance of lavish praise. Her sweet dark eyes gaze up at Asherel. I know the look of adoration has more to do with the cheese in Asherel's hand than the attachment to her human, but nonetheless, it is touching.

The huge Borzoi dog with its knifelike snout, wearing a pumpkin hat for Halloween, sticks his razor sharp face in hers. She looks at him and wags. Now before I grow too cocky about her progress, it is possible she doesn't realize it is a dog, and mistakes him for a garden trowel. Still, her transformation is certainly advancing. The big hurdle remaining is how to get her in an agility class. Asherel doesn't complain, but has asked when we will be able to take a real agility class. She tells me Honeybun can't wait much longer.

When we get home, I return to my trusty computer and do a Google search on Agility Training in the Charlotte region. The first facility has closed its program as the trainer has moved to Mexico. More jobs fleeing our punitive taxes on entrepreneurs, I grumble. The next one is further away- a full forty minutes. This trainer is a little more expensive, and when I call, tells me that it usually takes a full year for a dog to be ready to compete in Agility trials.

"You mean take a class, and then practice for a year?" I clarify.

"No, I mean a year of classes."

I do the math quickly. That will cost more than the original estimate for removing Honeybun's sty. What a racket this dog training trap is! These trainers are making more than the president of the United States on an hourly basis. I know there is no way we can do a year of classes. I look for the loophole, the shortcut, the lazy dog out.

"Does everyone take classes for a year? How about if the dog and owner are really smart and really diligent? Could they just learn the rules, take a class, and do it on their own?"

In my heart, I am sure I know the answer to that. I am a homeschooling mom. I know that teachers are a luxury, but that a motivated student can learn anything on her own, given enough initial guidance and resources. There are a few exceptions.... like brain surgery. It might be good to have at least a few classes to master that. But Agility training is not brain surgery. We can get the final few materials Asherel needs for her agility course out back. She has already built weave poles, dog walk, jumps, see saw, tunnel, and pause table. All she needs are the tire jumps and A-frame. The rules are all posted on-line. I am confident that with one class, she could do it.

"Some people do take breaks between classes," says Deborah, the trainer, “It just depends on how motivated the dog and the owner are in how quickly they advance." She doesn’t seem very convinced that anyone with less than a doctorate in Agility has a ghost of a prayer of entering a trial successfully though.

I explain to Deb how exceptionally motivated Asherel is; how she has built an entire agility course herself. Upon learning that Asherel has done this at the ripe old age of eleven, Deb seems impressed enough that she suggests a half hour private lesson to assess whether Asherel might already know enough to skip right into Beginner Two class. Now she is talking my language. I would prefer she offer to put her immediately in the Expert Class, but am willing to back off for now.

Meanwhile, as I plot her future, Asherel is out back with the dogs, developing her new "doggy play corner". I glance out back. Honeybun and Lucky are each sitting on a lounge chair, watching Asherel as she rakes a path in the small bamboo forest. The chairs are padded, and the dogs are leaning back eyes half closed. All they need is a cigar in their mouths and a Mimosa in their paws. Along the path, Asherel has set up a "doggy restaurant"- a tall table with snacks on it. The dogs stand on their hind legs, paws on the restaurant bar, choose a treat, and then are escorted to a clearing with a pad where they lie down and eat the chosen morsel. This is a far cry from the earth den Honeybun had probably been huddling in against the rain just a few months back. Some kids Asherel's age are doing drugs and piercing places where sharp pins have no right to be poking. Maybe $1000 for agility classes is not a bad exchange.

On our next free Saturday afternoon, with great excitement, Asherel, Honeybun, and I drive to Deborah's home, where she runs her small business with the agility course in her backyard. We pull into the driveway, and stretched before us is a field with nighttime spotlights, and agility equipment sparkling with the allure of diamonds. It is Nirvana to my daughter. Honeybun sniffs the air. Dogs live here, that is clear to her, and there are treats in Asherel's bag. No doubt this will be more entertaining than the recent vet trip. As we get out of the car, Deborah greets us. She wisely ignores Honeybun, and opens the backyard gate for Asherel. Honeybun sniffs the yard, nostrils dilated and sucking in great gulps of air, redolent with the scent of dogs having fun. Even treats don't bring her nose away from the cacophony of doggish smells emanating from every blade of grass.

Deborah first instructs Asherel to send Honeybun over the jumps. Somehow, with her nose hugging the ground, Honeybun easily hops over the line of three jumps. Next, Deborah directs them to the weave poles. The weave poles are six to twelve vertical poles closely spaced, and the dog needs to weave in and out of them in sequence as quickly as possible. Honeybun slowly weaves, with great difficulty. Deborah brings out a wire guide and everything changes. Honeybun whips through the weave poles. I snap several photos, knowing we will need to build a similar wire guide. Next she has Honeybun scamper up the A-frame. The A-frame is a steep inverted V structure, which the dog climbs and descends, being sure to touch all four paws on the bottom third (painted yellow) before leaping off. Asherel is instructed to have Honeybun sit as she reaches the bottom, at which point she is richly rewarded with treats. In a trial, she would be disqualified if all four paws did not touch the bottom yellow section. Honeybun rockets up the A- frame easily, and fairly quickly learns to sit at the bottom of the descent. She shows no fear, which Deb seems to think is a good thing. Her only fear is that we might forget to feed her dinner, but I keep that to myself.

The next apparatus is the tunnel. Honeybun has practiced on the much smaller tunnel we have at home, so despite the triple length, she easily zips through the tunnel. Well, she doesn't actually zip. With how long it takes her to emerge, I suspect she was foraging for food somewhere in the middle part, but she does eventually saunter out. Next, she has to do the Dog walk - a thin plank suspended high in the air with an up and down slender ramp to get on and off. For months, every time we went to a nearby park, Asherel had practiced making Honeybun climb on thin metal bleachers there. I had had no idea she was preparing her for a Dog walk. I peer at this determined little girl. As a result of all that preparation with the bleachers, Honeybun gleefully prances across the Dog walk though it is the first time she has ever stepped on one. I watch Asherel with deepening respect. She has been doggedly working towards this goal quietly and persistently, even beyond what I had seen. Despite all her reticence and quietness, she has been busily building a bridge to a dream.

The teeter is the most challenging. The dog has to walk across a plank until it pivots, where she pauses to let it tip slowly, and then walks down, again being sure all paws touch the yellow bottom third. Honeybun quickly learns the pivot point, and then cavorts down the slope to collect her treat.

The final apparatus is the chute. This is a tunnel with a collapsed silk chute. The dog has to fly through the tunnel and then the chute, billowing it open with her body as she runs through. I thought this would disturb her, having never done it, but she passes through with no fear. I have always loved this apparatus - it is like watching a snake swallow and disgorge a dog.

The half hour session is quickly ending, and Deb's husband has come out to watch. Deb turns to me, "Well, she has mastered the level one class already. She would fit right in with the Beginner Two class, starting in three weeks. If you are interested, I want to bring my dog out, and watch how Honeybun responds to another dog moving quickly."

Deb emerges from her house with a delightful, exuberant border collie. The little collie races across the yard, flying over the apparatus. Honeybun is interested, but calm, and still. She shows no aggression, and remains peacefully still, with slack leash at Asherel's side.

"She is fine," asserts Deb's husband. Deb nods. Honeybun has passed all tests. Asherel, cheeks pink with the cooling evening and exertion looks confident and happy. Classes start in three weeks, and Honeybun has catapulted past the beginner class. All we have to do is send the check. We are one step closer to Asherel's dream. Honeybun is just happy to be heading home to dinner which is an hour overdue.

Things begin to snowball now. The very next day, Carolyn offers us a tire jump, since her son's good intentions for agility training with their dog evaporated in direct relationship to his flood of interest in karate. Asherel and Arvo traipse to Lowes Home Improvement store with her drawings and list of the last few things she needs to complete her backyard agility course. She has gone on-line to research exact dimensions. Arvo, off of a 60+ hour work week is less than thrilled as we head off to Lowes. We assure him that in the long run, making the equipment will save us money. He grumpily acquiesces. It is not his idea of a relaxing weekend. Asherel clutches her list and does not back down.

"I will pay for it," she offers. She is nothing, if not determined.

Arvo studies her sketch of the A-frame.

"This is 9 feet tall!" he exclaims.

She nods.

"No," he counters, "We can't have a 9 foot tall thing in the middle of our backyard."

Asherel glances at me. I can tell she is fighting back tears, but she stands her ground bravely, "The dogs have to practice on the same stuff they will compete on."

"Was the one at Deborah's that big?" I ask.

"Yes," insists Asherel.

"Well, she won't need a full size one to learn how to do it," I advise gently, “Look at how well she did with Deb's tunnel which was 3 times bigger than the one you trained her on."

Asherel is silent. She knows how to use a pregnant silence to full advantage.

Arvo sighs.

"Let's go," he says resignedly, "We will find a way to make this work."

Plywood pieces are eight foot long, so Asherel is willing to concede a foot. She has worked out her supply list with amazing accuracy, down to the eyebolts, hinges, and chains she will need. She selects bright purple and yellow paint.

"Do you have to paint it two colors?" argues Arvo.

"Yes," persists Asherel, "The bottom third is yellow. That is the contact zone. The dog knows all its paws have to touch there." (I wonder *how* they knew that, being as dogs are color blind, but Asherel is doing so well wrapping us around her little finger that I do not bother to ask.)

$135 later, we walk out of the store. Arvo is ominously silent. I suspect he is beginning to add up how much this "free" dog is costing us, and is not liking how many times he is carrying numbers to columns parading leftward. However, as he unloads the purchases, he begins to metamorphosize. He likes to build things. It is dark, but he advises Asherel to come out with him now and they will get the A-frame started to the point where she can do the rest herself. By porch light, they install the hinges, the eyebolts, and the chain to keep it from collapsing. They finish the bright red taping of the weave poles.

With still a half hour till bedtime, Asherel collects some green material and the sewing machine, and makes Honeybun an elf cap. The Kennel Club is having Christmas photos taken for the dog's graduation from class next week. Asherel will wear a Santa hat, but she wants Honeybun to be an elf, her helper. The little green cap with its zigzag edges, bell on top, and elastic to hold it on is a work of art. Honeybun raises a sleepy head as Asherel tries it on her. She looks at me, the bell on her hat slightly jingling.

She does not seem at all nonplussed by wearing an elf cap. She had accepted with equanimity the little doggy sweater Asherel made a few weeks ago, complete with the embroidered words, "Dogmatic Dingo" on the side. Honeybun has become the model of patient sufferance. She seems to have an uncanny grasp of what is worth getting upset about. A dog stealing dinner is worth killing over, but wearing an elf hat is only a minor annoyance.

We are already gone to our field trip on the day Will comes to pick Honeybun up for her sty removal. We return home to Lucky, alone, looking a little confused, but happy to see us. We are amazed at how silent the house is without the excited prancing and clicking of Honeybun's toenails on the wood floor. No waggling wildly gyrating body, licking us for the only moment of the day that her enthusiasm becomes so overwhelming that she has to lick. I write to Malta:

"Help! Someone has kidnapped our valuable Carolina Dog! Do you have any knowledge of the perpetrator of this crime? The only evidence we see is a trail of blood leading from the dog door."

Malta writes back that she has effectively proven our house can be easily burglarized.

"Honeybun barked, and then ran, and Will grabbed her. Lucky just stood by watching... no barking, no attempt to save his sister. So much for your attack dog biting the intruder."

I guess every victory involves a loss. She continues with her email, telling me Honeybun is mingling with the other dogs, like she has always been there. Malta will bring her to the vet in the morning.

Meanwhile, we have little time to worry about the morning and Honeybun's upcoming ordeal. The next day is Election Day, and I have run a Kids' Voting booth for fifteen years. Asherel and I are volunteering all day on this historic Election Day. As an American, I am always excited by the blessing of freedom and being able to vote. I call the vet midday, and am assured all has gone well, Honeybun is fine, and on her way back to Malta's. I am instructed to put some antibiotic cream in her eye four times a day, and take her back to our Charlotte vet for the stitches out in two weeks.

Will returns Honeybun the following morning. She looks fine, with just a little swelling in the eyelid. We watch her carefully to see whether she needs the Elizabethan torture collar to keep her from scratching out her stitches. Alas, she starts rubbing at her eye, and we have to put the collar on. That is easy compared to putting the antibiotic goop in her eye. I cuddle her on my lap and put her head under my arm in a vise grip. She looks at me woefully, but is silent and still. I squeeze a drop in, and the sweet, long-suffering Honeybun blinks and lays still for whatever further torture I might care to inflict.

That evening, she will be required to wear her elf hat for her Christmas portrait. She lays her head down as the big plastic cone around her neck rustles, and heaves a long deep sigh. I hope she is not remembering fondly the good old days when ticks in the ear and starvation were the only atrocities she had to suffer.

When we were first dealing with all the issues of aggression, and working with Malta regularly, eager to heal everything and be done, I asked her countless times when we would overcome completely whatever issue we happened to be discussing. How will I know when I can let her loose when strangers arrive....how will I know when I can feed the dogs with Honeybun off leash.....how will I know when she will be safe to let children pet her....etc?

Malta, with barely restrained patience sighs and tells me, "You will just know. I can't tell you when that will happen for you. But you will know."

Yes, but what should I look for? What behavior will be the tip off? How long do such cases typically take?

"You will just know," Malta repeats. I know from what she has often said about how she has to be diplomatic with all the idiots in the world, that at these moments, I am another one of these babbling idiots. It doesn't matter. I do not need Malta's approval as much as I need a checklist. Tell me what to expect and when, and let me check it off. It works for groceries, and household chores. Surely it holds true for killer dogs.

Sigh. "Vicky, if it were me, I would let her off right now. But if it makes you nervous, you need to wait till you are not nervous or she will pick up on that and do exactly the awful thing you expect her to do. Trust me. You will know."

I know I do not look convinced.

"You will learn to read her body language," Malta offers.

Finally, while Honeybun's eye is recuperating, her top-heavy cone head drooping in the E-collar, I just *know* at last! I can feed the dogs separated, but off leash. After all, even if Honeybun attacks Lucky, the cone will smash into him and her teeth will not even get close. I put down Honeybun's bowl, and guide her cone around the bowl. It is very sad to watch her try to eat her food with the cone on if no one helps her. She has to center it exactly right on the bowl, or she is stopped a tantalizing few inches from the food, by the edge of the cone resting on the bowl. Sometimes as she struggles to reach it she tips the bowl over. I center her and shove her head into the food, and then call Lucky to his corner of the kitchen and put down his food. He looks pointedly at me, and then at Honeybun, and starts to run away. If he had full command of English, he would be saying, "You idiot! Do you not remember how that she-devil tried to kill me over my kibbles just three short months ago? Have you lost your mind? Why is she not restrained?"

I catch Lucky and bring him back to his food. He eats, with one eye on Honeybun. She finishes, and with the telltale whapping sound of her cone crashing into the wall as she turns from her food, Lucky is out the dog door. Honestly, I cannot blame him. He clearly does not trust her off leash.

The next day, while putting down Lucky's food as he prepares to run, I add some chicken broth to his bowl. He loves chicken broth. If it were to be his last meal, so be it, he says, as he settles down to eat.

Honeybun finishes- she always finishes first, and then thwaps her cone head into the wall, and sits down. She looks at me, and then stares at Lucky. She doesn’t get up, or approach him, but her unblinking gaze never wavers. Lucky slurps up the last morsels, licks his bowl, and turns away. Honeybun then walks over to the empty bowl. I cheer. She clearly understands she is not to go near his bowl till he finishes, and she shows no aggression. I honestly had thought she would never be trustworthy around food. This is bountiful grace and mercy to a poor stumbling fool! I am feeling so confident, I may even be ready to try poaching an egg, a skill that is tantalizingly elusive.

Meanwhile, as the dreary cone-head days drag interminably on, Asherel continues working on the A-frame. She glues the struts on, and then Arvo helps her set it up so she can paint. The top 2/3rds will be a lovely purple, and the "contact zone" a bright lemon yellow. It is a glorious fall day.

She is intently measuring and drawing; the paint cans at her side. I take the dogs on a walk, to give Honeybun a respite from her e-collar, and upon returning notice that Asherel has completed the purple section. After I read the paper, I peek out and the yellow contact zone is painted. I wonder what the neighbors are thinking, watching the lawn slowly metastasizing into something out of the Animal Planet channel. Right on our border stands the eight foot A-frame, bright purple and yellow. Hopefully the neighbors will think of it as modern art.

The next to last rally class day arrives, and despite her newly stitched eye, Honeybun is anxious and happy to go to class. Picture day! She trots in, wearing the green elf cap Asherel has made her, and Asherel is dressed in her Santa hat and red and green holiday sweater. This is my shy, fade into the woodwork daughter. The transformation is not just happening to the wild dingo.

It is also the day for the official rally test, with Lloyd scoring the contestants on an official rally course and official rally sheet. Honeybun, with her weeping stitched eye and elf cap is certainly not in top condition for this.

"Ready?' asks Lloyd to Santa Asherel and Elf Honeybun.

"Ready," declares Santa confidently. There is a little jingle as the elf glances up and nods.

Honeybun prances next to Asherel, her elf hat tinkling. It is a demanding course, with spirals, and "fronts" and "finishes".... and 270 degree turns..... Asherel looks imperturbable in her Santa hat. As she trots off the course, Lloyd hands her the score. She receives a single one point deduction because Honeybun sat before lying down on the down command, but otherwise, a perfect score.

It is hard not to fall to my knees and stretch my arms heavenward. Little victories are all the sweeter for having been fought so recently with so little hope of success. The little wild dog wags her tail as I nuzzle against her. Asherel smiles, giving her some cheese.

With the paint dry on the giant A-frame, it is time to test it. Asherel and I excitedly hurry out and hoist it upright from its side-lying position, hooking the chain on one side to keep it at the steep angle. It promptly falls over. We look at each other. Accompanied with the inconvenient tendency of not remaining upright, it flexes when any weight is put on it. Asherel is crestfallen. All that time, effort, and planning to no avail. Oh bitter reality. However she is not one to give in easily to despair. This is surprising considering the genes she has received on her maternal side.

“We could nail a support board on the bottom to hold it upright," she suggests.

I suspect we need another whole piece of plywood nailed to the bottom of each section, and a support on the bottom. Honeybun is curious though and wants to walk up it. She tries, but it is so slick, and steep, and wobbly, that she slides right off.

"And we need sand in the paint," adds Asherel.

She had told Arvo earlier she needed sand to give the dog traction, and he told her she could scoop it up out of the dirt where the sand box used to be. Asherel was silent. Later, as I tucked her into bed that night, she piped up quietly, "Mom, won't the dirt in the sand make the paint dirty?"

"Yes," I whispered, "We can find you a small bag of clean sand." She smiled and snuggled into her covers, her vision still intact.

But for now, the A-frame is not working. The required fixes seem endless, the process never ending. The parallel between the dog equipment and the dog rehabilitation is too obvious to miss. Doesn't God ever get sick of sending messages about patience and perseverance? Isn't once enough?

"I think it is too steep for her to start on," I offer.

So we try lying it across the little doghouse we bought years ago that Lucky never uses, which supports its middle, and keeps the slope gradual, more doable for the scrambling dog. Honeybun successfully navigates on the more gentle slope and even Lucky climbs it though with less alacrity. It is not ideal, but it will suffice for now.

Meanwhile, I am busily planning a field trip for my Sunday school class of sixth grade girls. We are going to Last Chance Rescue, to do whatever Malta needs doing. Ten kids have already signed up, and I write Malta joyfully, eager to give back in some small way all she has done for us.

"*Okey dokey*," she replies, "*I will have snacks and juice for the kids, vodka and brie for the adults.*"

Should I tell her to study some phrases without swear words in them? Nah... to ask Malta to stifle any part of her might destroy the totality of her effect. An alpha wolf can't go soft, or in the canine world, she will be eaten. I know it will be an experience these young ladies will never forget, and having never been to the farm yet myself, am very eager to see this haven of last chances, this place where the creatures no one wants find home.

Dear Lord,

I have been so impatient for success, and you have been granting it all along, slowly…I begin to understand that sometimes you can't rush growth. I suppose that would be like you closing the door to heaven right now, with so many people who don't know Jesus and don't know the path He lights to you. It was really not so long ago that I was blind, didn't see you, didn't even want to. But you waited for me and beckoned to me, and persistently held a lantern to light my way. If you had lost patience, I would have remained lost.

How easily I fall prey to despair, when things don't seem to go along the path I had envisioned, or the obstacles are too many and too unfamiliar. Ha! I never really thought of how my journey is like Honeybun learning to run the agility course. None of those obstacles or convoluted paths must make sense to her... and her progress is slow and she is often stymied. But she is learning that if she keeps her eye on her master, she will be guided and directed. I take my eyes off of you too often Lord. I hit the first obstacle and lose faith that you can guide me even over this! I cry and despair, and look at that frightening path before me and all the obstacles yet to scale.... And want to lie down and scratch fleas.

And you have been so gentle reminding me that every hair of my head is numbered, every step that I stumble has been counted, and every trial that I face has strengthened me and helped me understand a little better the One I am however so poorly staggering towards.

Help me keep my eyes on you Jesus, as I run the course.

Amen

PS: I think we have learned the lesson about how to be poor. What about the lesson on how to be rich? I think I am ready for that one now.

CHAPTER 9

Persistence

The last day of Rally Class arrives. Honeybun's graduation treat, meatballs, are carefully sliced and packed. She still has another day of the E-collar, and then stitches come out, and she will be a graduate of both novice rally, and coneheadness. She dances around my feet, sniffing the air, and salivating with the meatball scent drifting through the house. Asherel is sure she knows this is rally night.

"Dogs have a finely developed sense of time," she informs me.

Whatever. Certainly not worth arguing the merits of that observation. I send Asherel out with the dog, the meatballs, and the keys to the car.

"Load her up," I say, "And I will give Lucky this bone so he doesn't feel left out."

Asherel and Honeybun trot into the night. I feed Lucky the bone which he finishes before I reach the car. I know that, since he is already out the dog door and at the back fence watching us with accusatory eyes as we back out. He really has nothing to complain about. Since Honeybun entered our lives, we now do at least two walks a day, and often three. He is trained in agility by the indefatigable Asherel right after Honeybun's session, and he has had some discipline instilled in his sorely wanting character. And while her companionship was not necessarily on the plus side of the ledger until recently, Honeybun now likes him, and he likes her. While we are pack members, we don't speak the language and for all her history of malice towards him, she *does* know what he is saying in his native tongue. He rarely attempts escapes from the yard anymore, suggesting that he is happier with what he now finds in his fenced-in world. They often sit together in front of the glass door, watching the passersby, and with united ear splitting barks, practice breaking the sound barrier.

"Got the meatballs?" I ask.

"Yep," she asserts, and adds, "Look Mom! She knows where we are going. She is smiling!"

I glance in the mirror. I don't see a smile. I see dog hair and dirt all over the seat she is on, and I see endless Wednesday nights devoted to endless expensive classes when my heart longs for long soaking baths and inspiring books about patience and kindness.

When we arrive, Asherel begins to gather her things and asks for the light so she can find the meatballs.

"Where are the meatballs?" she asks, sunshine still sparkling in her voice.

I freeze.

"You told me you had the meatballs," I accuse.

"They must be here," she says cheerfully, and proceeds to rip through the many "emergency" items always stored under seats - blankets, jackets, mittens, jack knives, hand cranked radios, ropes, tool kits, flashlights, plastic bags....... everything except meatballs.

"I know they are here," she calls muffled beneath the pile, a little less confidently.

I hop into the back and forage through the piles of useful items. Nowhere is the one item of use.... the meatballs are clearly not in the car.

Honeybun is watching us, trusting us, wagging at us, knowing that this is the place where she gets fed a gazillion delectable treats. This is the highlight of her week. She is happy to be alive.

"She does like praise," pipes Asherel hopefully.

Not as much as meatballs.... the meatballs she thinks we are bringing. For some reason, it is almost the saddest thing I have seen yet in all the traumas she has endured, watching her prance in, her eyes riveted on Asherel, head eagerly raised. The meatball scent is still on Asherel's hands and Honeybun senses the specialness of this graduation night. She has worked hard over the past two months and she seems to understand tonight is a celebration. Of course, any night when meatballs are on the menu is a celebration for a dog.

There is a festive air, the soon to be graduate dogs all expertly going through the various courses and classes. There are sign- up sheets for next class, class evaluations to be filled out, and excited chatter about the AKC dog show that weekend.

Asherel and I are subdued.... the unsuspecting Honey still prancing.

"Go on and practice the course," urges Lloyd.

"What do I do about treats?" she asks me quietly.

"There isn't much you can do," I lament, "Just do your best."

Both she and I are devastated. What is supposed to be the glorious last night of class is suddenly going to be one of disappointment and torture to the little dog I had fed only half a dinner in expectation of the volumes of meatballs she would consume. Funny how life can swing on the hinge of a meatball.

Asherel takes Honeybun out on the course, and she is perfect, going through her paces with her eyes still glued on

Asherel. I can't bear to watch.

"She's doing great," commends the kind lady who owns Max, the corgi.

"Yes, for now," I agree, "But we lost our snacks for tonight so I don't know for how long."

Lloyd overhears me, "All of them?"

"Yes," I admit miserably, "They must have fallen out of the car when we got in."

In a flicker of an eye, three people have poured goodies into Asherel's hand. These are not just any old snack. These are graduation night "high value cookies." Asherel beams and thanks them all profusely. I can barely speak, and blink several times. Something must have gotten in my eyes, maybe angel dust.

While Asherel and Honeybun go through the course, I overhear Lloyd telling Nina, the assistant instructor, what a shame it is that Honeybun cannot do AKC rally that weekend. Meanwhile, I chat with Vicci, his wife who will be leading the agility class in January. They have decided to allow people to take the agility class without a prerequisite.

We had told Deb we would join her class, but now, watching my daughter with her pockets bulging with the offerings of her compassionate classmates, I wanted more than anything to be able to reach our goal with them watching. I thought Deb would understand.

"Is it too late to get in the agility class?" I ask. Vicci and Lloyd assure me they will get my application in on time.

Vicci warns me that we should work on clicker use for her class. Asherel had just informed me that clickers are essential for agility. Neither of us knows why, but we are obedient students who will dutifully get the clicker.

We admit we don't have one yet, but intend to get one tomorrow. A few minutes later, she hands Asherel a brand new clicker she'd had in the car, telling her it is an extra one. Honeybun rubs against Vicci, as Asherel clutches the clicker and smiles. It is very kind of Vicci, but already I am thinking of all the practice we now have to fit in on clicker use. We will just have to find the time. What can I cut out? Maybe I could clean the toilets just *once* a month. It is a huge sacrifice of course, but the goal is worthy.

Now with the meatball crisis averted, class is indeed a celebration. Honeybun and Asherel eagerly navigate the rally course, effervescent with success. At the end, Lloyd brings out a big bag of dog toys and invites the happy graduates to all pick one. Asherel picks a yellow stuffed star and throws it to Honeybun, who does not know how to play. Honeybun lunges at it, and throws it joyfully in the air. Then she tosses it and catches it in her paws, and skitters across the floor with it. She is so delightedly engaged with it, that when it is her turn to do the course one last time, she won't leave her toy. Instead of treats for her victory lap, the toy keeps her slack leashed at Asherel's side, sitting, staying, downing, circling, spiraling, and finishing with her tail straight up and wagging, a clarion of triumph and joy.

"Before we dismiss," said Nina, "There is one special award I would like to give."

We all turn to her, Lloyd smiling beside her. Honeybun is busily removing the stuffing from her star. Asherel and I are transfixed by the incredulous vision of our dog playing.

"For the award of Most Improved - Honeybun!"

What? We look up stunned. Honeybun has stuffing hanging out of her mouth. Nina pulls out a stuffed pig dog toy and hands it to Asherel. I barely recognize the smiley-faced, grateful, confident little girl that accepts her award and then hands it to her dog. Honeybun throws the pig in the air and then pounces on it, vigorously chewing, then tossing again, and ripping at it with her paws in exuberant delight.

"Maybe," smiles Nina, "When she is done with it you can collect the pieces and put them on her trophy shelf."

Collecting pieces to put on trophy shelves. I like that

symbol very much - every ugly little piece, lovingly collected and put in a place of honor.

Honeybun is like a flower whose hard shell of spring bud has been discarded and the glorious unfolding of the true nature within bursts forth in all its beauty. Her coat is smooth and sleek, her newly cleared eyes, sparkling. Her worried brow furrows less and less. She often explodes now into a frenzy of playfulness, finding a toy and bringing it to us hopefully. After a tug of war, she lets us take it and throw it for endless games of retrieval. She paws at Lucky, trying to lure him into a chase. He complies briefly, but still is not ready to trust her, and at her first playful growl, he stops.

Agility training continues in our backyard Mecca. We decide it would be wise to take a few private classes with Deborah, the expert agility instructor, in preparation for the Agility class at our training club. Deb promises to teach Asherel enough that we should be able to do the more advanced class with our increasingly beloved dog club. Asherel proposes she will pay for the classes herself, and lines up some dog sitting jobs to be able to do so.

I ask Deb if after this private work and the one class we will be ready to do an official Agility Trial. She laughs. I ask Vicci the same thing. She winces. I ask Honeybun, who then digs a snout pit and goes to sleep. Asherel just shrugs.

This wait and see attitude is shortening my life by the minute. Nonetheless, I have to admit the slow unfolding of a miracle has enjoyable moments. The slow crescendo of accomplishment edging towards fulfillment is not as easy to endure as instant victory, but maybe produces a deeper contentment.

Meanwhile, twenty girls have now signed up for the Sunday school field trip to Malta's farm by the time the day arrives. The drive is long, an hour and a half, but the first catastrophe is quickly dealt with. One girl had not brought her lunch - a miscommunication or missed email.... and was dangerously about to dissolve in tears. Fortunately, I have recently started keeping a gallon baggie of food in the car to hand out to homeless people, so I raid my homeless food bag, and the tears are stopped in their tracks. Within a few minutes we are in the boondocks. Malta's farm is situated in the middle of Nowhere, South Carolina. We pass small, sleepy, ramshackle towns, and soon are driving through farmland and pastures. The fall leaves, while past their peak, are still lovely on this crisp autumn sunny day, and the girls are content playing a car alphabet game.

Our caravan of girls finally lumbers onto Malta's farm. There are rolling, open pastures, forested at the perimeter, dotted with horses. I take a deep breath of the clean air, and listen happily to the silence, no sounds of industry, or traffic. But as I slam the car door, at least twenty dogs begin barking in an assortment of octaves. Big dogs boom and little dogs yip. We pile out of the car, and Malta emerges from her home with a sweet-faced brown dog on leash. I am changing into my muck boots as the girls gather around her. The girls have brought dog food, carrots, and donations. Horses and cows and goats are picturesquely dappling the fields. It is a bucolic world. The girls run happily towards the dog and Malta.

Malta snaps sternly, "This is a working farm, with animals in varying stages of rehabilitation. There will be no loud screaming, shouting, or running, and if you go anywhere I have not explicitly permitted you to go, you will likely die."

The girls screech to a halt and ask if they can pet the dog. As they quietly, respectfully pet the little brown dog, Malta tells them, "This is Melissa. She was used as a fighter dog. She was covered with wounds in both body and spirit when she came to us."

This sweet little dog letting twenty girls pet her is a pit bull, I realize walking over, having donned my boots. While claiming to be open-minded, I hold deep prejudice against pit bulls. I certainly don't advocate cruelty towards them, but see no reason for them to exist. I have similar feelings about pistol shrimp that stun victims by creating a sound louder than a jet engine. Why mar creation with that kind of creature? Or the blue ringed octopus, the deadliest per square inch creature on earth. Its body is less than 5 cm. long, yet carries enough venom to kill 26 adult humans within minutes. Pit bull jaws have the force of 1500 pounds per square inch. In laymen's terms, this means they can bite through concrete. In my opinion, this is overkill. *No one* needs jaws that strong.

Yet, I can tell just by looking at Sweet Melissa that my blanket condemnation of the breed might be unfair. Her almond eyes are gentle, and her little tail thumps ferociously as she licks the girls. I know that just three months ago, she had been the dog Malta had dragged home, furious with the callous owners that had trained her to fight other dogs. I understand why Malta chooses Melissa to be her greeting committee. Nothing, she is telling us, *nothing* created by God is irredeemable. All creatures deserve a chance at life and love, and our preconceptions about worth are about to be shattered. I hope and pray she doesn't rescue Blue Ringed Octopi as well.

One girl points to the long horse whip in Malta's hand.

"What is that for?" she asks.

"I use it on children who run or shout when I have told them not to," she quips. Some of the kids gulp.

"Nah," she laughs," I just use it to guide a dog out of the way, or warn an animal that is not behaving."

She hands the leash to Will and asks him to return Sweet Melissa to her crate. Then she asks if anyone needs to use the bathroom. Several of us peanut bladder folk raise our hands, a little timidly, subdued by the whip.

"Now," barks Malta, "There are twenty dogs in the house. Do not reach out and touch them. There is a little cute Chihuahua on the couch. If you touch her, she *will* bite you. We will go in groups of four." It sounds like we are commandos infiltrating enemy territory.

I enter with trepidation, envisioning circling sharks ready to devour in a feeding frenzy at the first sign of blood. Malta walks in with us, long whip in hand. The dogs sniff, and some wag. I squelch my natural desire to pet them, knowing the folly of disobeying Malta. There are dogs everywhere, but surprisingly, Malta's house is spotless. It does not smell like a farm, or dirty dogs. The dogs are clean, and the floors are scrubbed. I cannot imagine how she manages this with twenty dogs.

One girl points to a large multicolored dog and asks, "What kind is that?"

"That," exclaims Malta proudly, "Is a Great American Black, White, and Brown Dog." The girl looks impressed.

Gathered again out front, she commands, "Now I will take you to meet the farm animals. Now notice there is a band of cloth at the top of the fences. That is electrified. If you touch it, you will be electrocuted. While that is quite entertaining, I would not recommend it."

We all walk to the fence, and the girls wisely choose to stay about ten feet from it. Malta nickers and the herd gallops to the fence. One of the adults in amazement whispers to me, "This is like Dr. Doolittle.....I have never seen horses come galloping over when called."

Malta explains these horses were used as "nurse mares". The breeders kill the foals, the un-registered, less desirable foals, and then use the mares as nursemaids to the more highly prized foals of race horses. Every year, Malta and Will used to buy a few discarded foals from those despicable places. They can't house any more horses for now, and are raising the ones they have for eventual adoption.

"Now we will go pet some deer," she announces, "The deer are very shy. Timmy and Bonnie were found as fawns. Well meaning people thought the mother had left them, so they brought them to us. However, mother deer leave their fawns to go forage, but most of the time will return. These deer cannot be returned to the wild anymore. They would walk right up to a hunter and ask for an apple. Now since they are not used to mobs of people, we need to approach them quietly. Remember no running."

The girls are allowed to go in to pet the deer in small groups. Their fur is soft like a bunny, and they nibble on our zipper pulls and coat bottoms. Their eyes are dark and huge.

"Now we will meet some turkeys," declares Malta.

A large rainbow colored turkey and smaller white turkey fan their impressive feathers as we approach. Their necks and head change color as the turkey shows off for us. Malta affirms they too are friendly, and one by one we are allowed to pet them. One girl approaches the huge turkey step by step, haltingly.

No nonsense Malta trumpets, "Go on, you are not *stalking* him. You are *petting* him."

After each girl has pet the turkey in worshipful silence, Malta quips, "That was nice for him, because we will be eating him Thursday for Thanksgiving."

Every girl's eyes widen, and Malta laughs, "No we won't!" She winks at me.

A large sleeping pig snores nearby.

"Don't pet him," Malta warns, "He is a senior citizen and cranky."

She points up to the hillside. Suddenly she erupts into bleating, that is indistinguishable from the responding bleat high atop the hills. The discussion between the goats and Malta continues for a few minutes. One of the adults leans over and whispers, "This is like Walt Disney World."

"Malta is an animal whisperer," I respond, "She speaks all their languages."

We meet two young cows, saved from the veal platter, and finally it is time to get to work. Malta hands out rakes and shovels and brushes. Some girls rake the turkey pen, some groom the dogs, and some shovel dirt into pits the dogs have dug throughout the yard. Some are placed on poop pickup detail. Her yard is understandably covered with poop, with some twenty dogs roaming it.

One dog with a bandaged, casted back leg recently operated on for a clubfoot, playfully races around the yard. He is not supposed to be out using the foot, but finally Malta decided the joy of romping with all those children was maybe as helpful in his healing as resting the leg. He finds Mariah, one of the girls, to be his special friend and keeps tugging at her work gloves. She tries to shake him off, but he continues till he has pulled off the glove and then bounds around the yard on three legs, gleefully holding the glove in his mouth like a banner. We catch him, retrieve Mariah's glove, and continue working.

"Who wants to groom a horse?" calls Malta. Six girls shoot over, Asherel in the lead. Malta corrals Will's patient horse, Sequoia, and the six little girls all commence brushing her. I am pretty sure she doesn't need brushing, but Malta understands all animals, even little girls.

4:30 arrives all too soon, and it is time for us to go. Malta walks with me to my car.

"I hope we were some help," I say, "You were awfully nice showing them all the animals. This was wonderful."

"They are good kids," she concedes, "Not like some of the hellions we get out here. They are just like all creatures; you just have to figure out what they need."

"This is a wonderful place," I observe, "Every child needs to be connected with nature. We have lost that. We have lost our connection in the animal world."

Malta is quiet. I think we have worn her out.

We all pile back in our vans, and drive off in the waning autumn day. The sun sparkles briefly on the few remaining golden leaves and then drops behind the mountain. We drive over the bridge across Lake Wylie just as the last magenta and orange rays are splashing across the tranquil water.

"I wish we could've stayed longer," breathes Lucy, one of the girls in my car.

Night descends and as the girls play another wild, raucous alphabet game, I drive quietly, nestled deep in my thoughts.

Right before we left Last Chance Rescue, I told Malta that this was an incredible educational opportunity.

"You know," I said earnestly, "You could charge admission to do a field trip just like you are giving us. Homeschool groups would pay for this."

"We are thinking along those lines," she said, "But I wouldn't know how to start."

"I can help you there," I suggested.

The next day, I send a thank you note to Malta, with a reminder that I am ready and willing to send an ad to the homeschool newsletters. She quickly responds.

Thank you for sending the photos.... please tell the girls that it was nice to have them here and thank them again for the biscuits and treats for the animals. They did an awesome job too! Very polite and well mannered children. We are working on a regular farm day tour scheduled monthly event. (Minus the poop pick up for paying people) Same as what you experienced.

I hope the kids got something out of it.... I have to wonder how many will go home and harass their parents over cooking a turkey for thanksgiving! LOL!

Rebekah will probably be in touch with you to discuss the home school group tours and such. This is not my forte. You know if you are interested we are currently seeking out

our 2009 board members....Think about it....not much to it. No costs involved
Malta

I certainly do not need to take on any more responsibility. I am already too busy, with homeschooling, two dogs, my small art teaching business, my own art career, running the Destination Imagination group, teaching Sunday school, and occasionally vacuuming and dusting. Can I possibly add LCR board member to the list?

As I am rereading the emails and pondering, the early morning sun is streaming through the front window, broken into geometric splashes of gold splattered across the rocking chairs and piano. Honeybun comes up to me dipping her head and wagging her tail. She has already greeted me that morning. In the past, she always wanted to be near, but she rarely sought attention. She clearly likes us in her presence, but that is enough. Lucky, on the other hand, is constantly begging to be pet, or snuggled close to us, lifting his head and ramming it against us, entreating us to wrap every molecule of ourselves around him. But lately, Honeybun comes and wags and looks at me as though she wants something. So I pause in my work, and with an impulsive flood of love for the little dog, scoop her up and lay her on my lap. She is not really a lap dog. She is forty pounds, and doesn't love being picked up, particularly belly up. But, she lays there, her brows furrowed, and I smell a fishy smell. The vet told me that dogs express those notorious anal glands when nervous. Well, at least that saves a $20 vet visit.....

I begin scootching her belly and rubbing her neck. She never quite relaxes, but she doesn't struggle. When I put her down, she scurries away and crashes down on her bed near me. She looks at me with dark, unblinking eyes. This evening, Matt will be home for Thanksgiving. She has not seen him since late August. Will she remember him? Will she waggle for him the way she greets us... or will she growl and bark like she still does with strangers? And Christmas is coming soon. How will she respond to my dear Anders, my towering, quiet beloved first born whom she has never met? He comes home so rarely. I care a great deal how welcoming she will be. Will she sense or smell the family connection?

While wondering....I am inexplicably not worried. I have the whip if needed and will deal with what catastrophes are sure to develop when they happen. Uncharacteristically, I don't have a checklist of behaviors that need overcoming in the next month, with little boxes to check off. However, we do have a lot to do over the next few weeks and the calendar is full of scribbled events. The new dog classes start soon, another commitment.

Asherel walks in and sees Honeybun curled up in her wicker basket, near me. She sits down next to her dog and scratches her near her tail. Honeybun stretches languorously.

"Look Mom!" Asherel calls, "She likes this. She's smiling."

I peer over at the little dog and I don't see a smile. I see the holidays before us and the uncertainty of newly controlled aggression. I see the calendar filled with obligations, and cold nights coming while standing watching her on the agility field, ready to fend off any potential mauling or marauding. I am far too busy to think about adding a new responsibility. Still, we *have* made progress. Me and Asherel…and Arvo, and Malta, and Will, and Lloyd, and Vicci, and Deb, and Nina….and my neighbors and my friends.

I decide at that moment to accept the Board of Directors offer.

Dear Father,

Please guide me as I ponder taking on more responsibility in an overfull life. I have loved my family well, but I wonder if I have reached out to help others even as willingly as I reached out to help this dog…And I guess it is no secret to you that "willing" did not always describe my attitude even then. Help me overcome my selfish grasp on my time and energy.

Thank you for pushing me to persevere. I never envisioned Honeybun winning an award. I think we are both slowly improving, aren't we? I hope so anyway. I don't think I have ever had to persist at a task for so long as helping this dog with so little skill and so little chance of success. I am beginning to understand how weary you must be with us thick headed creations who take so long to learn the lessons you so lovingly place before us.

I didn't expect a pitbull to ever give me a lesson about tolerance or worth. You really don't make junk, though. I shouldn't be surprised by what you use to get through to me at this point. I know I have not looked deeply enough at any of your creation, marveled at each human being as bearing your image, your mark.

I grow so impatient when my prayers are seemingly unanswered. My parents grow old and as far as I know, have not asked Jesus into their lives. I beg and pour tears across my pillow, but still friends get sick or even die. But I begin to see that the hand that holds me dear holds every creature near, and longs for all of us to raise our eyes and look upon Him with love. We are chewed up, broken, ugly things... but you have placed us on a Trophy shelf, lovingly patted our broken pieces together, and loved us anyway.

Help me to love like that, to persist like that, to value like that.

And thank you for what this confounded dog is teaching me about you.

Amen.

CHAPTER 10

Selflessness

Honeybun greets Matt joyfully as he crashes through the door laden with schoolbooks and dirty laundry. She remembers him, or else she is simply healed enough that strangers are welcome, as they invariably mean treats for her. Interestingly, as she is settling deeper into normalcy, Lucky is tending towards psychoses. It is highly likely that Lucky always had that in him, but it took the advent of Honeybun to expose his weak links.

He has been ricocheting out the dog door when the toaster pops for some time now. Asherel's desensitizing techniques are not working. We watched the Dog Whisperer show on a similar issue. Unbelievably, there is more than one dog that has Toaster Fear. Cesar, the Dog Whisperer, had the owner put the dog on leash and keep him at her side as she went through her breakfast prep routine. So, Asherel puts Lucky's leash on, and then sits by the toaster. She pops it repeatedly. He flinches and tries to run away each time it snaps up with that terrifying sound toasters make.

"Pair it with treats," I suggest, "Then maybe he will link the toaster sound with something good."

Asherel spends the next several minutes popping the toaster, and stuffing a treat in Lucky's mouth. When she finally lets him off leash, he sprints outside. She repeats the same session every morning.

I have been feeding Honeybun off leash for a couple of months by this time. She is very respectful of Lucky, who is a slower eater. She sits nearby, but doesn't approach until he finishes. She stares at him, those dark predator eyes unblinking, licking her chops after her own hastily engulfed breakfast. The toaster problem is only indirectly caused by Honeybun. We never used to feed Lucky breakfast. He always had food available, and nibbled at it all day. I have since learned this is what dopes who don't read dog care books do. With Honeybun's food issues, it becomes critical that we feed the dogs at the same time. Lucky quickly discerns that if he doesn't gobble his kibble *post haste*, the demon dog will arrive with salivary glands dripping like artillery fire.

Any way, now his breakfast coincides with our breakfast, and he is subjected to those horrifying toaster noises. He gulps a few mouthfuls of food and then runs outside. I pull him back inside, and make some munching sounds to entice him to eat. Sometimes I add some chicken broth, which he loves, and he eats, though warily. When he tries to run away, which he does more and more frequently, I block him and lead him back to his food. Then he stands there, nose in the dog food bowl, but not eating. He is a condemned prisoner, being forced to have breakfast.

"Eat!"I command.

He nibbles one bite, and then stands there, head hanging, tail lowered.

"You can't force him to eat," cautions Arvo, "Have you called Malta?"

Amazingly, though it seems impossible, our strange dog becomes even stranger. As soon as Asherel appears in the morning, Lucky no longer greets her joyfully as he did in the past. Instead, he leaps out of a sound sleep and gallops to the back yard. With drooping ears, he cowers at the far back edges of the lawn, looking at us, as we stand at the back door wondering what on earth is going on in that nutty terrier brain. I hold up his food bowl and call him in. Honeybun sits nearby, ears perked, begging me to let her eat the stupid one's food. I can't feed her until Lucky is in or she will certainly be sitting nearby, ready to pounce while he eats. That is not a relaxing dining atmosphere for him. Eventually, he comes inside, and I put down the food bowls. He sniffs, glances at us, and then bolts again.

I can't figure it out. Since we shop at a wholesale store and get huge bulk bags of dog food, perhaps by the late stages of the bag, he is just sick of the food. I begin shopping in regular grocery stores and buying smaller bags of food to keep him interested. I even succumb to purchasing his very favorite food; one that our vet has warned is not as healthy as the ones we had been buying… the equivalent of Captain Crunch for dogs.

It doesn't matter. His behavior continues, such that he is eating only every other breakfast. Dinner seems thus far unaffected. I pick up his breakfast bowl, and he gets no more food until dinner. His backbone becomes more prominent, and I know he is hungry. He looks eager while waiting for the breakfast bowl, but as soon as it is set down, he skedaddles out the dog door. Then he begins doing the same crazy antics with his dinner.

"Have you asked Malta what to do?" asks Asherel.

"I am afraid to," I admit, "She will scream at me."

I know what Malta will say. A dog will eat if it gets hungry enough. Ignore the stupid behavior, put down the bowl at food time, pick it up in a few minutes and case closed. He will not starve.

The day before Thanksgiving, I always make most of the meal ahead of time, so on turkey day itself, all that is left to prepare is the turkey and stuffing, and everything else just has to be warmed. I am indeed feeling a little bad about the turkey, picturing Malta's brightly colored Tom strutting and letting the little girls pet him. I had been a vegetarian for fifteen years or so in my young adulthood, just for that reason. I love animals, and would prefer not to eat them, however developed some very strong food allergies. My allergist told me I needed to return to my carnivore roots.

This thanksgiving, I am making a fresh cranberry relish that my sister Amy raves about. Unfortunately, my only food processor is a tiny one cup model. I try using a very old, weak blender, which makes sad whirring noises, and chugs, but doesn't really chop many cranberries. With no other options, the tiny food processor mulches a half cup at a time and the blender tries as hard as its old motor will allow. The going is slow and arduous, another symbol of patient slogging of which my life is currently replete. I remove the cover from the blender to see how it is doing as it chug chugs sluggishly through the cranberries. Suddenly it surges, and spews a mess of staining red cranberry bits all over the floor, the counter, and the couch in the room beside the kitchen. Julia Child, I am not.

"Mom?" calls Asherel, who is nearby as I am teaching her to cook. Someday I want to be sure she also knows how to spew cranberry bits all over two adjoining rooms just in time for her Thanksgiving guests. Learn at the hands of the master, little one….

"Why is Lucky trembling?" she asks.

I glance up from my cranberry disaster. Lucky is standing outside the dog door, looking in, and trembling all over, visibly shaking like the shuddering blender.

Asherel scurries over and hauls him inside. She tugs him onto her lap. Lucky is not a lap dog, indeed at fifty pounds he is even less of a lap dog than Honeybun. However, unlike Honeybun, Lucky loves sitting on our laps. So he curls on her lap (with parts of him off her lap), shaking and trembling. Evidently, his neurosis is growing. No longer is his malady restricted to Toaster Fear. We now have full blown Appliance Fear Syndrome.

Lucky is in for a rough day. The cranberry debacle takes well over an hour. There is still to come the sweet potato mashing, the bake ahead mashed potato casserole mashing, and then finally the blending for the corn bread casserole. I am in the kitchen most of the day running various appliances. Lucky spends much of the day standing on the deck, watching and shivering in the brisk cold. It is clear the disease has progressed to the point where I need professional advice.

Dear Malta,

Having successfully with much gnashing of teeth healed the vicious attack dog Honeybun, I am now faced with a new and even more daunting issue. Lucky has developed a severe case of Appliance Fear Syndrome (AFS). At first, he would just be terrified and run outside if the toaster popped up. Asherel put him on leash and fed him treats while popping the toaster over and over again, for about a week. Then Lucky started racing out of the house every morning as soon as he saw Asherel. During my Thanksgiving cooking yesterday, I was running all kinds of appliances... blenders, food processors....and Lucky was trembling in absolute fear. He almost never eats his breakfast anymore, though he seems eager for it. When I put it down, (in the kitchen where the dreaded toaster is), he looks at the food and then races outside. I am pretty sure it is connected to AFS. I am hopeful that in your many years of dog rehab, you have encountered AFS before. Do you have any suggestions?

Blessings, and Happy Thanksgiving!
Vicky

Vicky,

Yep we can fix this....I have a fear of chainsaws....saw Texas chainsaw massacre when I was about 6....LMAO! True. You may have to germ up your toaster a bit to get him used to it. Sniffs and licks and such. On the other hand you could use the toaster as a control tool....carry your toaster out on walks with you... when he misbehaves just whip it out in front of his face. LOL! You need to formally introduce him to the toaster... Toaster this is Lucky...Lucky meet toaster.... and then introduce him to the rest of the appliance family. You do this casual like... put the toaster or blender in a high traffic area... or just the blender base... later add pitcher part and lid..... Couple of hours... interacting with the blender/appliance in a passive way... (Not running/turned on). When he can be around them not running and he ignores them we will go from there. (Good place would be by the front door where he has to pass them for walks... or where he likes to walk by most often) Don't plug it in in case he pees on it. (Ultimate dog revenge) lol! Happy T day to you and the fam! No turkey eatin' here!!! Malta

The next morning, I set out Lucky's food bowl, mixing in warm turkey broth to entice him. Honeybun inhales her meal with gusto. Lucky looks at the bowl, and then scuttles out back. I scramble after him, dragging him back inside.

"Eat," I command, pointing at the food.

He quakes in his paws and looks at me with terror in his eyes. I stare back. As soon as I turn, he shoots past me, back out the dog door. He is truly psychotic, I grumble to myself fumbling for his leash. I catch him, cowering on the back steps, and heave him back over to the kitchen, tying his leash to the closet door near his food. He quivers, every part of him shaking to the tip of his stupid tail. I wait with him. After about ten minutes of shaking, he lies down, still not eating. It is time to put a modified Malta plan into action. Unplugging the toaster and knocking out the crumbs, I put it on the floor near him. Then I grab a doggie snack, and balance it on the toaster lever. Lucky approaches the toaster, nosing it cautiously. Then he pushes it with his nose followed by violent shoving. Repeatedly, angrily, Lucky accosts the dangerous toaster which almost falls over with his savage pushes. With fury, he shoves his face into his food, flipping it wildly onto the floor with his nose. I watch, speechless. It certainly looks like a temper tantrum. It also looks a little bit like Lucky thinks the toaster is alive. He is not going to take it anymore. He is not going to be prey to this nasty toaster anymore. I know it is mean, but I am laughing now, and it does not escape my keen mind that so many of my fears have been 'toasters' in my life as well.

He finally stops and looks at me. The shaking abates.

Gathering the other appliances, the blender and the mixer, I line them up next to the toaster. He sniffs them, shoves the blender a little, and ignores the mixer. Then he returns to his food bowl and eats every last morsel. He licks the bowl, devours the food he has dumped on the floor, and lies down to go to sleep.

The next morning, I call the dogs in for breakfast. As usual, Honeybun is there faster than a squirrel with its tail on fire, sitting before me with smoke coming off her paws as she skids to a stop. Honeybun is never coy about food. Lucky ambles over, wagging his tail. This looks promising. I have prepared a deluxe day-after-Thanksgiving special - turkey broth mixed in with their kibbles.

Then I put Honeybun's bowl down, and she submerges her snout before taking another wasted breath. Anxiously, I put the bowl down for Lucky. He begins eating, slowly wagging his tail. I slip over to the toaster and open my breadbox near it. This is the first sign for Lucky that the world is ending and the toaster is about to come alive. He knows that if he doesn't dart out back as fast as possible, he may die a horrible death either being toasted or just lightly browned. Remarkably, he continues slurping turkey juice. Next the toaster lever slowly lowers. Lucky remains unfazed. The smell of toast permeates even the turkey smells, but still Lucky laps contentedly. When the toast is almost done, I put my finger on the lever so that the pop is softer, but still quite audible. Lucky keeps eating. Problem solved, as Malta so often says.

This is a miracle. Who would have thought I would find delight in my dog coexisting peacefully with a toaster? Who would think I would find God in a paranoid dog cured of toaster fear? It is my own parting of the Red Sea.

Another little miracle is unfolding before me as well. Wendy, my dog-hating sister, writes and asks how she can vote for Malta's farm on the current Favorite Animal Rescue Contest. The winning organization can win thousands of dollars, and we are allowed to vote every day for a month. I put out a plea to all of my email friends and know one or two have voted once. While a daily reminder helps me remember to vote every day, I doubt anyone else has done so. But then, unexpectedly, Wendy wants me to know that she is voting for Malta every day. Without knowing how much Wendy dislikes dogs, it is hard to imagine the improbability of this level of interest in Malta's hopeless mutts.

Although Wendy and I vote every day for over a month, Malta's standing never rises above seventeenth in SC. Malta doesn't win, doesn't even come close. But me and the dog- hating, cosmopolitan Wendy vote faithfully every day for a little, obscure animal rescue farm filled with dogs with no legs, no eyes, and no pedigrees. We know she hasn't a chance, but we keep voting anyway. Something is filling me besides the dander from two dogs. It feels suspiciously like character-molding from adversity, though of course I have little experience to recognize if this is the case or not. I have heard of this happening, but have always avoided adversity as best as possible. A little cockeyed-ear, dying bundle of adversity seems to have had other plans for me.....

Meanwhile, Lucky seems healed of his appliance fear but this only brings him marginally closer to normal. I don't dare tell Malta about how every time it rains, Lucky becomes highly anxious, racing around the house, nosing us for constant reassurance, and then darting outside to stand in the rain. I thought this was connected to the toaster issue, but on sunny days, he shows no anxiety with the toaster, so this craziness seems to be weather based. Since it rarely rains in NC for more than a day or two in succession, this issue is not a major one. The fear may have escalated when we had the sunroom built with its tin roof. The rain sounds like thousands of mass murderers lurking just above us, stomping and pounding to get in. I am unsure of exactly when Lucky started being nervous with rain. He didn't use to be, but since he is always crazy, added craziness sometimes slips in without notice. I find it highly amusing that the dog who has led a plush and perfect life from six weeks on is several stitches short of a sock, but the dog who for the first two years of life has probably known nothing but scraping to survive, is becoming a very healthy stable dog. I suspect that even in the canine world, hardships build character, and perhaps Lucky's life has been too easy. I know mine was, and while mourning its loss of ease….maybe there is something greater entering in. I find myself spending less time ruing the day I stopped to give Honeybun a drink.

Honeybun begins to figure out that humans are good for something other than food dispensing. They can scratch spots behind her ears that she can only swipe at ineffectually. She is less enthused with the value of kisses, but ceases to recoil when her nose is kissed. She never licks us, except in the brief first few seconds when we return home after a long absence. Her licks are more like nibbles. She understands eating us, but not showing affection.

On our walks early in her rehabilitation, she never reacted to our praise of her for quietly passing other dogs, or sitting when we stopped to talk with strangers. Now, she wags her tail briefly in acknowledgment of our commendations and glances at me. She does not seem to care that she is a *good* dog, as long as she is a *well fed* dog. Still, there seems to be a dawning awareness that being good earns extra biscuits and those lovely scratches on hard to reach spots.

Her relationship with Lucky is slowly becoming the doggy friendship I had hoped for. When we play with Lucky and chase him around the house, she watches, her expression eager, her tail wagging.

"Com'on Honeybun!" we encourage, "Play!"

And we clap our hands in front of her. She pauses, then dips down into play position, paws at Lucky and finally joins us in chasing him. As she growls playfully, Lucky remembers how just a few months back that sound preceded vampire teeth seeking blood and he backs away. Honeybun pivots before him, wagging and in play stance, barking for him to please cavort. Increasingly, Lucky throws caution to the wind and chases her. These times are brief, but growing more frequent.

She rarely leaves our side. I often absentmindedly jump up and step on her tail, as she is always underfoot. She never growls, or even tries to move - but patiently waits for me to remove my foot. I love her tail, and always feel very bad for trodding on it. Besides the lovely interplay of thick beige, white, and golden-red fur on her tail, it is a most unusual shape. Like her ear, it has what I suspect is a deformity that makes it curve in the opposite manner of typical dog tails. Most dog tails curve down at the base and then end in varying degrees of upward curves at the tip. Honeybun's does the reverse of that. Her tail has subtle curves that make it a straight up question mark. She always holds it erect, unless she's sleeping, the question mark of her nether region. What questions would this dog want answered as she shoots that constant query to the world?

"*Where is dinner*?" is certainly high on her list.

" *Is there anything edible in the vicinity? Why won't these humans let me eat the dangerous intruders who deliver packages on my doorstep? Why do they get upset when I lie on their comfy bed yet encourage me to lie on one of the three beds on the floor? Why do they keep taking away the pencils I so love to chew? Why does the big scaredy-cat dog not want to play with me? Why does the little human keep thrusting a stick in my path that she wants me to jump over?"*

Asherel has found a patient companion who will endure any new bizarre activity she concocts with dignified submission. Her latest craze is "freestyle dancing". She assures me Honeybun loves it. This is also what she claims when she puts humiliating costumes on the poor patient little dog. Since I refuse to buy dog clothes when there are starving children in Rwanda, Asherel resorts to sewing them.

"She loves dressing up, Mom," Asherel informs me, as Honeybun sits there in her elf hat with the jingle bells and the collar with little green and red elf flaps draped all around it.

"How can you tell?" I ask dubiously.

"Well look at her, she's smiling."

I look at the little elf dog. I don't see a smile. I see vet bills collecting like dandruff. But I do see that Asherel's sewing skills are improving in her constant quest to have the best dressed dog in Charlotte. The placid and kind little dog has come a long way from the circumstances she likely endured the Christmas before we found her. She is quite good-natured about whatever indignity Asherel wants to hoist upon her. Lucky only wears his Santa hat briefly before pulling it off. Honeybun sighs but resignedly sits there, waiting till Asherel tires of this game. Sometimes I find her curled up in her bed, elf hat and collar still on, Asherel nowhere in sight.

I remove the costume and scritch her behind her ears, and through her glorious thick ruff. No wonder her tail is constantly asking questions. What kind of loony tune home is she a part of? She snuggles into her thick warm bed as the record November cold knocks at the door, curling her questioning tail beneath her.

Meanwhile, on a mission, I send numerous emails to my various homeschool lists to advertise the Last Chance Rescue field trips. I am praying that there will be an outpouring of children eager to pay to come shovel dog poop and learn about the redemption of three legged dogs. Malta is skeptical. With Christmas just three weeks away, I assume there will not be much response till after the holidays are over. Everyone is too busy buying useless gifts and spending too much money. I am too, but continue sending emails hopefully.

One of my art class children has to drop out as the family can no longer afford the classes. But I know that art is one of the few joys in this silent and depressed child's life, and feel strongly that I need to offer the class for free. Winking at Honeybun, I remind her, "You would not be here if Malta hadn't helped us for free," since she is concerned that the reduced income will cut into her milkbone allotment.

In the midst of Christmas frenzy, I begin to receive little gifts from neighbors, and am stressing with all the time and money drain of this joyful season. I have no idea what to get my neighbors. I don't even know what to get Anders, my oldest son, who never wants or asks for anything. Arvo finally pins him down, cornering him in a phone call to summon some degree of greed and tell us what he wants.

"Anders wants socks for Christmas," he calls out as he

gets off the phone. Socks. I round out his gift of socks with silly things, like cow cell phone covers, and Bugs Bunny USB drives.....How does anyone ever survive this crazy season?

In the midst of all this shopping, I receive a letter in the mail from Last Chance Rescue. Malta is desperate. The twenty dogs she is rehabilitating have four blankets between them to sleep on, and her towels for drying them after baths are all rags. 210 pounds of dog food each week are consumed by the dogs, not to mention 400 pounds of livestock food, and 2100 pounds of hay for the livestock. Each week. She receives no government funds, and much of the operating expenses come out of her pocket or from the volunteers who love LCR. Can we organize a supply drive?

Now? At Christmas? When I have to go buy socks and find something my son will love that will make him want to come home more often? I remember the dogs I met at LCR - the crippled Chihuahua that can't walk, the three legged retriever, the dog with the gunshot wound healing....

So Asherel crafts an appeal letter and we make fifty copies. We trudge through the icy, cold day and put them in the mailboxes of all our neighbors. We print 50 more and distribute those the next day. We plan our collection time for two weeks hence, right before Christmas.

In the midst of all the holiday falderal, Asherel and I take a break to visit my sister Amy in Texas. I request all the Texas experiences....rodeos, cattle drives, horse cutting.... Amy and her remarkable husband, Jim, organize three days of Texas experiences. We see all my requests and then some, including armadillo races. The rodeo is certainly exciting, but I cannot help feeling very sorry for the bulls and the bucking broncos. The bulls are bucking wildly not only because they are not riding animals and want the intruder off their back, but also because a tight strap is cinched around their belly uncomfortably. Amy thinks it is cinched around their testicles. If this is true, then the cowboys should have a turn next with the belt cinched around *their* family jewels. True or not, it is unsettling to see these creatures prodded till they are crazed with anger, after which the rodeo clowns and their mounts risk their lives to divert the bull's attention and horns from the fallen cowboys. The announcer insists the animals are not being hurt, that this is what they would do in the wild......

I personally have never seen bulls in the wild trying to kick off a naturally occurring cinch around their belly or private parts. Maybe things are different in Texas. And the calf roping is even more disturbing. The poor baby cow is spooked into running top speed, roped by the brave cowboy, thrown off its feet as it slams to the end of the noose around its neck, and then hogtied while it lies there helplessly struggling. If this is so much fun, why aren't the rodeo cowboys doing this to their own babies?

One night, Amy sends me to bed with a book by Cleveland Amory about Black Beauty Ranch in Texas, a huge animal rescue ranch. Amy is a cat lover who until a recent spate of old cats dying had four cats. She rescues many strays. One of her favorite authors is Cleveland Amory, and she was delighted to find out that his ranch was near enough for her to visit. The book she gives me to read, Ranch of Dreams, is about a haven for animals that have been hurt, exploited, or nearly annihilated, as in the case of the Grand Canyon Burros. It is a heartbreaking book, but the hopeful message is clear. Helping the little you can is better than doing nothing; indeed at Black Beauty Ranch, it is *everything* for the few animals lucky enough to end up there. I now feel officially like scum of the earth for attending the rodeo. And of course, there were my past sins of indulging in entertainment with a blind eye to the plight of the animals. I had learned enough about the treatment of circus animals to know I should not, in good conscience, ever attend a circus... but what about all the events we *have* attended...steeplechases, show jumping, dressage, killer whale and dolphin shows? I am appalled by how much animals are used for human pleasure, with little thought to the best interests of the animal. Even the armadillo races were probably less fun for the armadillo than their natural activity of dashing across the desert roads dodging cars. I have a sudden urge to go free lobsters from restaurant fish tanks.

Upon returning home, I research rodeo cruelty, and am even more horrified. How have I missed the incredible suffering of these poor creatures for fifty years of my life? Honestly, I am ashamed that I paid money to support this animal exploitation - ashamed of my fellow human beings and myself. What are we thinking?

It is raining the day before our LCR collection drive. The rain matches my mood. And to top it off, the happy dog truce is growing stale. Asherel prepares to take Honeybun outside for her agility training. She has a handful of highly motivating ham. As she is gathering her shoes, both Lucky and Honey follow her, saliva dripping in tandem. And then Honeybun pivots and lunges at Lucky, snarling, and chases him from the room. I am walking by as the dogs streak through the room, nearly toppling me. With a shriek, I catch hold of Honeybun, and throw her to the ground in the "dreaded roll". To her credit, she instantly lies still, subdued. I have not had to do the dreaded roll in months. Reminded of how awful those early days had been as I let her up, I am very discouraged. So much need, so much work involved, and so much struggle...and it is all a drop in the bucket. I am hanging by a thread trying to save this dog. Malta is hanging by a thread trying to save her twenty dogs. Rodeos are happily raking in profits all over the west, while animals all over the world are discarded to the slaughter when they lose entertainment value.

"What are we going to give to the LCR collection?" asks Asherel, emerging from her room with a sunny smile.

It is easy to be discouraged. It is harder to keep at it and to try to make a difference in the face of so much ignorance, hopelessness, and despair.

"I have an old blanket and I have at least six old towels, and I can buy a bag of dogfood for Malta," I answer.

"Do you think she would want an elf hat?" asks Asherel.

When on the ground rolling Honeybun, I notice she smells nasty. Some awful smelling stuff seems to be emanating from her cockeyed ear. I open the flap and the smell knocks me over. There are crusted gobs of blood inside too. Lovely. This matches my mood perfectly. I clean the ear as best I can with a damp paper towel, and judging from the amount of disgusting goo, feel a professional (again!) needs to look at this. Oh goody. For Christmas, we will be giving each other vet bills.

We greet our beloved vet receptionist as Honeybun trots daintily up to the counter,

"Hello!" I say with a weak smile, "We are here for our weekly visit."

"What are we in for this time?" she asks.

"Something is going on with her ear," I answer, “Something that smells really bad."

First they weigh her. Forty-four pounds!!! That is three pounds above her ideal weight of forty-one at the last visit just two weeks ago. Our starving dog is getting fat. At this pace, she will weigh more than me by Christmas. I understand her obsession with food, but the good times clearly need to stop rolling.

The vet assistant is the same young man that had endured my tears when he told me the sty would cost $500. He pokes around in Honeybun's ear, and she is not happy about it, but suffers quietly. She lowers her tail to half mast, and looks miserable. The verdict after a microscopic analysis - a nasty bacterial and yeast infection producing lots of foul smelling gunk which they remove in the back room. I hear them exclaiming over the large volume of nasty smelling gunk.

As he enters the numbers of what this latest malady is

going to set us back, he turns the computer screen towards me, and then runs from the room. He is taking no chances that I will dissolve into an inconvenient crying mess in front of him again. It is a mere $100, though. Not enough to collapse over, just enough for a brief intake of extra oxygen.

"Usually dogs with upright ears don't get these," he mentions.

"Yeh, but that ear is damaged," I commiserate, "And it doesn't stay upright."
(The other one is pointing to God, I want to add, and I sure hope He intends to pay for it...)

He sends me home with a cleanser that should prevent these from recurring if squirted in her ear once a week. I add that to my burgeoning check list. Meanwhile, Asherel and Lucky went shopping in the store while we were with the vet. Asherel periodically returns with some cute outfit or bone that Lucky "has picked out", one of which is a little doggy raincoat, yellow with a print of little ducks on it.

"Wouldn't Honeybun look great in this? And you know how much it rains in North Carolina," she pitches.

"Asherel, she is a dog, not a toy," I sigh.

She smiles hopefully at me.

"How much is it?" I ask. (It actually *is* pretty cute.)

“$20," she discovers.

"Forget it."

She returns a short time later with a pink reversible to plaid mid weight coat.

"This is on sale for $6.99!" she exclaims, "And it is reflective and reversible."

There is much to be said for reversible things. If time were reversible, how far back would I need to go to not want to go back any further? At this point, I am thinking longingly of my days in the womb.

After telling Malta about Honeybun's ear; she offers to drop off her medicines so I don't need to buy any.

"No, we can afford it", I tell her, "You save your meds for your houseful of dogs."

She has given up drinking coffee to save money for the dogs, but she is offering me her medicines. My complaining spirit recognizes the need to stuff a cork in my soul.

With the rain unabated, I email my art class, my Sunday school class, and my Destination Imagination group with an appeal for blankets, towels, and dog food. There is no one else I can think to accost. Having never even sold Girl Scout cookies because I hate asking others to support anything I do, this somehow seems worthy enough to grovel and beg.

Sunday, LCR collection pick-up day, dawns overcast

and grey. Oh dear. I have been up from 12-4 a.m., unable to sleep. On my morning run, it sprinkles a little, which concerns me. Will people leave things out in the rain? After church, Asherel and I wait anxiously for 2:00 which is the designated pickup time. It is now sprinkling steadily outside. As I walk to the car, a neighbor drives up and hauls out a fifty pound bag of dog food.

"I didn't want it to get wet," she explains.

We drive around the block, spotting bags marked "LCR" sprinkled like wild flowers all along the route. I collect over two hundred pounds of dogfood, fifty towels and twenty blankets. On the porch is a little note with two cans of dog food and a bone. It's from a friend who is a pastor's wife. They are in the process of selling their home and the church building, as times are tough and money is rapidly vanishing. Funny how that tiny offering fills my van with the glow of heaven.

Dear Lord,

I am humbled by the kindness of others.Thank you for the outpouring of food by strangers to discarded dogs they have never seen.Thank you for the spirit of selflessness that I have perhaps not noticed often enough. Create in me a spirit that would seek to comfort others who have no hope of repaying me for the sheer delight of being more like you.

I pray for the dear widow and her family that I met this week. Thank you that I can offer something that is useful to them. I have to say, Father, I did not expect reducing my income purposefully to feel so good…

Thank you for helping Lucky overcome his fear of toasters. I suppose all fears look equally ridiculous to you. After all, if we truly believe that you love us, you who made heaven and earth and can silence any storm, then we really ought to understand that whatever you bring is for the best.Yet how much of my life is controlled by fear? Too much. I fear rejection so I don't tell others about you strongly enough. I fear failure so I don't start difficult tasks. I fear loss so I hold too tightly to what I really need to let go.

Please Lord, help Honeybun to let her fears go, to know that she no longer has to fear the strangers in her life. They are not there to kick her any more. She is safe, and beloved.

Oh my, dear Lord. So am I, aren't I?

Amen. Amen.

CHAPTER 11

Determination

Had I the heavens' embroidered cloths,
Enwrought with golden and silver light,
The blue and the dim and the dark cloths
Of night and light and the half light,
I would spread the cloths under your feet:
But I, being poor, have only my dreams;
I have spread my dreams under your feet;
Tread softly because you tread on my dreams.
William Butler Yeats

Asherel and Honeybun prepare to attend the third private agility class with Deb, but Asherel is worried. She has been faithfully working with Honeybun on her agility practice in the back yard, and for the past week, Honeybun seems disinterested. Asherel has a high value "cookie"- luncheon ham. That can't be the problem. But Honeybun lackadaisically trots up to the jumps, sometimes half-heartedly jumping, but often walking around them. She weaves at a snail's pace. She refuses to come when Asherel calls, and instead sniffs the grass. I glance outside a few times and wonder what is up with Honeybun.

Right before class, Asherel stumbles inside crying.

"She won't do it, Mom," she mutters, with little chokes of crying. It is clear she has been frustrated into tears for a while.

"Maybe she is tired," I suggest, "I did take her on a five mile run today. Maybe you should just work her on the weaves."

"I did!" wails Asherel, "She just stops and sniffs every one."

"I don't know what to tell you," I comfort helplessly, "Maybe it is her ear infection. Maybe the medicine makes her feel sick."

Or maybe she is just weary of all the demands of civilized life. I know I am. The long runs to exhaust the dogs, the constant surveillance reading any signs of imminent viciousness, the expensive classes and vet bills, the rolling, and whipping, and interminable future of never relaxing…I can see why Honeybun might be tempted to just pack her suitcase and return to the ticks and the swamp.

We traipse to class hoping Deb will spark some fire in

the disinterested dog. While hoping this is just a passing problem, I feel a little worried and sad for Asherel. She loves the prospect of Agility trials with this dog. She has been working towards this dream for years, with her attendance over the years at all the area Agility trials, working with Lucky, and finally Honeybun. What if Honeybun decides she just doesn't want the fame and fortune, the talk show circuit of world-renowned agility stars? What if all Asherel's determination leads to nothing?

We warn Deb that Honeybun seems under the weather. Surprisingly, Honeybun perks up and while still somewhat slowly lumbering through the course, she attempts everything. She looks better than she has all week, at least. Relieved, I realize how cautiously hopeful we have been rolling towards a goal. How very dismaying it would be to stop short of it. It is not such a big thing, entering an agility trial, but it is the spark that sometimes was all that lit a very dismaying darkness, and I want it now as much as Asherel.

Deb has the full sized A-frame set up, which is quite tall and quite steep. Honeybun has only done the smaller, tottering A-frame that Asherel built up to that point. Yet, Honeybun clambers up the steep side without pause. She has to scramble to make it over the apex, and then scramble again to keep from tumbling snoot over tail on the way down, but she does so fearlessly. Asherel resumes her more typically content and happy demeanor, and I exhale.

While the calmness and passivity might not be the right attitude for Agility, it is actually working in her favor in the rest of her life. She is becoming a stable, gentle, almost reliable dog. When we return home, a meat salesman rings the doorbell, and Honeybun skids into the door and leaps up on it, barking as usual. I walk over calmly, smack the whip, and order her back. I have the routine down pat. I dream about smacking whips and rolling dogs. I cautiously approach the door.

"Just one moment," I say politely to the meat man, and then smack the whip again and command Honeybun to sit. Amazingly, she does. She wags her tail and makes little anxious moaning sounds, but she remains sitting while I open the door. The salesman looks concerned.

"I don't hit her with this," I explain, waving the whip, "She is in training."

He still looks worried, as the door is open, but says tremulously, "Well good luck with that."

As he makes his pitch, my eye remains on Honeybun. Every time she twitches as though to stand, I point the whip at her, warning her to stay. She has never listened to me off leash with such a tempting intruder like a salesman, but she is listening this time. The poor meat man doesn't know that I have no intention of buying his meat but am just enjoying the opportunity to train our dog. Strangers are hard to come by. He keeps a wary eye on her, while trying to sail gracefully and convincingly through his spiel. Finally, I put both him and Honeybun out of their misery.

"Thank you, but I don't eat meat," I say, and he hurries gratefully away.

At that point, as the door closes, I release Honeybun, telling her what a good dog she is. She remains quiet as she watches the meat man drive away. Why, if she is so good, did I not buy her a small sirloin?

This day is also the final art class for the year. Asherel asks if she can put Honeybun on leash during class, and not crate her since she has been doing so well. I agree. As the kids file in, Honeybun doesn't even bark. She wags her tail, sniffs all the kids, and then lies at Asherel's feet. This is all very encouraging. Anders will be home in two days, and all signs are pointing to Honeybun not sucking out his eyeballs. That will be the final test for me of Honeybun's complete rehabilitation. If she sweetly welcomes Anders, then I am ready to call her completely cured. At that point, I will book a flight to Tahiti, and reserve a hotel that doesn't allow dogs.

The day finally arrives when he flies home for Christmas. Anders works in Boston in a start-up business he and three MIT friends are developing. We last saw him in June, when we attended his graduation from MIT. I have been sending weekly updates on Honeybun and our trials and tribulations. He is busy starting the new business working nonstop, and it is likely he has not read any of the emails, however. Even if our life was remotely interesting, he is too swamped with the demands of this new job to read my many updates.

Anders has a sweet gentle core, but sometimes you have to be willing to dig a little to find it. His exterior demeanor comes across a tad differently. He is very quiet, and very serious. Though keenly intelligent with perceptiveness that often surprises me, he is not interested in most conversations. He can be curt, and gruff, and distant. He doesn't seem very people oriented at all, but I may misread him at times. As with Honeybun, I don't always read the signs correctly. And as with Honeybun, I am determined to get past his bite.

His world is of the intellect. Most of social intercourse confuses and bores him. He has always been silently communicative with babies and animals, but people in general hold little interest for him…at least people who don't know what a "release candidate kernel" is, which is 99.999% of the world. He is a very tall young man - just the sort of threatening presence Honeybun displays her remaining aggression towards.

As we drive back from the airport, we prep Anders on how to greet Honeybun.

"She is really very sweet," I assure him, and myself, "But she can be funny when meeting people, especially when they first walk in. So, we will go in first and put her on leash. You wait outside until we tell you it is ok."

He nods.

"She has never bitten anyone," I assert (but not because she hasn't tried, I don't add.) I urge him to ignore her when he enters the laboratory, er, home.

Anders quietly stands on the porch as the dogs come crashing to the door, barking and leaping for joy. Honeybun stands with her nose pressed against the window, wagging her tail. Asherel enters first, like the Marines, and snaps the leash on the overjoyed Honeybun. Lucky squishes between her legs and races over to Anders. It has been a year since Lucky last saw Anders, and he is beside himself with delight.

"OK," I say, holding open the door, "Come on in, Anders."

Honeybun is busy licking all of us, dashing from one

to the other, when she looks up and sees Anders. She moves toward him, that piercing still look on her face, tail still wagging. His face was the same unperturbed look he has worn since babyhood.

"Hello Honeybun," he says.

She licks his hand.

Despite my instructions to ignore her, a second later, he is kneeling and petting her. Funny how animals see right through all the flotsam and jetsam of the outer rings of character. Honeybun ignores the gruff, silent, and towering exterior and plows right through to the kindness of his soul that reveals itself cautiously and rarely. Later, I see him silently returning her stare, and am about to warn him to stop, that that is perceived as a challenge to a dog, but then she leans against him, and he pets her.

I am taking notes in my head. What is it about the dog that is bringing out such a quiet gentleness in my gruff son? I suspect it is her unquestioning and unconditional acceptance of who he is. She is not telling him he looks like a wet mop with those shoulder length corkscrew curls. She is not asking him if he is content, financially solvent, or has brushed his teeth. She is just leaning against him with her silky soft presence.

It is almost Christmas, near the end of one of the most challenging years of my life. It seems a lifetime ago that we found Honeybun. All those struggles so sharp and cutting early on are blurring to a softened haze of memory, morphing to the image that fills my heart now. She is not perfect, but then who is? It is an incomparable joy for me to have all my children home, however briefly. Anders goes right to work fixing all the things that have gone wrong with all our computers since he last fixed them for us. I sit nearby with a good book, while Matt, Asherel, and Arvo watch a football game. Lucky tries to inch his way up on the forbidden couch, and Honeybun lies near Anders' feet, her unblinking eyes watching him. One ear is cockeyed, and one ear is up, alert, listening. I try to mimic her as much as I can this visit, and it is largely peaceful, though flies by in near silence. This is difficult for me and I cry as his plane whisks him back to Boston, so much unsaid. Goodbye son. Honeybun gently licks me, a rare gift, when I return home.

Things are going so well that I begin to open the door to friends without leashing Honeybun. I tell her "back", smack the whip on the ground and hold it threateningly. Lucky nearly always manages to get around me. I need eyes all around my head and ten arms to keep both dogs under control. Since Honeybun is the less reliable in terms of aggression, I focus on her. Sometimes I even open the door to children without my whip in hand. She seems to universally like kids now. That is a huge worry off my heart.

I schedule a farm field trip, and add my services as an art teacher to entice more students. We will draw one of the farm animals under my instruction. The information is sent out to all my email groups, and my homeschool network. An immediate flood of responses pour back. Ten kids sign up the first day, at $15 per person. Malta can accommodate twenty. Maybe I *can* be useful! That is $150 already for the farm, and a likely $300 by the time the field trip deadline rolls around. That feeds Malta's animals for at least a week…

With Malta and Will now working seventy hour weeks, seven days a week, she does not have the time to work with her rescued horses. They need a "humane horse trainer", whom she is willing to train. She sends an email plea to her "farm friends" list. I write back instantly intrigued.

"Do Asherel and I qualify as a humane horse trainer? She has worked with horses since age 5, and I worked with them a lot when I was growing up, and was on the college riding team. I am rusty, but I think I could relearn pretty quickly. I am making no promises, but can you tell me what is involved?"

Malta quickly responds,

"Safety is the big issue. You would need helmets. I can

train you in an hour and you could come whenever you were able. It involves basic building trust with humans- no dressage for a while... things like feeding, brushing, picking hooves. Sadie won't even let anyone touch her yet. I just don't have the time to work with her. She needs to learn that not all humans are monsters."

We meet in a week to go over the details. After informing Arvo that Asherel and I will be volunteering to work with the horses since Malta doesn't have time, he yelps, "My daughter will be working with *wild* horses?"

"No, not wild, just *psychotic*."

"Great," he answers.

"We will be wearing helmets," I assure him.

Meanwhile, we decide that with the economy in shambles and interest rates at an all time low, it is time to refinance. The appraiser shows up at lunch time. We are ready with Honeybun on leash. When she sees Chad the appraiser, she reverts to the fiend she had been months ago. She lunges, snaps, snarls, and barks. The only thing she doesn't do is pull out a gun, and I think if she had opposable thumbs, she would have. We jerk her back like Malta taught us, yelling "Enough!" in deep baritones. Will my life never be normal again?

"She *does* have some aggression issues, doesn't she?" notes Chad.

“Oh she is much better,” I claim. He can of course see that for himself.

The entire half hour he is at our house, Honeybun unveils her wild demon. Sometimes Asherel has the leash, and when Chad is within biting range, I take over. She sits quietly when he is in the room a while, but each time he moves, she flies into a rage of barking and lunging. She gags as I snap her back, time after time.

When Chad leaves and I reattach my arm, Asherel pets her and proclaims cheerily, "That went well. She was pretty good."

I stare at Asherel.

"Good for what? A convicted murderer?"

Writing to Malta, I inform her that her Honeybun training days are not over. She writes back and assures me the problem will be easily solved, but is too busy to think straight right now. I am getting the sense that Malta is cutting me loose. She has given me the tools and now I am required to plow forward on my own. I have been puffing up a little too much, and now is deflation time. A needle in my pride is not welcome, but some would argue, necessary at times. We have had this dog over six months now, and there is still so much work to be done. I have no choice but to be patient. Stick with the program. Stop whining.

However, I am feeling a little overwhelmed yet again. So much to do. On top of all the demands of home school, I am busy with my various roles as team manager for DI, Sunday school teacher, and art class teacher.

"Sometimes I wonder why I teach this class," I complain to Asherel, "I just don't have the time with homeschooling and all the other things we are doing!"

With this admirable attitude, I open the door to my little art group. They set busily and happily to work, when one straggler comes in - quiet, late, subdued. She is normally cheerful and talks a mile a minute. Not today. She has also forgotten to bring a picture to draw from. So I give her my pile of photos saved for such emergencies, and she quietly leafs through them. She chooses a beautiful peaceful scene and tells me this reminds her of Texas and so she will draw this one. I give her some instructions and am about to scurry on to the next child amidst the controlled mayhem of the chattering class, when she asks if she can tell me why she chose that particular picture.

"It reminds me of Texas, when my dad was alive. Four years ago he passed away, and today is his birthday," she says sadly, "I want to do it as a memorial for him."

The class is silent. What do you say to that?

Putting my arm around her shoulder, I tell her I know that it must be a very hard day for her, and I will help her make it a lovely picture to honor her dad.

And then I commence feeling like a dung beetle for all my kvetching about how I am too busy to run my art classes or train my dog. We are all called upon to be "guard geese" at times, looking beyond ourselves to the needs of the gaggle. And sometimes it can be in the form of something as mundane as an art class or saving a wounded beast. The little girl does not speak the whole class period, just silently and mournfully spreads pastel fog and water across her paper of grief and comfort.

The private lessons with Deb end, and we have a brief respite before the classes at the dog club will begin. Asherel is signed up for a class called “Contacts”, which means that she will be working with Honeybun over the A-frame, teeter, weaves, pause table, and dog walk. Deb told us she is far beyond beginner level at this point, and will be the star of the class. I am not so sure, since there will be many dogs around. She has never done agility work with other dogs. However, Asherel is now feeling very confident.

The first class is an informational meeting, just like the first Rally class had been. This time when we walk in, we feel entirely different than we had those many months ago when we had first entered the building. Asherel is still one of only two people there not dependent on Medicare, but this time, we greet many familiar faces.

The general meeting reiterates all the soothing points about all dogs not being friendly, stay out of other dog's "personal space", ask before petting, have fun, etc… Then we break to our small group settings for the specific class in which we are registered. Asherel and I know Vicci, Lloyd's wife, who is the assistant instructor. We have met Bit, the lead instructor, and respect her just from watching the perfect obedience of her chocolate lab. The first thing out of Bit's mouth is to warn the whole class that Honeybun does not like other dogs in her face, and that everyone is to respect that. Asherel and I stand there like lepers as the others gawk at us.

"But my dog loves everyone," complains one lady, "She will want to race up to play."

"But you will have perfect recall, as required in this class," admonishes Bit sternly, "So that won't be an issue."

Perfect recall? I don't remember that as being a prerequisite. Asherel and I studiously avoid looking at each other.

"Remember," reminds Bit, "This class assumes a level of obedience before the dog is ready for performance work. It must be able to come consistently. There will be a lot of distractions and other dogs. Most of our work will be off leash."

Vicci is smiling, like she always does, and looking encouragingly at me and Asherel, nodding like a bobble head doll. I avoid her gaze. Perfect recall? Come consistently? Level of obedience? All those ominous phrases are clanging in my head. Bit asks how many dogs have any experience on agility equipment. Finally, something we can look her in the eyes to respond to!

Vicci pipes up, "Honeybun has been working with Deb K."

Bit looks impressed, "What has she done?"

Asherel lists the full array of equipment, but admits Honeybun is slow through the weaves.

The other members have also had agility training. One dog is new to agility, but his owner has competed with other agility dogs. Far from being the hopeful star of the class, it looks like Honeybun will be the dog with imperfect, inconsistent, maybe even *absent* recall and no more training than anyone else there in agility.

As we drive home, Asherel perkily chatters, "I can't wait for next week when we start!"

I am lost in the miasma of doom and gloom, envisioning being handed a yellow paper with giant letters saying "Excused from class by reason of nonexistent recall and gross misrepresentation."

"I am not sure about that perfect recall bit," I say morosely.

Asherel admits that might be a cause for concern.

"But you have a week... If you work on it really hard every day..." My words trail off.

So she starts the next day working very hard on perfect recall. She takes Honeybun out back and within seconds, I hear Honeybun inside, skittering across the floor. Asherel is standing outside, looking in through the sliding glass door.

"Maybe we should do an obedience class instead?" she calls, tapping on the door.

"Maybe we should write to Bit in the spirit of full disclosure and tell her we don't have perfect recall. What do you think?"

Asherel nods.

I email Bit admitting that we had thought the class started with the dog on leash, and while Honeybun does come consistently indoors with no distractions and lots of yummy treats, she does not have anything remotely resembling perfect recall. We do not want to set her up for failure, and if Bit recommends we do a different class, we will certainly consider her suggestion.

Bit writes back. Actually, the class description *had* specified off leash and consistent recall essential, but that was mostly to ensure there weren't dogs running all over the place, out of control, wasting class time. She wants to give Honeybun a shot, let her try… she may surprise us. She may indeed, I think, I hope it is a *pleasant* surprise.

Class day is bitter cold. Worse yet, our class doesn't start till 6:30 that evening. We bundle up and gather the very best treats we can find - honey baked ham, chicken cordon bleu, and Italian meatballs. Honeybun is salivating the whole car drive. We arrive a half hour early - not knowing how traffic will be at that time of the evening. The leaders are busy dragging out the heavy agility equipment. We introduce Bit to Honeybun, who wags her tail, and Asherel lets Honeybun sniff the surroundings while I help set up. Asherel is nervous. I am too. Can I be prosecuted for murder if I knowingly unleash a dog with imperfect recall? Honeybun has come a long way but she has never been off leash around other dogs. At 6:30, only one other dog has shown up. Despite praying this will be all that come, the other five dogs meander in. I am then praying that God will remove all Honeybun's teeth painlessly, miraculously, and quickly.

Bit asks who wants to go first, and I nudge Asherel forward. I cannot stand the suspense any longer figuring it is best to get the carnage over as quickly as possible. Asherel glares at me as she stumbles forward.

The first piece of equipment is the A-frame. Asherel keeps Honeybun on leash and runs beside her. Honeybun scales the A-frame admirably, but as soon as she finishes, Bit asks, "Has she done it off leash?"

"Yes," says Asherel.

"Well then do it again off leash," commands Bit.

She notices a look of concern on Asherel's face, pauses and asks, "She won't go after the other dogs, will she?"

"I don't *think* so," answers Asherel slowly.

Bit looks troubled, but the next dog is already going over the A-frame, and her attention is diverted. When Asherel's turn comes again, she unsnaps the leash, while I wait on the other side of the A-frame, per Bit's instructions.

"Grab her collar if you need to," warns Bit.

Honeybun knows I have the mega-value treats in my hand, and she flies over the A-frame, and skids to sit in front of me. I snatch her collar and wipe my palms, mysteriously sweaty in the frigid night.

"Very good!" calls Bit.

The next piece of equipment we will defy death and destruction on is the dog walk.

"Has she done this one?" asks Bit.

"Oh yes, she loves the dogwalk!" answers Asherel.

Honeybun actually looks like a real agility dog on the dog walk. She zips across the plank at top speed and sits at the end, to gobble her ham from me.

By the time we are ready to try the weaves, we are almost enjoying ourselves. Honeybun has shown no interest in attacking anything but the ham and meatballs. She scampers through the weave poles, and then class is over. It has raced by.

Asherel and I walk cheerily back to the car. As we leave the enclosure, Vicci and Bit both tell us how well Honeybun has done. This is the beauty of low expectations. She is not the star of the class, by any means. The other dogs *like* other dogs, are very obedient, and dash over every piece of equipment with ease. The other owners have all competed in agility and know what they are doing. But Honeybun has not hurt anyone or their dog, and she has tried every piece of equipment without fear. Asherel has done all that is requested of her with a smile, and cheerful understanding. There are no hospital bills to pay or lawsuits to litigate.

"That went much better than I expected," says Asherel. I nod, too worn out to speak.

"And Honeybun had fun. Look Mom, she's smiling!"

I glance in the mirror. I don't see a smile. I see endless cold nights tensely poised to grab a canine missile should it target innocent flesh. I see class after expensive class en route to a goal we may never be able to reach. But she does look content, sitting in the middle seat, chewing on an empty cracker wrapper. I have to admit, the class was fun for me too, once past the torturous aspect of uncertainty. Progress has been slow, but it is still progress. It is like a canoe ride rather than a motor boat, and I am beginning to enjoy the scenery along the way.

We don't have long to rest on our laurels. The next day we head out to Last Chance Rescue to work with the psychotic horse. I am battling a cold, but feel well enough to go, and Asherel is gurgling with excitement over working with the horses. So we pack our schoolbooks for the long drive and off we venture to blaze these unfamiliar trails. Malta greets us with ten barking dogs. They all crowd around us, anxious to be petted. One of them, with a face carved in sweetness and love, plants his paws around my waist and leans his head against me. I haven't had a hug like this in years. This is why I love dogs - no matter how old and wrinkled and ugly you are, you are still the one who operates the can opener…Whenever I move, he moves with me. If I didn't already have two dogs at home, I would've snatched him up.

On the pillow of a chair with food next to her, lies a tiny Chihuahua. This is the dog we had been warned not to touch when we were there for the fieldtrip. She doesn't look dangerous, no bigger than a teacup. I watch as Malta gives her filtered water from her glass.

"Why is her food right on the chair?"

"She can't walk," answers Malta. Malnutrition in her long life has crippled her legs. She can only crawl. So she reigns like a queen from her chair, waited on hand and foot by Malta and Will. And she terrorizes the big dogs if they bug her. She is a Great Dane in a Chihuahua body. Dogs have Napoleonic complexes too.

Malta grabs a halter, and we head out to the paddock.

"I'm gonna start you on an easy horse to show you what to do," Malta explains, as we pass through the deer enclosure. Timmy and Bonnie watch us with their huge doe eyes, and ears like serving platters. As Malta unlocks the gate to the paddock, having gathered our brushes, hoof pick, and lots of treats, she warns us about the little pony that crowds near.

"Look at his ears. What do they tell you?"

“That he is not happy,” I answer, glancing at his ears flattened back.

"That's right, this is Bob and he is mean. If you turn your back on him, he will bite you. And then he will hide. He terrorizes the other horses too."

She waves the lead rope at him, swooshing him away.

"You will work with Sequoia, Will's horse. She is nice and I won't worry at all. That one, the palomino, is Sadie. She is the one that I want you to try to help."

Sadie stands nearby, watching us, but when Malta reaches out a hand, Sadie skitters away. Meanwhile, as we lead Sequoia into a center enclosed ring to work with her, Bob is raising a ruckus with another group of horses along the fence, baring his teeth, flattening his ears and kicking.

"Why do you have Bob?" I ask.

"Because when I was at a farm picking up a dog, the owner was about to shoot Bob because he was so mean. So I took him too. He almost killed me in the horse trailer when I tried to tie him in. I understand why the owner wanted to shoot him, but...He is much better now."

I can't imagine what he was like then when he first arrived.

The first thing Malta teaches us is to always have an escape route. This of course does not fill me with warm and fuzzy feelings. I suspect we are not embarking on the most carefully thought out adventure we have ever attempted if plotting escape routes is the first goal. She instructs Asherel to scan her surroundings and decide where she would flee if the horses start to go crazy. I am wondering if we should perform a preemptive flee now. Next, she teaches her how to get the 1000 pound animal to follow the 100 pound girl's directions.

"You won't be able to overpower her, right?" says Malta as Asherel pulls fruitlessly on the lead, and Sequoia plants her feet, "So you have to outthink her."

As Malta enlightens us on various ways to be smarter than a horse, Sadie is growing interested in what is happening in the ring, and she approaches the fence right behind me. I grab a snack from my pocket and offer it to her. She stretches her neck full length towards me, slowly, then reaches out with her muzzle, knocking it to the ground. I offer another. This time she takes a step closer and nibbles it directly from my hand.

"What is the story with Sadie?" I ask.

"She is a Mustang. For three years she was left in a pasture. Never touched, groomed, or bothered with. Then when someone finally got a halter on her and tied her, she got stung by a wasp and went crazy. No one could get near her again. The owner just came one day, and left her at our farm."

"She's never been ridden?"

"No, she is basically wild. For three years, she has lived as a feral horse."

So Malta *does* want us to tame a wild Mustang. Won't Arvo be excited! I have about as much experience doing that as I'd had before Honeybun in taming a wild, vicious dog. I reach out to pet her muzzle, but she skitters away again.

With basic training in Horse Groundwork 101 completed, Malta announces we can now groom Sequoia and practice what she has shown us, for as long as we can stand the cold. She reminds us that when we are done, just pop back in the house to drop off the halter. Be sure to close all the fences behind us. She trudges away, her multiple broken bones gathered over the years aching in the bitter cold. Someday, I will ask how she broke the bones, wondering if that is Bob's contribution to her health and well-being.

Bob, innocent of my misgivings about him, stands outside the pen watching us the whole time. I offer him a treat through the fence. He perks his ears forward and takes it as I stroke his nose. His ears are still back, with a grumpy look on his face, but he seems to like the attention. Petting him, I realize that I am meeting up with many examples lately of crusty exteriors hiding soft, needy spirits within. I am even beginning to feel a budding tolerance and sympathy. Maybe some of the human pitbulls and Bob's of the world deserve a closer look. I promise myself I will practice loving the unlovable on the next telemarketer that calls, instead of telling him that I am unable to talk right now due to a brain transplant that has severely affected my hearing.

We practice not being killed by a horse for another hour and then decide to head back. I still have over an hour drive home, and my very sore throat is definitely getting worse.

But first, to leave the circular pen, we have to get by Bob. Sequoia does not seem anxious to walk out the gate back to the field where Bob waits. We shoo Bob away, and he moves back a few feet. Sequoia looks at us and doesn't budge. She obviously knows something about Bob, and is taking no chances. I consider calling for help, but recoil from the display of weakness; one little pony so befuddling us. I swat the lead rope at Bob again, and he grudgingly moves away, far enough to entice Sequoia to safely leave the pen. As we head to the paddock gate, glancing repeatedly at Bob, all three horses follow us with Sadie in the rear.

After popping through the gate and locking it, all three horses stand near looking at us. I reach in my pocket and offer Sadie another treat. She comes closer and nibbles it gingerly from my hand, her muzzle stretched as far as she can reach in her timidity. Muzzles are amazingly elastic, like a snake uncoiling. Asherel reaches out her hand, palm flat with a treat, and Sadie pecks it quickly from her hand. We both remain several minutes, feeding the three horses, and crooning to them till we are out of treats. Then I reach out to pet Sadie's nose. She stands still and I stroke it twice before she backs away. Asherel continues talking gently to her, and also pets her. We caress her soft muzzle for a few minutes, though she is nervous and only lets us touch her a few seconds each time before pulling away.

When we drop the halter back at Malta's house and inform her that Sadie let us pet her, she is surprised.

"That's more than she has ever let me do with her," smiles Malta, "Sadie is yours to work with. Have at her!"

We drive home, blasting the car heater. It is funny how simple some of the pleasures of life can be. Something as inconsequential as petting the nose of a horse that has not endured human touch in three years, a few seconds of soft hair against one's palm. The first tentative touch of friendship between species has just made my day.

Dear Lord,

I am determined to look beyond the externals and see what is inside the creatures you have placed in my midst.

Thank you that you have given me such an assortment of crochety, untamed, skittish, and withdrawn characters to learn to see depth and soul. Oh Father, as often as I have been misunderstood and my motives misinterpreted...I must have done to others as well! I know my fellow humans should be more comprehensible than wild dogs or psychotic horses, but how often do I misjudge and hurt relationships that I should be nurturing? I struggle to relate well to my own son!

I am a person of deep emotions, of words. How hard it is for me to comprehend silence, or reticence to share feelings! It was wise of you to let me practice on a dog first. I might be ready now to move on to a human. I think perhaps you had to send Jesus as a man. How else could we hope to relate or begin to comprehend God? It is so hard to step outside of our own skin. Of course, a man who walks on water is a little outside my experience too, but easier to wrap my brain around than eternal and infinite.

Thank you for your determination to follow me, to keep me in your sights, even though I walked away so many times. I know I have a prickly outer coating myself but you never give up on me. Sanding my edges hurts, Father, but I suppose it is the only way I will take on a heavenly polish.

Amen.

CHAPTER 12

Perseverance

We visit Sadie only a couple of times a month as the drive is too far to do on a regular basis with all the demands of homeschool, dog training, and the Destination Imagination team I coach. You may have noticed this is the umpteenth time I have mentioned this list of all I do. This is my way of making sure you know how special and important I am, but also to excuse our slow progress. I really want to do it all, but the constraints of time are dragging me down mightily.

The second visit progresses much as the first had, with Sadie seeming more interested in us, and letting us touch her nose a little longer. However, our third visit advances our taming exponentially. Malta and Will are not there, but are off at their "money making job" which is how the farm survives. Asherel and I are on our own, definitely reducing my performance anxiety. Malta never criticizes, but I am always more relaxed when no one is watching and wincing.

As we approach, Sadie's ears perk up and she trots over to us. This is indeed a good sign, though it is connected to the delicious treats we always ply her with. Like Honeybun, her heart seems to be directly linked to her stomach.

"Our plan of attack," I instruct my side-kick, "Is to put the halter on Bob and groom him in the ring. When Sadie comes near we will feed her, and then we will leave Bob in the ring and work with Sadie more closely."

This is necessary because we don't know what we are doing, and Bob is unpredictable. I have learned through the benefit of prior disasters that ineptitude and unpredictability when commingled can produce results that are often not ideal.

Also, Bob is not nice to the other horses, and when they come near to see what goodies we are offering, Bob flattens his ears (even further than they are habitually) and charges. The other horses swirl, and sometimes kick out, and I don't want me or Asherel caught in the ensuing maelstrom. As expected, Bob meets us at the fence, ears back, but still seems happy we are there. I deduce this from the fact that he is not biting us. I easily halter him this time, pulling his ears forward as I put the strap behind them.

"See?" I prod him, "This is happy horse expression. Ears forward to make friends and influence people."

As I release his ears, they snap back, the equine equivalent of a scowl. Sadie and Sequoia scatter as I lead Bob to the enclosed pen, and then follow at a safe distance. If Sequoia wanders near, Sadie flicks back her ears, swishes her tail, and lunges at her. Poor Sequoia rushes away, and watches from a distance. I hate that horses do that to each other. Whoever thinks that animal communities are any sweeter to each other than humans hasn't watched animals very long. The one thing they *do* have over human interaction is honesty. There is no doubt that Bob is a mean crank towards other horses and will kick them if they come too close. He never puts on a pious front.

Bob is happy in the enclosed pen, as he knows our pockets are bulging with treats. He also seems to like the attention, and I am sure in horse language is putting on an air of superiority to the horses standing outside the pen. Sadie comes to the pen fence and stretches her muzzle towards us. Leaving Asherel in charge of Bob, I move slowly to the fence and she allows me to stroke her long nose and soft muzzle. She puffs air out her nostrils, distending them in a high strung, nervous sort of way, but stands her ground as I pet her. She eagerly inhales the horse treats Malta has left for us. Bob consents to let us pick his hooves without much trouble, and brush out his coat, which is beginning to shed its winter lining. It is time now to work more directly with Sadie. Bob remains complacently in the pen, watching us, and closing his eyes in the warm, just beginning to beckon spring sunshine.

Asherel grooms Sequoia, leaving me free to charm Sadie. She surprisingly approaches me, and even lets me hold both hands on her nose. I have a little soft face brush in my hand. Sadie has not been groomed in years. Her long mane is knotted and matted, and her coat has dirt all over it. She looks healthy, just dirty. She thinks the face brush is food and tries to nibble it. I softly touch it to her face and manage a tentative swipe. She remains still, her skin quivering. I think she likes it. I don't see smiles, like Asherel does, but she isn't running away and that is an encouraging sign. I continue to brush her nose, and she remains poised to run, but stationary for now. Then as the brush moves to her neck, she skitters away, but when I call her, she returns.

As I brush her nose, her eyes half close, dreamily. Once again I slowly move to her neck, and this time get in a couple of quick brushes before she backs away. It is like a dance. She moves up to me, I brush her face, move to her neck, attempt two or three swipes, and she skitters away. Each time she returns, she is rewarded with a treat. I have no idea if this is what "humane horse trainers" do, but it seems to be working. She stands for longer and longer periods while I brush her neck. She won't let me near her mane, or her ears, but is happy to let me brush the dirt from her neck. After about a half hour, she skitters back and then canters away. She has had all the human touch she can tolerate that day, so we pack up our bags of brushes and halters. I am strangely peaceful. This must be what patience feels like. It is an alien feeling to me; this slowed heart rate, distant goals slowly approaching in the far distance, no boxes being checked on my ever-present list.

"Next time," I tell Asherel, "We will carry the halter on our arm, so she can get used to it being around while we brush her."

I will train her from the nose back. We have conquered the face, and most of the neck. Next time, we will move to the withers and chest, taming the wild mustang one body part at a time.

As we pass the deer pen, we notice Bonnie, the small female deer has two long lines of stitches across her shaved face, with wounds on her body too. When we arrive home I e-mail Malta, and tell her how much fun we had, how peaceful it is at Last Chance Rescue, and by the way, what happened to Bonnie?

Apparently, a stray dog had attacked the deer, trying to kill them. It broke Bonnie's nose before Will, hearing the commotion, raced out, tackled the dog and saved the deer. The dog was humanely euthanized. The deer were stitched up, put on heavy meds, and were recovering.

"*Peaceful here? LOL*!" she writes.

Meanwhile, dog agility classes are proceeding better than expected. The classes are at night, and the usually mild

NC winter is unusually frigid this winter. I shiver in my multiple layers of down and wool, nervously watching for any sign that Honeybun is about to attack during her periods off leash. I don't need to worry. She is fixated on the luscious treats we have packed for her, and her attention rarely wavers to the other dogs. Of course, our good fortune cannot continue forever. Next class, a rambunctious poodle slips his leash and races to Honeybun's reward dish. Honeybun has just completed the weaves and is collecting her treat. I am too far away to intervene, and watch in horror as the poodle sticks his nose in Honeybun's food. I am already picturing the intestines uncoiling across the field, the sirens as Asherel and Honeybun are dragged away, the angry eviction notice pinned to our dog. But amazingly, she just finishes her mouthful, and her tail keeps wagging. Asherel grabs her then, but not a growl has erupted.

After that heart-pausing incident, she scampers over the A-frame; literally leaping across the apex like it is a jump on her quest to collect her treat.

"Bravo!" cries Bit, the instructor, "That was beautiful!"

I laugh. Honeybun's "passion and enthusiasm" is all about getting to the food as fast as she can. She loves agility night, because it means lots of tender morsels that are withheld the rest of the week. On top of how delicious the agility snacks are, we reduce her dinner on training nights to ensure she will be motivated to keep her attention on Asherel.

One night, as we near the midpoint of the agility semester, Honeybun slips her collar. She has just finished the dogwalk, but quickly assesses that more food waits over by the A-frame. I watch ineffectually as she looks piercingly at the dog still scrambling over the A-frame, and determines that she can beat him to the reward. She gallops towards the food.

"She slipped her collar- she's loose Bit!" shrieks Vicci, the other instructor.

Bit is about to grab the dog from the A-frame, as I yell to Honeybun, "No! Stay!"

Honeybun stops in mid stride, screeching to a halt. Asherel grabs her.

"That was good!" exults Vicci.

I think that is what is referred to as "perfect recall" that dreaded skill we know our dog doesn't have. Yet somehow, out of the depths of her love for us (or at least the love of our treats) she has rummaged the ability to obey even in the face of such tantalizing prey.

While we still have four classes left, it is time to sign the dogs up for the next class. Honeybun has already leaped ahead, bypassing all the obedience classes, and all the "foundation" classes for agility. Reading over the choices, I see we can do the second level Foundation class, or the Handling Class, which requires all those prerequisites we don't have, or instructor approval. Handling class is for the dog that has a solid understanding and skill on all the equipment, and now is ready to prepare for competition with training in intricate handling techniques. It sounds unwise for us to even consider. I write to Vicci and Bit, asking what class they recommend Honey tackle next.

They both recommend the Handling Class. I sit back and gaze at the email, feeling like crying. Part of that is of course due to the $125 class fee, but the other part is that the vote of confidence moves me deeply. It is sometimes such a little thing that hope teeters on.

At church, I sit in the far back, my usual spot, unless someone steals my seat. I am there quite early, and hide behind the program, rereading the same paragraph hoping I will not have to talk to a stranger. Noticing a woman alone in the pew in front of me, I see her wipe a tear away. The church is still nearly empty, with ten minutes before the sermon will start. I know the woman very slightly. I think of Sadie, hurt by wasps and letting that one event color her world "danger", remembering the weeks spent just to touch her neck. Visions of Honeybun snarling at anyone approaching rather than risk being hurt…

I stand and tap the lady on her shoulder.

"Hi," I say smiling, "Is everything ok?"

No, it is not. Her daughter has not spoken to her in two years. She will not speak to her sister or her father either. She blames her mother for awful things, all untrue. The lady quietly wipes her eyes. She will never forgive her daughter for what she has done, the hurt is too great.

Sympathizing, I tell her I will pray for her, though that sounds insignificant even to my ears. But I tell her, remembering Honeybun, remembering Sadie, remembering Jesus; sometimes when we reach out in love to those who don't deserve it, or even want it, miracles happen. The choir starts singing and I return to my seat with a deep sigh, thinking of silent ones, hurts unvoiced, and words of love unspoken.

After completion of two classes with the kennel club, we are now eligible to apply for membership. Our membership is contingent on the board's approval, and if admitted, our classes are then half price. I have no idea what criteria they use to admit or deny membership. Applicants must have superior sense of smell? I didn't realize dog clubs are picky. I wonder if a non AKC non-breed dog like ours will be admitted to the oldest kennel club in Charlotte, an AKC bastion of beautiful champions.

Bit grabs me as we are starting class the fifth week and says, "Oh, by the way, as soon as you fill out a membership form, you are a member. We all voted you in last night."

I laugh, and smile at my new friends, our American Dingo, and my brave little girl. We haven't even applied yet. What a wonderful group of people we have landed in the midst of. So many kind souls rooting for us, taking risks for us, and extending so much grace and mercy to us.

"She's a great little dog," Bit adds, noting my incredulity.

With three classes left in our Contact class, Bit asks if we have registered Honeybun with an agility group.

"You mean like UKC?" I ask. I know her breed is accepted by UKC, though not AKC. I thought Bit just wants us to be able to brag that our dog is a recognized breed by a recognized club.

"No, I mean like USDAA for agility competition."

Asherel darts a sideways look at me, and I can tell she is simmering with excitement.

"I would register her now," says Bit.

The very next day, I search online for local or nearby USDAA agility trials. There are surprisingly quite a few within two or three hours from us. I read over the description of "starters" classes, and realize that Honeybun might indeed be ready for the novice contests. With mounting excitement, I call the USDAA representative, and register Honeybun. We are now an official US Dog Agility Association (USDAA) member with a number, poised to compete. We begin perusing the trial schedule to determine which we should enter and when.

The evening of the orientation meeting for the Agility Handling class arrives. We are instructed to bring our dogs if we desire. The socialization time will be valuable for Honeybun. Grabbing a bag of ham to keep her focused on us, and not the other dogs, we go with wagging tails. The instructor, Laura, explains that this class is for dogs that have advanced beyond basics, and are "elite athletes". The class members gather around her. Only one other member has brought her dog, a little white fluffy thing. Laura explains what we should expect from the class, and we are smug, being as we have now survived two agility classes and not put ourselves to shame. Honeybun has not killed any living creature thus far.

She will do anything for food, is highly motivated by the premium ham treats we bring to class, and has been a model of obedience. The other class member who brought her dog to orientation begins an extensive discussion of how her dog refused to eat in her first agility class, and thus training is so hard as she is not food motivated at all.

I glance at Honeybun, whose attention is riveted on Asherel and the baggie of ham in her hand. Laura is conducting a pointed discussion about how elite athletes are thin, so they can handle the rigors of agility training, and how all elite athletes can easily feel their ribs. She keeps looking right at us, and at Honeybun, who is drooling while watching every move the ham in Asherel's hand makes. I wish she wouldn't be in a collected sit position because it rounds out her belly in a way that I suspect an elite athlete would not be proud of.

The instructor continues, "You don't need to press to feel their ribs, or they will need to lose some weight. Do not be insulted if I tell you in class that your dog needs to shed a few pounds. It would be wise to feel their ribs and maybe in the next few weeks, work on getting their weight to a healthy level for agility."

Why is she harping on this rib thing? I smile as she looks right at us, and glance again at Honeybun. How inconvenient that she chooses that moment to be leaping on Asherel pawing at the ham.

Ok, she *used* to have ribs... I know they are there. But they are definitely not as prominent as I remember.

"Any questions?" asks the instructor.

There are none. We start to move away, when the instructor asks, "Would anyone like me to feel their dog's ribs?"

Being as there are only two dogs there - the recovering anorexic, and our dog.... I wonder who she is talking to? We continue to move towards the exit, and the instructor calls to us, “Your dog will need to lose a little weight."

Good grief. The dog we have rescued from the brink of starvation is too pudgy now. Our little elite athlete is still jumping up on Asherel trying to retrieve the premium ham piece.

"She's a rescue dog," I explain lamely, “She was nearly dead from starvation when we found her."

The class looks at our pudgy dog. It is clear they are all thinking she has not missed many meals since then.

We start both dogs on lean cuisine, “healthy weight dog food”, and I try to up their exercise level. Honeybun, in particular, is not pleased. Lucky, ever the resourceful one just supplements his diet with goose poop. Honeybun, on the other hand sits despondently at the door of the laundry room where we store the dog food. She looks at the door, and then pointedly at us. We ignore her, and she wanders to her empty dog bowl, licks it, and then looks accusingly at us. Seeing this brings no additional dinner, she decides it is time to learn to speak English. She comes to me as I work at the computer and mournfully says, "woooood!" I glance at her.

"Arrrrooffooood!" she moans. Asherel pokes her head around the corner.

"Our dog just spoke," I explain, "She asked me for food."

We crack, and give her a small extra scoop of the low calorie kibble.

"Mom," Asherel reproaches, "She's frowning."

I look at her. She looks hopefully at me again.

"Do you want an elite athlete or a chow hound? Remember, next week, Laura will be looking for her ribs."

I slip her a little extra food later. I cannot shake the image of the starving dog who never knew where her next meal would come from.

Agility training in the backyard continues, and we have one more week of Bit's class before she moves on to the handling class where we know Laura will be poking around for ribs. Honeybun is now off leash doing entire sequences on the agility equipment in class. She never shows any aggression or really even any interest in anything but what the *treat de jour* is. She is gaining skill on all the agility pieces, particularly the jumps and A-frame and dog walk. She is learning the teeter, and nonplussed by the tunnel. However, she is slow and seemingly clueless about the Weave poles. I do not see how Honeybun is ever going to master them but Bit assures us she eventually will. Fortunately, we can enter novice jumper classes and avoid the weaves at least for a while in agility trials. We are contemplating an end of summer competition in Virginia.

Unexpectedly, Nina from the Rally class that seemed years ago forwards me an email:

Effective April 10, 2010 mixed breeds will be able to compete in AKC obedience, agility, and rally. Unfortunately they must compete in separate classes, and only at trials not held in conjunction with conformation shows, but at least it's a step in the right direction.

This is very good news. There are many AKC trials, but quite a few less USDAA trials nearby. We seem to be on a path to actually reaching our goal, step by step. I push on Honeybun's side. No ribs yet. Well, we still have a week……

"Arrrrrroooofooooood!" Honeybun howls.

Concurrently, our horse training is proceeding well. Malta and Will are there when we visit Sadie the next time. They are building catch pen fencing, which will be nice for us in the future as we can separate the horses more easily. Malta is confident we will tame Sadie, but I am not sure her confidence is justified. And I am not sure that we are wise and discerning in working with wild Sadie, and belligerent Bob. Some nights I go to sleep and see mangled, trampled bodies when my eyes close and wonder if perhaps we should seek tamer volunteer opportunities, like defanging rattlesnakes. But Asherel is having great fun.

Malta has not watched us work with Sadie for weeks. I am a little nervous, knowing I am bumbling along in ignorance. I bumble better without an audience. Malta's eyes are on me as Sadie eagerly tosses her head and pulls at my belly pack with her teeth. She knows we have treats in there. She lets us fiddle with her face, but still refuses to let us touch her neck or comb her tangled mane. Her nipping at our clothes, tugging at us with increasing excitement is not malicious, but she could miscalculate and nip skin. I don't want to reprimand her for fear of destroying all the good karma we have established with her.

As she nibbles at me, I pull the halter, dangling from my hand over her nose. She lets it sit there for a few seconds, then tosses her head and it slides off.

"That's right!" calls Malta, obviously unable to watch us stumbling neophytes any longer without comment. She strides over.

"Make her earn her treats now," commands Malta. She snatches the halter from me, and puts a treat under it, holding it under Sadie's nose. Sadie shakes her head and nibbles at Malta's arm, her teeth showing though not closing. Malta smacks her nose and Sadie skitters away.

"Don't let her show her teeth at you," Malta warns, "She will be back. She knows you are the food dispenser, but now you are the food dispenser with rules."

Sadie returns and licks her lips.

"Now you try it," orders Malta.

I give the treat to Asherel, then taking the halter, I instruct her to hold the treat under the dangling halter so that Sadie will be forced to slip her nose in if she wants the treat.

"Make her work for it!" calls Malta.

Sadie perks her ears, and then nibbles at my arm again. I flick my hand at her, and shout "No!" Sadie skitters away.

"That's ok!" insists Malta, "She'll be back!"

Sadie returns, circling slowly back to me. This time she sticks her nose in the halter, without nipping at us, and gobbles her treat.

"Good!" encourages Malta, and then like the gifted teacher that she is, she leaves to continue working on the fence. I know we are probably still being watched, but she is giving us space to learn in our own stumbling way. Asherel holds the treat while I fumble with the halter, but eventually we begin to coordinate our efforts well and we are consistently getting the halter halfway up Sadie's long nose. Once, she even allows the halter three fourths of the way on, calmly finishes her treat, and then licks her lips.

"GREAT!" calls Malta, "End there; end on a good note."

We saunter over, smiling with success.

"Did you see her licking her lip?" our teacher quizzes, "That means she has just learned something new. From now on, no more showing her teeth and she has to earn the treats. Next time I will get you the halter that clips on, so if you can get it over her ears, just leave it on. She will probably go a little crazy and run some, but just leave it on. Don't pull on it or anything yet, just let her get used to it."

I am happy to hear she feels we will get the halter on, but am envisioning the mad gallop that will ensue with us likely in the path. While talking a good talk, I am essentially a coward and the thought of a deranged mustang whisking about like an egg beater does not fill my heart with confidence. I am more willing now to step into completely uncharted waters with our success with Honeybun, but this is a thousand pounds heavier tub of water.

On our way out, we stop to pet the new baby foal in a nearby pen. Malta is not happy about the foal. Before they had one of their rescue stallions neutered, he managed to get to one of the mares. The result was this sweet foal. As Malta told the wide-eyed field trip class as they gazed at the new baby, "We do not rejoice in baby horses here. There are already too many horses being discarded and starved. The last thing the world needs is another horse."

Transfixed by the beautiful little foal, with her spindly legs and soft fuzzy mane and tail, I understand Malta's point. She is the one that has to struggle with the fallout of too many unwanted animals in the world. But I cannot say I don't rejoice in this little baby now that she is here. Honestly, there are too many people here too, but which one would you send back? The task switches at that point to finding someone who wants her. Malta would agree. She will cut off testicles faster than you can say "zero population growth", but once that animal is here, she will do everything in her power to make its stay here on Earth a pleasant one.

Handling Class starts as the spring begins to cascade, with oak leaves finally unfurling, the azalea bushes in full bloom, and little birds huddled in tiny nests in crooks of the tree out front. Honeybun looks marginally thinner, and she is distinctly not happy that we have reduced her intake.

We already know many of the people in the class, though the instructor does not know us except for that first brief introductory meeting. The classes will be conducted for eight weeks, and the largest hurdle for me will be staying awake. I am a notorious early to bed, early to rise kind of gal, and Honeybun too has settled into my circadian rhythm of life. At 9:00, she tiptoes daintily, nails clicking on the wood floor, over to Asherel's bed, where she leaps like a cat onto her side of the bed, and snuggles her head on the pillow. Asherel covers her with a sheet and blanket. Within seconds, this pampered pet closes her eyes and begins to snore.

Our new handling class starts at 8:15 and ends at 9:45. I begin hallucinating at 9:06. This class is well after all our bedtimes. And to make it even more tortuous, we only feed

Honeybun a teeny morsel of dinner so she will be more anxious to work the agility course for food. She sits at her bowl, and says, "You are not telling me this is all there is, are you?" She beseeches, begging us with her dark mournful eyes to notice how she is wasting away into nothingness.

We eagerly pile into the van early, as the sun is setting, to head out to our first class. Steak is the "cookie" tonight, as I want Honeybun's full attention on Asherel.

The class gathers, and Laura, our leader, marches in. Laura is a highly competent, fully knowledgeable, no nonsense teacher. She reminds me of Malta in that respect. And she knows dogs! Within seconds of meeting a rather lumbering Springer Spaniel, she tells the owner the dog is hesitant over the jumps because first of all, he doesn't want to be touched. The owner keeps trying to hug and touch him, and the dog would prefer to be left alone. The owner admits this is true. I am not sure I have ever considered that a dog might not want to be touched. Lucky can't be touched enough, but Honeybun does not seek out or love being pet for very long. I know people who don't like to be touched, namely me. I don't mind hugs from beloved family members, but in general I have a personal body space hedge of about 50 feet. If people get closer than that, I get nervous. I could relate to the poor dog who had inadequate English skills to tell the owner to get her hands off him.

Next, Laura wants to know if the dog has been examined to be sure that he is physically able to handle the jumps. I am perplexed. What makes her ask that? The dog is slow, but seems to jump perfectly well to me.

"He doesn't seem comfortable over the jumps," Laura explains.

"Well," the owner admits, "He did come up lame after our last trial." She pauses and adds, "But the vet cleared him for activity now."

Laura rolls her eyes, and takes a deep breath, "Look, our vets are not sports performance vets. Honestly, they just don't know the way a sports performance chiropractor would about agility dogs."

I laugh out loud thinking Laura has just made a joke. No one else is laughing, and they look at me like I am a Neanderthal. I blink. They appear to be serious. I see more dollar signs dancing across the sky. Dog chiropractors?

Laura continues, "Everyone should have their agility dog checked by a chiropractor. I have an eight year old, ten year old, and recently retired twelve year old dog that did agility for many years without troubles. If you want to have a long life of agility, you should have the dog followed by a trained chiropractor."

I glance around. Everyone is nodding. I don't know what these people do for a living, but *we* can't afford a human chiropractor, let alone a dog chiropractor. What will they suggest next? A dog masseuse? Indeed that is what they start discussing next and I am seriously worried now.

"Furthermore, you should be constantly assessing your dog's level of fitness, and sometimes that means adjusting towards a leaner weight..."

Here she looks pointedly at Honeybun. Honeybun is not offended as her eyes are locked solidly on Asherel's pouch of steak. Thankfully, Laura does not belabor the point and gives the class their beginning instructions.

"OK, I want to see where all of you are. I have set up a little pinwheel here..."

Pinwheel? I hope Asherel knows what that means, because I do not. First dog chiropractors, now pinwheels.

"Here is jump 1, 2, 3, 4, enter this end of tunnel, pinwheel to 5, 6, 7, 8, enter this tunnel, front cross and 9, 10, 11, and finish on 12."

Asherel glances at me. I detect a touch of terror.

"Did you get that?" I whisper.

She shakes her head no.

"Walk the course," dictates Laura.

Asherel rather reservedly marches out onto the pinwheel course. She shyly moves to each jump and then returns to me. The others, obviously veterans, walk confidently, and then run the way they will run their dog, complete with hand motions. I have learned by now that Asherel will warm to the task, and to push her to get over her tentativeness now will backfire.

"Do you know what to do?" I ask. It may seem a little thing to those Type B personalities out there to be able to step back and not shove your child into the fray, and not force her to do what she is hesitant to do. It is a major thing to us Type A obsessive perfectionists. If nothing else, Honeybun is teaching me that you can't force growth. Sometimes the process must unfold slowly. If by some miracle, I can summon the patience to wait, it happens without my direct intervention. I know this is a major character flaw that has been sorely tested in the year of Honeybun. I cling to the verse, "Be still, and know that I am God." Be still. I sit on my hands and am still.

This time she gives a quick nod. She seems to get this pinwheel concept.

"We'll go in height order. 8" dogs first."

This means jump height. Honeybun is a 16" dog. She is the third dog in line. I watch with trepidation as Asherel prepares Honeybun. She tells her, “Sit,” and then moves three jumps away. I am screaming inside, but practicing that “be still” verse, and sitting on my tongue. Three jumps away! How will Honeybun know where to go? What is Asherel thinking? How does she expect Honeybun to sit that long? And worse still, Honeybun is looking around, her attention not on Asherel at all. My tongue is still, but my mental speech is diuretic.

"OK, Honey!" Asherel shouts, "Jump!"

Honeybun explodes, and to my utter shock, correctly clears the first line of three jumps. Then she circles back to clear number four.

"Out!" calls Asherel. (She doesn’t know “out” I am screaming mentally.)Amazingly, the little dog circles, following Asherel's signal and clears the jump.

"Tunnel!" commands Asherel.

Honeybun pauses at the entrance, glances at Asherel who repeats the command, and then skitters into the tunnel.

"Over!"

Honeybun sails over the next line of jumps, now reverse order from the first line.

"Tunnel!"

This time she doesn't hesitate but races through the tunnel.

Asherel is ready for her at the other end, "Jump!"

Honeybun races over the last three jumps, and the class cheers.

"Very good!" exclaims Laura.

Asherel and Honeybun trot back to me, both grinning. Maybe there is something to this "be still" strategy after all. I am wondering where all this quiet confidence is springing from. Honeybun glances at me and reminds me that not every eleven year old would dare take a wild dog, and trot her over park bleachers in anticipation of a distant goal no one has the audacity to envision. I look deep into the wise eyes of this ancient breed. What a curious vehicle God has sent redemption in.

"I didn't know she could do that," I say, "Great job."

Next, Laura has a simple exercise for us that she claims will be a good thing to practice every day. With the jumps lowered to just off the ground, the handler will send the dog to the jump without moving towards it. The dog is to learn to watch the hand and body language alone of the trainer.

"Otherwise," explains Laura, "All you are doing is teaching the dog to heel over jumps. She needs to learn to follow your hand and your voice, as you send her out over jumps."

I am no longer quite as surprised when Honeybun does it perfectly.

"She did very well," says Laura. Then, she demonstrates better handling cues and sends Asherel over the course again. Even I see the difference. Somehow those changes more clearly communicate to Honeybun exactly what she needs to know.

"If a dog messes up," says Laura, "It is because you have not given her the right information."

The Springer Spaniel is next.

His owner commands him to go out, and he lumbers a little ways, and then circles back to her, sniffing and disinterested.

"Pay him!" calls Laura. (This is handler lingo for give the dog food.)

The owner looks horrified.

"But he didn't do it," she counters.

"Pay him whether he does it or not," says Laura.

The owner could not look more disgusted.

"Even if he does it wrong?" she asks incredulously.

"Right."

Even I am with the owner on this one. Why pay the dog for doing it wrong? I am not getting this strategy at all. When Asherel doesn't do her school work, I raise the standard. It occurs to me as I watch the glum, apathetic dog that Asherel responds similarly at times.

The owner shrugs and tells her dog to go out. The dog repeats the same apathetic walk to the jump, and then returns.

"Pay him!"

While the owner and I squint at Laura in ongoing skepticism, the owner gives her dog a morsel. He wags his tail.

"Again!"

"Go jump!" says the owner.

The dog, wagging his tail hops over the jump and returns.

"Good boy!" calls Laura, "Pay him big! Then do it again."

"Go jump!"

This time the dog races over the jump and comes bounding back. I pick my jaw up off the grass and realize I have just seen an epiphany. It doesn’t take much gray matter to connect my method of schooling an apathetic child with the apathetic dog. I again glance at Honeybun who is watching me closely to be sure I have learned the proper application.

"Good job, now you have a happy and interested dog. See class," instructs Laura, "I want to be sure you get this. If your dog shows up for work, you pay him."

She turns to the Spaniel's owner, "You were horrified when I told you to pay him right or wrong, weren't you?"

"Well yes," she admits, "He just doesn't show much interest, and I don't want to reward that."

"If he isn't showing interest," she said, "You have not made it worth his while, or you are asking too much of him."

My brain explodes with thoughts, most of them shaming me. So many times I recall not getting what I want from my kids educationally, and my tactic has often been to raise the bar, raise the expectation. I have been doing to them exactly what the owner of the Spaniel has been doing. I have made the problem worse. I listen carefully to Laura.

"If I show up to work, and my boss gives me a nickel for every hour I am there, by the end of the day, I am not going to be willing to stay and finish the job," she says, "Or, let's say I have a problem with being late. If I show up five minutes LESS late than the day before, and I am rewarded for that, I will make a little more effort to not be late. Get this people. Reward your dogs. Reward them lavishly. You cannot motivate them too much. And don't just reward them at the end. Reward at different times, or they will only work at the end."

Again I am only there in body. My mind is remembering our child rearing and home school. So often the reward comes at the end of a long project, or maybe even not till the end of the school year. I look at the bored and lumbering Spaniel, and the tentative excitement starting to show as he looks at his owner. What embers have I lost over the years? What fires have not roared? Honeybun sits eagerly before Asherel, wagging her tail. Asherel slips her a piece of steak. I would have dissolved into a mess of self-reproaching tears, but Honeybun chose that moment to expel gas and the moment passes.

Class ends and we hop in the car. Honeybun instantly curls up on the seat.

"She had fun," says Asherel.

"How can you tell?" I ask.

"Well look at her, she's smiling."

I put on my seat belt and turn to gaze at the tired dog. I don't see a smile, and I don't see ribs either. I see more strict enforcement of food restrictions, and maybe a dog chiropractor if we continue down this crazy path.

As we drive home in the now chilled evening, I tell Asherel, "I learned so much tonight. About how to homeschool better. I don't think I have rewarded you enough for just showing up."

"You mean in the morning when I come out for school you should be giving me a cinnamon roll every day?" she asks happily, her bright cheeks glowing from the fresh air and cool evening.

I laugh and feel a quiet joy for unquenchable spirits, glancing at Honeybun who has snuggled peacefully into the seat. She looks at me knowingly and within a minute is snoring.

Dear Lord Jesus,

I understand that for someone who has the vantage point of eternity, months to get a horse to let you touch her neck or for a dog to learn to squelch aggression may be but a blink of an eye. For me, it has been a long and tormenting slow journey. It is often hard to persevere, especially through the plateaus of progress. I am recognizing something however that I bet you thought I would never get. The longer it takes to reach a goal, the more valued that prize becomes. I sometimes wish that I had met you as a child, and that I would not have made so many mistakes in life.... Well yes, ok, they are sins. There, I said it. But I guess as soon as I commit even one sin, and even now that usually occurs within fifteen minutes of waking up, Jesus would have had to die. I am still grappling with that concept, that a Holy sinless God cannot share even one molecule with a sinful creature in His presence.

What I do understand, at least a little, is that poor lady in church, and how desperately she hurts and longs for her child to return. She doesn't want to force her love, of course, or it wouldn't be love. If the child returns with no sense of the hurt she has inflicted or the error of her ways, I suppose the mother might even suffer more. The only way the prodigal's return could bring joy and reconciliation is if it is her choice, and if she understands what a right relationship with her mother really is all about.

I am so sad to admit that I have been a prodigal daughter to you. I say I want to be near, but then struggle to find time to pray, or immerse myself in your word, or strain for righteousness. I probably grieve you more than even I grieved when Honeybun was ignoring my pleas for her to stop attacking. I followed you with Honeybun until I realized it was going to be hard… and then I wasn't quite so anxious to stick to your plan. And when I succeeded, I took my eyes off of the author of my success, and put them on me again.

But like all good teachers, you have rewarded me all along the way. You have brought me new friends, a new joy for my little girl, a new mission that helps others and fulfills my love for hurting creatures. And I am even beginning to dare to reach out to people. Though that is still hard.

I guess that long verse about perseverance leading to hope in Romans 5 is true. I am not sure I really got it before, because it starts out with suffering, and I try as hard as I can to avoid suffering. But this dog has caused suffering…. and that certainly led to perseverance,mostly because I had no choice. And if the verse is true… then perseverance is at work developing my character, and when I have character…. I have hope. It's funny. I do have hope. I don't know when I got it, but I have a growing sense that this isn't really about a dog…

is it? The dog is just your messenger reminding me to listen up, because my character needed a little spring cleaning.

Ok, Lord, I am listening. I am listening with broken ears, but at least now they are cocked in the right direction. Amen.

CHAPTER 13

Hope and Self Reflection

On one of the field trips, Malta goes through her story about the herd of nurse mare foals on her farm. I have listened before, but this time she makes the plight very real.

She asks for volunteers and pulls out four girls. She tells us one little girl is a very expensive foal, and another her mother. The other two girls are playing the parts of the inexpensive foal and mother.

The expensive mare is used solely to produce expensive foals. These expensive foals are overwhelmingly thoroughbreds, race horses.The normal gestation period of horses is about a year, and very shortly after birthing a foal, the mare is shipped back to the stud farm to get ready to produce another foal. At this point in her story, Malta takes the volunteer expensive mare and pushes her away.The volunteer expensive foal is now hungry, and without a mama or milk.

The Jockey Club does not allow race horses to be artificially inseminated, thus the mare has to be shipped to the stud farm. The new expensive foal however, is too small and vulnerable to be transported. The foal is quite valuable so the owner uses less expensive mares solely for the purpose of bringing them to milk.

Malta grabs the "cheap" volunteers and pushes them together.

"So," she continues, "the cheap mare is impregnated, has her foal, and now can produce milk. The owner takes the cheap mare, and brings her to the expensive foal."

Malta now walks the "cheap mare" volunteer over to the "expensive foal" volunteer, and tells her to drink up.

The remaining volunteer is a small skinny girl, now left all alone. Malta returns to her.

"Now this," she snaps, "Is the cheap foal. The owner takes her....," Malta grabs the arm of the little girl, "...and throws her in the ditch." She tosses the little girl to the side.

"If she is lucky, the owner will bash her over the head with a 2x4. If not, more often, she will be left to die of starvation. A very few will be rescued by places like us."

The little skinny girl stands off to the side, wringing her hands.

"Those horses in the field there," points Malta, "Are all nurse mare foals... well they are grown up now, but we still think of them as foals."

"Who pays for that?" asks one mother.

"Will," she answers, laughing, "And me. We have a business installing sound systems and most of our money goes into the farm."

"What can a regular person do to help this situation?" I ask, horror seeping in as I watch the skinny child still standing off to the side, alone.

"It's a catch-22," says Will, who rarely speaks, but obviously feels deeply for the horses, "Right now, some of the Nurse Mare farms will let people like us pay the ransom, and buy the discarded foals. If we raise a stink, they won't let us get to the foals. They will still operate, but more sneakily."

The little girl slowly edges her way closer, back to her mother.

What a world of grief I have been oblivious to! I know suffering is out there, but prefer the ostrich approach to overwhelming horror… I like to bury my head and come up in time for dinner. However, Honeybun is alive because once, I didn't. Maybe sometimes once is enough.

The other horses that live at Last Chance Rescue are mostly rescued PMU mares. A PMU mare is one whose urine is collected to provide postmenopausal women with hormone replacement therapy. The urine is used in the medicine. The mares are stacked side by side in standing stalls sometimes no more than three feet wide, and hooked up to a urine collection device for six months or more of their gestational period. They have minimal or no human interaction or relief from the boredom of the stall. Just before foaling, the mares are removed from the device, allowed to birth the foal, and then the whole process begins again. The foal, as wanted as the discarded nurse mare foal, often meets the same fate. When the PMU mare has reached the end of her useful life producing urine so human woman can avoid hot flashes, they are often sent overseas for use as food, or their hides are used for purses and other goods.

We look out over the field of the PMU mares. Clouds gather overhead, but the rain holds off till the field trip ends. Malta speaks to the group, but keeps looking my way. I have the uncomfortable feeling that she is speaking to me directly. What more can I do? Sure I have hot flashes but I have never used hormones to deal with it, and now that I know to do so would be the equivalent of drinking horse pee, I sure won't start.

We drive home past the billboard announcing the upcoming Steeplechase. Asherel and I attend that event every year. Beautiful thoroughbreds race and jump over various obstacles. We make a day of it. We go early, pack a picnic, bring chairs and camp out right alongside the track, at a break in the foliage. If we wanted to snap off our arms, we could reach out and touch the horses thundering by. Last summer, we watched two go down. One got up very slowly. I don't think the other got up at all. I had just ignored the obvious dangers to the horses…And had not known that for many of those beautiful animals, there was a discarded "cheap foal".

Asherel glances at the billboard, and asks if we will be able to go to the Steeplechase. I had hoped she wouldn't see it, wouldn't ask. I don't want to break her heart. A conscience can be a terrible thing.

"I will leave this up to you," I quietly answer, "But I have to tell you, I have an icky feeling about it. You know that those horses are there because of nurse mares…And many foals are thrown away so that the prize thoroughbred can have the cheap baby's milk…."

"Then we don't go," said Asherel with finality. This is one of her favorite events of the year, one we love, and attend with great preparation and joy. I know she does not relinquish it lightly, and I am proud of her. We drive on past the billboard. The sun is finally breaking through the clouds, briefly with strands of gold in a blanket of grey.

I am writing grants with a vengeance in preparation for the yearly fundraiser for Last Chance Rescue. I have no experience writing grants, but lately every undertaking in my life involves things I am completely unqualified to attempt. The farm hoe-down fund raiser is thus far not gaining a single donation. Considering the expertise of the grant writer, this should be no big surprise. There is one organization, a manufacturer of horse conditioner, whose initial response is promising. When Malta first sends me the link to the horse conditioner, I laugh, figuring it is a mistake, or a joke, along the same lines as dog chiropractors. Horses need hair conditioner? But it is not a joke. Indeed there are many such companies. I wonder what starving third world companies think of our country where businesses thrive selling products that makes horse manes tangle free.

They write back after I send them the grant plea letter. This is the first semi-positive response I have received. They ask if we are willing to spend the $30 shipping fee. I write back that as long as the donated goods exceed $30, we are willing, then send them Malta's email and tell her it looks like finally we are going to land a deal!

A short time later, I receive an email from Malta. She rants about how the horse conditioner company turned us down. She is livid.

We *are not a horse breeding activity like a breeder's show where people are encouraged to make more horses for the world to then discard. They only have money to fund people like the American Quarter Horse Association, (AQHA) which slaughters horses.*

This is news to me. I do a little Google research, and find, as usual, Malta seems to be correct. Apparently, many have speculated about the connection between the AQHA and their promotion of horse slaughter. According to the website I find, PMU breeders work out a deal with the AQHA to register the foals that are produced as a result of the PMU industry (usually a cross between a Quarter Horse and a Draft). This seems strange to me- but it really boils down to making money.... the love of which is indeed the culprit behind much evil. The article alleges that the AQHA profits by registering more horses and the PMU industry profits by selling the foals for more money to individuals and introducing a preferred breed for the slaughter industry. I don't know how much of this is true, but Malta seems convinced of it.

Malta is not done with her disgust with the human race for the day. She sends me a notice that Michael Vick, the NFL player who had been sent to prison for his pit bull dog fighting business, is about to be paroled, after serving twenty-three months in jail. Upon release, the NFL commissioner is considering his reinstatement into the NFL. Countless dogs were slaughtered in his callous disregard of the law and decency. I could not find if he had sent money to rescue organizations, or attempted in any way to make amends to the victims of his crime...yet here he is about to be restored to his multimillion dollar contracts and life, a role model for the youth of America.

I spend the day working on grants, with several back and forth emails with Malta.

It is an art class day, so at 2:00, I finish my work on the grant writing, and tell Asherel to put Honeybun in the back room.

"It will be easier, if I don't have to deal with her," I say.

It is not that I don't trust her around the kids. But the art class enters through the back yard gate, which I leave open, so Honeybun would have to be tied so she can't escape from the yard.

"Oh please!" begs Asherel, "Let's just leash her in here so she can see the kids."

I agree, since class is due to start any minute and I am worn out from all the animal despair I have dealt with thus far this day.

I tie Honeybun to an end table leg that is wedged in the corner of the sunroom between two large couches. She can't reach the kids, but will be able to be with them and see them, promoting positive socialization.

She watches the first kid clump up the deck stairs, and begins barking like a maniac. I run to get the whip, and smack it down in front of her, yelling, "Enough!"

She quiets momentarily, so I hurry to the next room to gather supplies. The next few seconds are a blur. Another child comes in the door. Honeybun lunges, and there is an awful cracking sound. A whirl of golden fur races towards the child, the leash towing a broken off table leg. There is nothing I can do but watch.

The child freezes, and then Honeybun is upon her...licking her and wagging her tail. She has broken a table leg off in her desire to lick a child. The rest of the class floods in, and Honeybun greets them all, waggling like a Mexican jumping bean and licking them, towing the table leg behind her.

This is a dog that no one wanted. This dog would certainly have been euthanized if we had called Animal Control to collect her. And now, a crowd of little children gather around her, laughing and petting her. I take the table leg off her leash and try to stick it back on the table.

Malta's response later when I tell her:
I guess we can declare her "cured"? Of course now you should get rid of her for ruining furniture!

Honeybun has her own epiphany at the next Handling Class. We arrive to hear that the temporary field lights have finally blown a fuse, and with the sun already setting, we are urged to get moving through four various stations quickly, before darkness huddles too closely around us. The "pay" today is left-over pot roast. I dribbled the gravy in the bag so it covered the less scrumptious hot dogs. Honeybun is prancing as soon as we hit the field. She knows her "salary" has just gone up, and she is eager to work some overtime.

The first station is set up in a circuit, with a u-shaped tunnel at both ends and two jumps in between. Honeybun does not understand the word, "tunnel" at first, but after four or five circuits, she begins to comprehend, and is racing through the course, collecting her paycheck eagerly at the end of the tunnel.

The next course is two sets of weaves, and a pause table. Her job here is to race through the weaves, sail onto the pause table, sit for at least a count of five, and then pirouette through the next set of weaves. Weave poles are her nemesis. To do the weaves well, the dog must first understand always to enter from the right, and second, that she must weave in and out of the poles without missing one, as fast as possible. However, to go fast, she has to do flying lead changes, or skips, between each pole. It is not a natural motion for a dog, and really kind of silly being as a dog generally chooses the shortest path to pot roast. I watch my girl and dog with skepticism.

"This one will not be easy," I comment.

Asherel wisely ignores my lack of confidence and pulls out her morsel of pot roast. She unsnaps the leash. Fortunately, the weaves are set up for beginners. They are "channel weaves", which are poles on movable platforms that can be placed in a straight line for the expert dog, but spread out for the less experienced. In this way, the middle channel becomes a wide path. At their extreme outer placement, the dog doesn't have to weave at all, but can run down the middle clear path. This is where Asherel places the poles for her first run through. Even this set up is difficult for Honeybun, however. There are no impenetrable walls, and since she doesn't quite understand her mission here, she often runs off to the side.

"Weave!" commands Asherel.

Honeybun races down the clear middle path, and leaps onto the pause table.

"Good girl! Now weave!" and off she darts for the new set.

The second set of poles are a little closer together on

the channel, so she has to do a very slight weave pattern to stay on the path. Miraculously she does so. Asherel lavishly rewards her, and then kicks the channels closer in.

"Are you sure you want to do that so soon?" I ask.

The team ignores me and marches back to the pause table.

"Go weave!"

This time she clearly has to do a near skip between poles. She misses one. Asherel still gives her some pot roast.

"You want to reward that?" I ask.

Again, I am ignored. The impending darkness appears to have affected my girl's hearing. Asherel kicks the poles in further. Now they are almost in a straight line. Never has Honeybun remotely weaved with them so close together.

Once more, Asherel directs her to go weave. Honeybun shoots through the weaves, and before our very eyes, she suddenly understands. I watch in amazement as she does flying lead changes, doesn't miss a pole, and weaves like a dog from Animal Planet. Asherel gives her mounds of pot roast, and smiles at me. There may have been a touch of "I told you so, oh ye of little faith" in her look, but I forgive her smugness.

As darkness descends, she works on "front and rear crosses" until the light is too distant a memory to safely continue. As we leave class, thanking Laura, Asherel notifies me, "I think she gets it now."

Of all the things an agility dog must learn, the weaves seem to me the most tortuous. I honestly didn't think she would ever figure out how to do them. Of course, I never thought I would like a pit bull, or be able to prevent Honeybun from killing Lucky. I think "improbable but not impossible" may be my new mantra.

Meanwhile, we have finished the homeschool year, and have a free afternoon to head out to Last Chance Rescue. I forewarn Malta we will be there for a few hours, so get her list ready.

Malta still wants us to spend the bulk of our time with Sadie, but has a few "easy" chores for us as well. First she wants us to give the monthly flea and tick meds to the "Ru's".

"The Ru's?" I ask.

"Rufus, and Ruru, the 3 legged dog," she says, obviously incredulous that I still don't know the names of the dogs, given all the times I have been there.

"I can do that," I say, having dispensed those medicines to my own dogs. At last, a task that I am qualified to perform! We head to the Ru pen. Ruru, the 3 legged dog, has intense stranger anxiety. She cowers in her dog house, at the furthest back corner when anyone new approaches. Asherel and I climb over the fence, meds in hand. Rufus, a big dopey mixed -breed greets us joyfully. He slobbers all over me as he gobbles up his medicine. Easy. I am feeling confident. Ruru cowers, her dark eyes pinpoints of light in the furthest recesses of her doghouse. The flea vial is different from the kind I use at home, and it takes me five minutes to figure out how to puncture the seal. My confidence falters a bit. I hope Malta is not peering out at us in disgust. As I finally conquer this technological challenge, a little medicine spurts out all over my hand. I glance at the house. No Malta wondering what is taking so long. I squish out half of the meds on Rufus's neck, and now hold the tube upright so it won't leak, calling Ruru. Ruru stares at me; head slightly averted, and trembles.

I sit on the ground nearby and make encouraging noises. Rufus is all over me, licking me, and climbing in my lap.

"Would you help me here?" I snap to my accomplice.

Asherel tries to entice Rufus to her, but he is much more interested in dumping the medicine. I find a ball and toss it. Ruru, a retriever/border collie mix, cannot ignore a thrown object. She comes hopping out of her house and rockets on her three legs after the ball. She scoops it up joyfully and then turns, and screeches to a halt. The retriever in her is screaming to return the ball to me, while her stranger neurosis is crippling her far more than the loss of the leg. She scuttles away.

Asherel however has ingeniously placed herself in front of the dog house door. Ruru comes around the house from the back, and then slams to a stop. Oh no! A stranger, albeit a smaller one, is blocking her retreat. She looks at me, drops the ball, and runs around the back of the dog house, hiding. I pick up the ball, and toss it again. She races after it, and the same dilemma confronts her. Once more she drops the ball, and runs away. I grab the ball, and toss it.

Yet again, Ruru sprints after it. If I could not clearly see she's missing a leg, I would never have known. She moves quickly and effortlessly. We play this game several times, until finally in the 85 degree heat, she brings the ball to a shady spot by the dog house and collapses, tongue lolling, sides heaving. We have been out there a good half hour now. Malta has to be wondering if we have given up and gone home. I creep over to the tired and hot dog.

"Good girl," I pant, reaching out.

She lowers her head, but she doesn't run, and I pet her. Finally, I squirt the medicine in between her shoulder blades, and scratch behind her ears. We are friends now. We bring the tube back to Malta's house to throw it away.

"Success!" I trumpet. Malta does not seem impressed.

It would've taken her one minute, but that was a minute the overextended Malta doesn't have. Still, I keenly perceive that she may consider us dimwits. My pride has taken a major beating since acquiring Honeybun. I used to consider myself skilled with animals, and competent with new tasks. The list is growing of things I only succeed at because I outlast resistance.

We head out to visit Sadie. She trots over instantly, and quickly drops her muzzle into the halter to smack up the treat. However, she won't allow the halter any further up her nose than last time, and seems less willing to let us anywhere near her neck or ears.

"Sing to her!" suggests Asherel.

We start with "Sadie Sadie, give me your answer, do. I'm half crazy all for the love of you," to the tune of *Bicycle Built for Two*, since we know she likes that one. We had already attempted this unorthodox method of humane horse training during the preceding visit. She lets us stroke her forehead, and her nose dips deeper into the halter.

"Try another," Asherel chirps.

I start an off key rendition of the hymn "*Just as I Am*". Sadie puts her ears back.

"She doesn't like that one," Asherel observes, "How about *He Leadeth Me*?"

I can never remember the words, even of beloved songs, so I make up words when my memory lapses. Sadie pricks her ears forward, and her nose sinks so deeply into the halter that I get it over one ear. With a slight rear, she jerks back and throws it off, but it is a success of sorts. She circles back as I continue singing, and she paws at the ground. She wants the treats, and she likes the song, but she is less thrilled with this halter business. The next few times we get the halter nearly to her ears, and she remains calm. Best to end there, particularly since we are out of food.

"She likes your singing," notes Asherel, "Do a new one."

My favorite song is *The Sound of Music*, and having learned that as a child singing with my dad at the top of our lungs on our weekly Sunday drives, I do remember all those words. Sadie stands still, as I sing. She is transfixed as we rub her cheek, then her neck. She watches me but doesn't move as I press my hand all over her neck. She has never let us do that before. And then as my hand moves to her withers, her skin twitches, but she doesn't run. Asherel, hot and tired, sits at the base of the tree, while I sing and pet the wild Mustang. Music is soothing the savage beast.

We pop back in to ask Malta if she has a last half hour task for us. She does. We scoop dog poop while a pack of twenty lonely, attention-starved dogs romp around us, nibbling at my clothes as I shovel the poop.

As we labor in the hot sun, I ask Asherel if she still wants to own a farm.

"Of course," she answers.

We have been there four hours, and have barely touched the to-do list Malta and Will tackle every day. When we say goodbye, Malta barely glances up. When she finishes her paperwork, it will be time to start the nighttime feeding of the hundred animals. If I am helping her out with hopes of effusive gratitude, I will need to find another facility. The work is overwhelming and never-ending. Malta is too worn out to expend much energy to prop our egos.

It is ok, however. I feel a great sense of satisfaction, an oozing peace, applause from another source. Or maybe it is just sore muscles. We moved a lot of poop that day.

As we pull away in our car, the twenty dogs line up at the fence and watch us go, tails wagging in unison. Malta's head is still bent over her paperwork. The farm is bathed in a hot golden sun. The music is swirling in my head of hills alive in song while animals cock an ear to listen.

After our work at LCR, I write to Malta and tell her how Asherel still wants to own a farm even after the less desirable poop scooping detail. Malta's response is typical:

Perhaps Asherel should have been here this morning to wake up to the smell of 2 explosive butt dogs... Smelled so bad it woke me up out of a dead sleep. On the walls and all over the living room. Who knew dogs could aim? Makes me want to live in a beach front condo with a pet hermit crab... a stuffed one.

Meanwhile, the agility handling class is going remarkably well. Honeybun is off leash for extended periods of time, and continues to ignore the other dogs, and gleefully jumps, weaves, tunnels, and climbs as directed to grab her gustatory salary. Sometimes when Asherel pauses to listen to Laura's instructions for a length of time, Honeybun gazes at her hopefully, and wags her tail to indicate the need to be slipped a goody. If food is still not forthcoming, she pops over a few nearby jumps on her own, and then returns with expectant outreached paws.

Despite countless times of my conceit getting the best of me, I begin to feel boastful. At this stage in my life, I should have known better. Like a dog returns to its vomit, so go my prideful tendencies. This is such an ingrained character defect that I am actually feeling proud about how I am not prideful with all we have done. The problem with puffing up is it often leads to bursting.

I like to recite my list of accomplishments to myself, or to anyone who might like to commend me. This dog, rescued like Eliza Doolittle from the depths of poverty and despair, *we* have taught to behave like a high class citizen. She now comports herself like all the other AKC champions. She has a full wardrobe of beautiful clothes, courtesy of Asherel. She goes to bed every night lying like a queen on the soft bed next to Asherel, covered with silken sheets. She has three different collars for various events, and a beautiful leather leash Asherel won at one of the Agility raffles. She obeys better than some of the veterans, dogs that have actually entered and qualified in agility trials. She never barks, or lunges after the other dogs in the class.

After class one evening, we thank Laura who is giving some final critiques to another handler and her dog. The rambunctious dog lunges at Honeybun, anxious to play and sniff, but all of us tense and shout, knowing this is always a potential fight trigger. Everyone has been warned long ago that Honeybun has a large personal space, which is a nice way of saying she might rip the nose off of any dog who comes too close. Surprisingly, Honeybun just stands there, wagging her tail. Not a single growl.

"I am so proud of her," I boast, though of course I am not bragging, but simply stating facts. I like stating facts, especially the self-congratulatory ones.

"She has done really well," agrees Laura.

"I know," I continue modestly, shining my ego on my sleeve, "That is just the sort of situation that we were so afraid she would not be able to handle."

"And it was my dog's fault for getting in her face - he would've deserved a snarl," says the other handler humbly.

"But she has to get used to that, because dogs do that," I say, full of my wisdom, the resident dog training miracle lady. If I had been a balloon, I would've been floating.

We drive home and I am giddy with my expertise and skill. I have transformed this dog, and I must be sure to tell as many people as I can, for their edification and good.

A few days later, we finish lunch, and the ultimate dog tidbit is left - bacon. Honeybun loves bacon maybe best of all the delicacies that are now frequent parts of her charmed life. I grab two pieces to do our "sit-stay-come" training which we practice often. I command both dogs to sit and stay in the kitchen. When I call out "come" from the living room, both dogs barrel around the corner, and Lucky crashes into a little wire table with a tall lamp and various knick knacks on it. Asherel is following on the dogs' heels and in a miracle of dexterity, catches the lamp. The table and knick knacks crash over with a tumultuous bang. Lucky skids into Honeybun.

In a whirl, Honeybun turns on him and in a horrible rehash of those early days, begins ripping at his neck and back, pulling out mouthfuls of hair. Lucky is on his side, having gone down with the table, and can't get back up, while Honeybun is relentlessly attacking. She stabs at his belly with her teeth again and again. Then she lunges at his throat. Lucky is unsure the bacon is worth this…..

I scream and smack at Honeybun's flank. She does not stop immediately but pauses long enough for Lucky to get up, at which point I grab her and throw her over in the "Dreaded Roll"- a move we have not had to do in months. I claw my fingers on her throat, and scream at her, holding her down. For a brief second, I believe it is possible she is thinking of biting me, but then she goes limp, and lays her head down.

"Don't choke her," scolds Matt, who has come running out of his room in the ruckus.

"She has to feel like she is going to die," I explain. I don't admit I want to kill her. She has exposed me for the boastful arrogant fool I am, and I am almost angrier over that than the fact that she wanted to eat Lucky's kidney raw. I hold her down for another minute, and then throw her in the back bedroom and slam the door.

I remember Malta told me not to be discouraged if Honeybun has moments of reverting to her old behavior. She told me it is certain to happen again. I realize with crushing dismay that I thought I was so talented, that I had squelched all unwanted behavior forever. I don't like the image of myself I am remembering from the class that week. Humble Pie is not tasty.

If there is any good from any of this, Lucky has not been hurt, though there are scattered tufts of hair floating in the room. I don't think Honeybun will be trying that again anytime soon, as she had been pretty scared by my fury and unexpectedly successful wolf roll. My sense of certainty has been shaken, however. *Maybe* this will heal her (again) and me (again) of my always too near the surface arrogance. I hate these lessons with a passion. I also understand that they are necessary. Grrrrrr.

I remember Laura's lessons with the apathetic dog, and wonder why Honeybun reacted so strongly. I understand there is always a reason for dog behavior, convoluted as it may be. She must have felt threatened. She didn't know Lucky wasn't attacking when he slammed into her. She may have felt justified in protecting herself. I know most of the struggles in our family interactions stem from not understanding each other. From misperceiving motives. "A gentle word turneth away wrath" is sage advice. It is another lesson that both Honeybun and me are slow to absorb. We give Lucky a bone, and after an hour, open the bedroom door.

"Don't welcome her back into the pack," I command the troops, "Just continue to ignore her."

Honeybun comes out contritely, subdued. Lucky immediately approaches her, tail wagging. He touches his nose to hers. He doesn't care what I say; he is welcoming her back into the pack. After all, he *did* get a bone out of the whole ordeal. I hope she is as impressed as I am by his forgiving heart. How much these dogs have to teach, and all the while I'm thinking we are the trainers.

Dear Lord,

Just when I think I have everything figured out and am ready to move on, we are back to square one. I guess we really are never done arriving until we arrive. Don't worry. I am not too discouraged, at least not totally. Maybe the issues never completely go away, but there is change. At least she broke the leg off the chair to lick a kid, not bite her.

I know it is a little thing, but I really am grateful that I was nice to the telemarketer today. It would be better, I know, if my thoughts were "held captive" too, and I had more charitable feelings while holding my tongue… But Honeybun is teaching me to focus on how far I have come… not how far I still have to go.

I guess we are both learning "weaves" in a sense. It is not a natural movement for a dog and has to be practiced every day, or that skill disappears faster than Honeybun's dinner. And it is not natural for me to curb my impatience at interruptions in my schedule, or be kind when all I really feel is annoyed. I have to practice it every day…. And learn to ask you for strength to overcome a little more regularly.

Even that nutty dog Lucky is teaching me something I am not always so good at - forgiving. He stood there at the door ready to forgive Honeybun long before she was sorry. That is not easy… but you did that for me. The moment Jesus died on the cross, I was forgiven. Not only had I not said I was sorry, but I hadn't even recognized I helped put Him there.

And even through that, you loved me.

I know I have nothing to offer you, but my love in return. And my gratitude. Thank you Lord. I am wagging my tail!

Amen.

CHAPTER 14

Forgiveness, Humility

Malta is enraged. She has received an email from a dog owner who is panicked as her dog, Molly, has developed such severe separation anxiety that the owner is no longer able to keep her. Molly has ripped apart a door sill, clawing off all the paint, and chewing it, and then ripping the screen in her frantic efforts to go find her owner, who has left the house. The owner tells Malta that after three years of this "wonderful" dog, this new behavior is impossible for her to live with, and though she "loves" Molly, she must now find a new home for her. Will Malta help?

Malta's first email back assures the owner she is willing to help, but the "inn is full" and the owner will need to hang on to Molly for another three or four weeks. In the meantime, Malta will give her strategies to help.

Molly's owner emails back that she has contacted all the no-kill rescues and shelters, and none will take Molly. She is forced to bring her to animal control, which will euthanize her in twenty-four hours. "*Thanks a lot, Last Chance Rescue. It is your fault I had to bring her to Animal Control. If you have half a heart, you will go get her from Animal Control."*

Seething, Malta shoots back an email,

Animal control will probably only keep Molly for 3 days max. Most owner turn-ins are euthanized on the spot. Rescue groups like ours have 50+ Mollys a day. List after list sent to us asking us to take dogs that will be euthanized in a matter of hours by animal control. This is not lashing out at you... just a bit of reality. You could have boarded her for a few weeks. And as for not knowing what you have gone through - we deal with dogs like this every day... we deal with the pain of not being able to help dogs like Molly because there is no room. Your email pegged rescue groups at fault for your choice. It is not our fault nor the fault of any group that you chose not to hold onto her until a rescue had room for her. And who would you have liked me to call at 10 pm? And where should we put Molly? No rescue group on the face of this earth is responsible for your decision to take her to Animal Control. We have jobs - we have homes that dogs chew window sills off of, and we repair them. We have dogs that have serious issues. I do know your story... I do know what you go through.... we hear it, see it, live it 24/7 365 days a year. The world is brimming with Molly and Brenda stories. My response is because of your "guilt trip" email you sent. "Molly and I are more than just an email" - so are the other 100 Mollys and Brendas. And the dog starving in the ditch doesn't even have a Brenda - we see those on a daily basis and do our best to help them too. Go save your dog... board her until there is room- you expect us to do it, yet you are not willing to do that yourself? That would be your part of responsibility in this matter. Live with your choice. But don't blame us or any other group for your choice. Don't blame animal control either for euthanizing her if that is what happens.This is your choice not theirs. And don't lay guilt trips on people that go the extra mile to help dogs like Molly. I hope you find some peace with this or maybe you will go get Molly and board her until there is room? Either way my heart goes out to Molly and all the Mollys out there.

Malta then sends all the board of directors the updated intake policy for LCR. It clearly outlines some of the issues that Brenda and Molly have raised. I read it over, hearing the anger pouring out of Malta. I am angry too, knowing she has not had a vacation in years, and that she often goes without meals or sleep because she is dealing with yet another animal emergency. I know she has also not had new shoes in eons, because every spare dollar goes to the rescue farm. I read her policy, increasingly in awe of what her rescue farm deals with every day. How dare that tyrant Brenda speak to her in that way! But as I am reading, my own words to countless rescue agencies six months ago come back to me with alarming similarity to Brenda's rants. Surely *I* am not the jerk Brenda is… am I?

I realize with shame that I had not been a whole lot different from Brenda in her perception of animal rescues when Honeybun first entered our lives. I had been dismayed and shocked that none of the animal rescues wanted to help me. I was broke, and wanted to help the dog, but had no resources, no knowledge, and was quite anxious to act compassionate, but shift the responsibility to someone else. It was Malta's first rude but direct email that kicked me in the derriere and told me in no uncertain terms that compassion is a big fat fraud unless you are willing to do what it takes to actually save the animal you claim to feel so much angst over. I wanted to give up and let Malta take the problem away... and then feel really good about myself because of how much I had "cared" by rescuing the dog and bringing her to Malta. I love Malta's line- "*That is not rescue... that is transportation.*" How could I condemn Brenda, much as my deflated ego longed to, when I *was* a Brenda six months ago? It was everyone *else's* fault that I couldn't find someone to help the dying dog. It is Honeybun teaching me sometimes the one who needs to help the most to save the world is standing right behind my nose. A red, sniffling nose, at this point.

We spend the day helping at our club Agility Trial. Our jobs, replacing dropped bars on the jumps when the dogs knock them, afford us front row views of owners and dogs as they enter and leave the ring. What happens in between is not nearly so revealing of the character of the owner, than how she enters and how she leaves. I study this carefully, realizing quickly what kind of person I am in comparison, and which I want to be.

When the handler enters the ring, she removes the dog's leash and then tosses it nearby. A leash runner takes it and deposits it on the exit end of the ring. Most owners just toss the leash. A very few take the time to look the leash runner in the eye, say "Thank you" and hand them the leash. (over the course of a class or two, you'd be amazed how sore one gets bending over time and time again to pick up the leash). Those owners already receive points from me, though it is hardly an expected courtesy, and most handlers are far too focused or nervous to be considerate of the leash runner.

Next, the owners position their dogs for their run, and it is as varied as the handlers. Most are very no-nonsense, with stern commands to the dog to wait as the handler marches a few jumps away. A very few kiss the dog's snout, muss his fur, and laugh, telling the dog how wonderful he is and what an adventure they are about to have. They are often, but not always the handlers that hand the leash runner the leash instead of tossing it on the ground. Again, those are the owners I now award more points to.

Then the dog runs the course. I am planted in between the entrance and exit, and help with setting jumps and leash running. While seeing portions of the dog's run, my focus is on the start and end. However, I do notice which dogs clear everything (no jumps for me to reset) and the dogs that blow everything, going off course, not listening, dumping bars....

Now the handler and dog exit, having completed their run. Of course, every owner whose dog did fantastically well scoops the dog up and jumps for joy and runs to get him goodies galore. That is expected and easy. However, the most interesting scenarios involve the handler of the dog that let her down. That saga begins in the last few seconds of the run. Some handlers, obviously disgusted, send the dog over the last jump, which he may or may not jump since he is clearly not doing his best that day. Then the handler snaps the leash on gruffly, and marches out without speaking to the dog. The dog invariably is looking hopefully at his master, his ears lowered because he knows he has not met expectations.

And then there is the other type of handler. As the dog has crashed into every jump, done the course in reverse, and lost hundreds of points, in the last few seconds of the run, the handler finds a jump or obstacle he knows the dog will successfully clear. He sends the dog victoriously over that one jump, and as they cross the finish, he falls to his knees, kisses the dog and tells him he is the most wonderful creature on earth, and what a fantastic job he did! The dog is leaping for joy and all is right with the world, though he has just garnered the worst score in the history of Agility Trials. Dog and owner race off to get goodies with a bubble of love and joy casting iridescent rainbows around them. Those are the handlers that get the most points from me. They may have lost the agility trial, but they won a prize much, much more valuable.

I think of my children, especially of the one who is most distant and hardest to reach emotionally. Have I always discerned something to shout "Good job!" about, even when he fails? Have I found the full side of the glass? Have I looked beyond my own needs with compassion and understanding for others? Introspection can be a troubling activity. Upon arriving home from the trial, I write him a note, letting him know how wonderful and beloved he is.

Finally, it is time to board Lucky and Honeybun with Malta while I bring my Destination Imagination team to the "Global Final" in Knoxville. They placed first in the state earlier in the year, a feat that was no less wonderful for the grudgingly admitted fact that they were the *only* team in the state in their division. I am exhausted from four days of herding children to the various events they have to attend, and getting little sleep. My team does better than expected, placing thirteenth in the world. We are assured this is phenomenal for a first year manager, first year team. The team dances and does cartwheels later at the party, chanting, "Thirteenth in the world!!!"

I am happy, and they are ecstatic. It is a nice kudos after a difficult year, with the advent of Honeybun coinciding with my first year coaching a team. Early the next morning after the exhilarating awards ceremony, I travel directly from Knoxville with Asherel to our family vacation in Hilton Head. Arvo and Matt have arrived a day earlier while we finish up in Knoxville. Once a year, unlike Malta, we do get a family vacation, and we cherish that week at the beach.

I email Malta upon arriving in Hilton Head, asking how the dogs are doing. Lucky has peed on her wall, and Honeybun is covered in mud from playing with the other dogs. They are both loose with her core pack, and she describes

Honeybun as happy and good, but Lucky as "puffy" and with an "attitude".

"*No wonder Honeybun felt she had to fight him*," Malta writes.

I feel a little bad for Lucky, not believing he is as bad as Malta seems to feel he is. He is just socially inept. I can relate, actually. He has never peed indoors before. He is likely just marking territory in that den of twenty-five dogs. I cannot believe it is "passive aggressive", as Malta describes it. I doubt dogs know how to be passive aggressive. But both dogs seem to be doing fine, once Lucky gets over his "attitude"...and I am very excited to read that Honeybun is joyously playing with other dogs. Hard to fathom that happy, beloved dog had been a hair breadth away from being another Molly story.

While resting in Hilton Head, I receive a second email exchange from Malta with Brenda, and learn that Molly has been euthanized....and Brenda blames Malta. Malta, who has never laid eyes on Brenda's pet of three years, is responsible for Molly's death.

The second morning in Hilton Head, I awaken with the sun, and pedal away on an early bike ride. Noticing a teeny little creature struggling across the beach towards the surf, I stop to see that it is a little baby sea turtle, courageously traveling across the sand to the siren call of the ocean. He ignores me, stretching his neck forward, and his legs scampering as fast as they can go. His shell is beautiful with a design made by heaven. A Hilton Head resident stops and tells me she has lived here her whole life and never seen a sea turtle. We watch the baby, and finally he reaches the water. He races forward, and then the incoming tide sweeps him up, and deposits him way back on the beach, near where we had first seen him. Since the tide is coming in, every time he makes it to the water edge, a new wave carries him back further than he started, but doggedly, he keeps racing forward. Finally, I can stand his struggle no more, and pick him up, pitching him past the surf. I hope my helping him along doesn't disrupt some great cosmic plan.

I have felt like that little sea turtle - life circumstances sometimes carrying me back further than I have advanced. It gives me great joy to watch that little baby, no bigger than the first digit of my thumb, so determined to reach the ocean against all odds. Some must make it even without my help, or there would be no sea turtles. They get past hungry gulls on the beach, hungry fish in the surf, hungry sharks in the ocean depths, and some grow to be magnificent creatures. I think only about one in ten make it to adulthood, maybe less. I hope my little turtle makes it... maybe the thirteenth in the world to find the ocean that day.

On our fourth day in Hilton Head, I receive another email from Malta. She tells me her guest, Stickybun, (as she calls Honeybun) has renovated her crate, adding an east facing window in the three hours they were out. She includes a photo. It shows Honeybun, one ear up, one ear down, alertly looking directly at the camera; with her head fully out of a hole she has chewed in the side of the crate. It looks like she is stuck, unable to go further out or back in. Her head is like a living trophy, mounted on the side of the crate.

"*Too funny*!" writes Malta.

It *is* funny, but that is a $50 crate my dog has just ruined, that now needs to be replaced for the never demanding, but always financially strapped rescue farm. Like a sea turtle's march to the sea go our finances, one step forward, and two steps back.

This morning, I traipse off on my morning bike ride beneath a threatening sky and sprinkles. Thunderclouds blossom just off the beach, and it looks likely I am going to get drenched at some point on this ride. Turning onto the hard sand of low tide, I glance back and spy a rainbow, arcing over the dark blue cloud-scape. Another symbol of hope, glad tidings! First the sea turtle, and now a rainbow. What lovely omens of light in a stormy and troubled world! I am feeling very blessed by the symbols of hope God seems to be tossing my way, singled out, special, loved.

The next morning dawns lovely and sunny, without a cloud in the azure sky. I am awake, as usual, long before the rest of my family. I watch the sun come up with my coffee steam drifting its blessed aroma through the still air, and then hurry off on my bike to the beach.

It is low tide again, and very few people are out yet. The air is still. A Blue Heron poses near the surf line, poking his saber beak at some unlucky fish. Another glorious symbol! Blue Herons are so shy and elusive, rarely seen.Whenever one appears, I stop to watch, considering him a gift from God. With glowing optimism for the good all these small miracles portend, I bike on. Picturing Honeybun with her head stuck in the hole she has chewed out of the crate, happy chuckles bubble out of me.

Hilton Head Island is shaped like a foot. We are staying in a condo near the instep. The toe is about a forty minute bike ride when going into the wind, and that is where I head. Reaching the toe, I see a Beach Patrol truck pull over near the dunes, next to a large mound in the sand. I hurry over to discover it is a huge sea turtle… what is left of it. The shell is intact, but the turtle has been partially eaten. The head and flippers are gone. I take a picture, knowing this might be the closest I will ever get to an adult sea turtle.

"What do you think got it?" I ask the Beach patrolman, who is snapping pictures of the shell.

"Something ate it," he answers, "Maybe a while ago. It just washed up overnight."

"That's sad," I say, watching him take the photos.

He dons some gloves.

"I'm going to bring it back to the museum so they can keep the shell."

I nod, watching him, then tell him, “I saw a baby sea turtle two days ago."

"No you didn't."

My eyes bulge wider at his audacity, and I insist, "Yes I did. On his way to the ocean. I walked him to the surf." (I didn’t tell him about pitching it in the ocean, as that might be illegal.)

"How big?"

I spread my thumb and forefinger a couple of inches apart.

"That wasn't a sea turtle," he says smiling, "They are just nesting now. It takes fifty to sixty days for the eggs to hatch."

"But couldn't he have been an early bird?"

"No... it was probably a fresh water turtle. They won't survive in salt water."

My face falls in horror. Not only have I not seen a sea turtle, my symbol of hope and survival against impossible odds, but instead have killed the turtle I *did* see. He notices my distress, because he comments, “It might have been a diamond terrapin. They live in sea water."

"I have a photo of it on my camera."

"Oh, let me see."

"I don't know if I want to know if it is not a sea turtle," I concede sadly, but pull out my camera.

While I scroll through my pictures looking for the faux sea turtle photo, he heaves the dead sea turtle into a plastic bag, and with a grunt, lifts it into his truck bed. Tossing the gloves in a garbage bag, he peers at the photo I show him.

"That's a Terrapin," he concludes, "It lives in sea water. I have one as a pet. I found one today with an eye pecked out, and brought it to the vet. It will be my other pet. See these claws? Sea Turtles have flippers...maybe one claw. But they don't have clawed toes like this."

Of course.... how did I miss that? I so wanted it to be sea turtle.

"But you didn't kill it," he adds kindly, “They like the

sea water."

Discouraged, I hop on my bike and head back. So what kind of symbolism does this distressing turn of events evoke? Delusion? False hope? Rescue that isn't rescue at all? I so hate it when reality gets in the way of what my world should be.

But to cheer me up, I get an email from Malta later that makes me spit my cracker all over the computer from laughing. She tells me she has been dealing all week with "a monkey woman".

Sad sad sad. And she is destroying a dog. The dog will bite the kids. She doesn't want to hear that. Children flopping all over the sofa, crying, can't even have a conversation... no control over the kids, no control over the dog...Accident waiting to happen... and she refuses to acknowledge it even though the dog has already nipped at the kids many times, chases cars, rolls and pins the cat, won't come when called. I yelled at the little heathens, " ***Sit down and be quiet",.****in dog voice. My house is not Chucky Cheese. Total disrespect by her and her kids. She told me, "Being tough is not my strong point." Oh really... didn't notice (eye roll). It's easier to give in to that little brat child, isn't it? Being tough takes energy and is not always pleasant. Rules and boundaries take energy to enforce. Throwing a lollipop is much easier.*

Same thing as you had with Sticky but she cannot realize that she doesn't have nor wants to have what it takes to make changes in her life to fix it. She thinks the kids can train the dog. The kids or neighbor kids are going to get bit. She ain't no Vicky. You know when dogs come here they behave...they just do... even the crate eaters. It is not a trick or a quick fix. It is an overall attitude. She fails... no way it will work. She doesn't have what it takes. You can tell by people's dogs and kids what the parents are. The nippy angel dog is not ours but another rescue... I don't know what is going to happen with this ordeal... she was supposed to pick up on Friday. I have no idea what the rescue has decided to do with the dog. I said to repossess him.

I send Malta my story about the sea turtle saga, and she writes back:

Ya know the whole turtle thing just represents life itself to me. Birth, struggle, death...You didn't see the fun parts though... the swimming around. People often forget the swimming part because it isn't as tangible as birth, struggle, and death...Sswimming is the most important part. IMHO.

That is true. The swimming around is the most important part, and I hadn't seen that. I had seen the birth (or thought I had), and the death, but missed the main event... the swimming. There had been lots of that. It was a large turtle, had lived a long life, and probably enjoyed a good bit of swimming. Maybe the turtle symbol is one of hope after all, and maybe my focus is on the wrong thing.

On the morning of our departure day, I awake very early so I will have time for a final bike ride on the beach. Melancholy always nips my heels when our beach week comes to a close. The cool morning breeze wafts through the sun-stained air like silk across my warm skin. The heron is there again, this time standing just feet from an ocean fisherman, undoubtedly waiting for handouts. They look like friends, the waves crashing around their double pair of thin legs.

Reaching the toe of the island, the same place the turtle shell had washed ashore, I see wide tracks, like something being dragged, from the low tide line all the way up to the sand dunes. I stop and look more closely. All along the edge of the flattened path are sharp, deep slashes diagonally pressed into the sand. With sudden delight, I picture the mama sea turtle, dragging her cumbrous body the hundreds of feet from the ocean edge to her nesting place in the secluded sea grass and dune. Orange tape marks the turtle nests, warning people to stay away. I have not seen a live sea turtle, but it is unmistakably her tracks. Judging from how close her tracks come to where the tide now settles at its lowest point of the morning, I know I have not missed her by more than a couple of hours. Joy nudges away the despondency I have been fighting. I would've preferred to have seen her in the flesh, but her tracks printed on the sand creak and groan with her effort and her presence. Sometimes all I see of God are His tracks as well, and it must suffice.

"I hear you!" I cry to the wind and the sky.

I bike with the breeze at my back, and see a pink bellied baby dolphin leap into the air, the sun cascading in rivulets from his sleek form. I don't stop to hunt for any more shells or shark teeth. Instead, I take in the larger view, the sun just above the horizon, already blindingly bright against the silver sea and white sand.

Dear Lord,

Thank you for reminding me that faith may be defined as the presence of things not seen, but the evidence of your presence is as unmistakable as the evidence of the sea turtle by her tracks. Help me not to lose hope because things are not always what they seem to be.

Help me to have a spirit of forgiveness even to the undeserving. I guess the key to that is humility. If I can humbly admit that your forgiveness is not through anything I have done, but all through what Jesus has done, it is easier to extend that forgiveness to others.

It is easy to condemn others, but it really is harder to do so when I know I am just as guilty. If I am all puffed up, which happens as you sadly know far too often, I can't see my feet and that I am walking straight into self-righteousness. I can't say I love the lesson, but you showed me a few thousand times that every time I boast about my success with Honeybun, she proves me a liar.

I never really thought of that before - the connection between forgiveness and humility. I hope I can hold onto this lesson Lord. It is maybe the one I need the most.

Amen.

CHAPTER 15

Faith

We return just in time for Honeybun's birthday. We do not really know when she was born, but since Lucky was born June 2, and Asherel's birthday is June 3, she decides to call June 1 Honeybun's birthday. It has also been almost exactly a year since we found her.

Asherel dresses her up in her pink birthday bandana and we mix sirloin tip dog food in with her dry kibble. Lucky wears a green bandana, and gets the birthday dinner as well. Neither dog seems very impressed by the birthday outfit, but enjoys the dinner.

Asherel takes her out back to her training agility course, and works through her front and rear crosses, and weave poles. Honey is excited, and watches her trainer with increasing understanding. Simple hand movements, or change in Asherel's posture are beginning to cue her now. If Asherel tells her to "go out", and then straightens up, Honeybun continues to move outward to the next jump. If Asherel crouches down after sending her out, Honey wraps back in towards Asherel. It astounds me to watch the communication growing between the two, and how easily Honeybun seems to read the signals.

"You need to go online and find a USDAA trial near us in August," I suggest.

"Will she be ready by August?" Asherel asks, uncharacteristically uncertain.

"I think so! Certainly for Novice Jumper."

"Will *I* be ready by August?"

"Ask Laura," I advise.

I have come down with a wretched cold, and am grateful it waited to assault me till after DI Globals and our vacation. We plan to visit Sadie Tuesday, but I am still too sick to go when Tuesday arrives. Meanwhile, Malta's generosity has backfired on her, and she is trembling with hurt and anger.

The woman she called “the Monkey lady”, a description formed while watching her children doing gymnastics on her couch like a monkey, has gone to court and claims Malta has refused to return her dog. The woman is obviously lying. She had brought the dog to Malta crying for help. The Humane Society recommended that Malta was the only person that *could* help her if *anyone* could. The family dog, recently adopted from that humane society, had suddenly become aggressive with the children, tried to kill the cat, and was uncontrollable. The children had bruises all over their arms from the dog. So the lady left the dog with Malta, with the understanding that Malta would further assess the situation to try to help her, and the lady was to return on Friday.

"The dog was perfect with us, Vicky," laments Malta, "The cat passed right under its nose, and no problems. The problem is not the dog. It is a fine dog, but it is an accident waiting to happen. Those kids are going to be bitten because the mother has no idea how to put limits on them, or on the dog."

Apparently, Malta's blunt appraisal of the "monkey lady's" lack of authority over her dog and children offended her. In spiteful deceit, she went to the magistrate judge and claimed Malta would not give her back her dog, and she feared for her life. Malta had no idea any of this was happening, and took the day off from work Friday so she could wait for the lady to show up to reclaim the dog. Malta was at the vet when she received a call from one of her volunteers that a cop was at the door, demanding that Malta relinquish someone's dog.

Malta scurried home, utterly dumbfounded. The policeman told Malta he had an order from the magistrate judge that she turn over the dog.

"What is this all about?" cried Malta, "I am happy to return the dog. She was coming today to get it. Take the dog! I don't want the dog!"

The officer began asking questions- do they have a business license, how many dogs do they house, how many kennels...?

Malta, who has a healthy fear of what a government gone power- crazed can do suspects the crazy lady told them horrible things about LCR.

"Come in and see for yourself," she demanded.

The officer told her no, he would wait outside.

"Look, if I am being accused of something, don't you think you should come in and see what kind of awful conditions my animals are housed in?"

The policeman entered the house. Twenty-five well behaved dogs, including the sweet pit bull, Melissa, greeted him. Malta's floors were as usual, spotless. Not a bit of clutter or anything out of place. Her counters were clear and scrubbed. The sun sparkled through her neat windows. It was like it always is.

"Do you take pit bulls?" asked the officer, who apparently has one he wants to save. So the officer, seemingly won over, took the crazy lady's dog, and Malta, dear tough Malta, is as close to despair and tears as I have ever known her to be. Later she talks to me for an hour, rehashing this attack on her refuge with deep hurt.

"She has sullied our name, all lies, and all because she

didn't want to hear the truth. I spent forty minutes beating around the bush trying to find a nice way to tell her she had no control of her kids. I never told her I would keep the dog from her. I don't need any more dogs! All I was trying to do was help her! You know how I have treated Asherel, or the field trip kids. I have never purposely hurt another human being. How could she do this? And what can I do now? A cop - she sends a *cop* to get the dog! And now a judge has in writing all her lies and accusations. This hurts the animals. And there is nothing I can do! She can lie all she wants, and defame LCR, and we have no recourse."

Later she writes to tell me she has contacted a lawyer friend who says defamation will be very hard to prove, and very expensive. He does not advise she attempt it. Instead he suggests she have the people and organizations who know her write letters on her behalf. I tell her I will write one the next day; just give me details on where to send it.

She writes back that she will send details tomorrow, "*For now I can't think about it anymore, I am to the boohoo point.*"

Never, *never* have I known Malta to be anything but strong, and assured.

Malta writes on, "*She is one very evil person. And I don't say that often about people... but I have never met a person willing to go through such lengths over their ego before. You know I forgive her though. I forgive simply because being angry and hateful does not serve the purpose of life. Not sure how long I have left on the planet so I gotta do what I can do to make it a little bit better place in my own way. Like chuckin' a turtle into the sea."*

I read her email and glance at Honeybun who is in her wicker basket, her pink bandanna neatly tied around her birthday neck. She is snoring. There lays the transformed wild dingo, rescued by the forthright talents of Malta, who feels herself drowning in this sea of troubles rising about her. It makes me feel to the "boohoo point" too.

Frequent spring storms delay the Handling Class from completion until mid summer. Honeybun always seems to remember that it is Wednesday night, and she trots over to me sitting on the couch, nails clicking on the wood floors, face hopefully furrowed, tail wagging. She stands before me, her chest gently heaving with her silent whine. If I continue to ignore her, she scampers over to the door and sits in front of it, immobile. Not a hair twitches as she sits, waiting for us to take her to class. I don't know if it is the anticipation of class, or of the delicious meatballs, but she clearly wants to go.

Laura's agility courses become increasingly complex. Asherel finally begins acquiescing to my pleas to walk the course with the other handlers, and she even begins to practice how she will turn to allow a front or rear cross. I may even observe her counting her strides, which the really excellent handlers do. She is always the first off the course, never walking it more than once. Most of the others walk it at least two or three times.

"Done so soon?" I ask, trying hard not to glare menacingly.

She nods at me briefly, eyes ahead, clearly not wanting to discuss tactics with me.

"You know what you need to do?"

"Yes," she clips.

And invariably, when it is Honeybun's turn, she knows what to do, at least sort of. As she clears one course with no errors, Bit, another class member, claps her hands and calls out, "Honeybun did everything right!"

It is time to look for a trial within driving distance. I surf online and find a USDAA event in Chapel Hill, just three hours away. It will entail a hotel, but I am willing to incur some cost if the trial seems like a good one for Honeybun to enter. I email the trial manager, and admit what neophytes we are, but anxious to enter our first trial.

The manager writes back immediately, filled with advice and encouragement. She mails me the application, a thirteen page form filled with information, much of it indecipherable to me who am not versed in the shockingly wide variety of events and titles.

I write back begging her to just tell us which classes we should attempt. She gives me a variety of choices that she feels our novice dog could handle. Asherel reads the entire document a couple of times and then we sit down to fill it out.

"Wait till the last minute to send it in," she advises, "I want to see if Honey will be ready." This from the ever optimistic Asherel is a surprise. I *am* ready. Somehow I know that our journey is nearing a conclusion, and we need to seize the moment.

"Starter" jumper classes are relatively easy. The only obstacles the dog needs to navigate are jumps and tunnels. Honeybun is fairly competent on those, but I agree with Asherel that we can wait and be sure she is fully ready before committing. We still have a month. One of my biggest concerns is the official measurement of the dog to determine jump heights. The jump height is figured by the height of the dog at the shoulders. We have measured Honeybun and she is tall enough for 16 inch jumps. We have been warned that our measure will not be accepted but that an official measurement will be taken at the first three trials she attends. The way this is done, we are told, is a metal apparatus is placed around the dog and a bar lowered over the shoulder to get a very accurate height. I do not know how Honeybun might react to this unfamiliar apparatus placed on her by a total stranger. I do know that "vicious" dogs will be evicted from the trial, and so hope she will take this new task sweetly. It would be embarrassing to be disqualified even before entering the field.

There are countless class choices a new dog can enter. Classes called Snookers, and Gamblers are apparently within her capabilities. I tell Asherel her duty is to go online and find out what these entail, mostly because when I read about them, my brain is spinning and has not worked this hard since completing calculus. Oh wait, I never *did* complete Calculus, but it I had, that is how hard my brain is spinning.

We download the USDAA rules book. In Gamblers classes, the dog accumulates points by running a course with varying obstacles in an allotted time. The handler can choose the obstacles, but the judge can impose restrictions on what order obstacles are performed or can give specific extra point challenges or "jokers", also called gambles. This sounds fun but confusing.

"Jumpers" class is a little less imposing. It is a course of jumps and tunnels, and sometimes weave poles. In Starters' Jumper class, which is what Asherel would compete in, there will be no weaves, which is good, as Honeybun is still very inconsistent in her weaving skill. The winner is determined by fewest penalties, and in case of a tie, time elapsed to complete the course.

Snooker is a class named after a British billiards game, and the goal is to gain as many points as possible by negotiating the obstacles in "snooker" sequence, defined by color. The colors cue the handler to the difficulty of the obstacle with red being relatively easy and black being the most difficult. The rules beyond this simplistic description can only be deciphered by someone with a post graduate education. After each "red" is a "color" obstacle and the dog is only allowed to attempt the color after clearing the red. Once all reds are performed successfully, the dog moves on to the closing sequence, which includes all the higher point value colors up to black. How points are determined is too confusing for me to even attempt to paraphrase, but as the USDAA rules book states:

“The maximum score possible in the opening sequence is determined by the number of "Reds" defined in the course plan by the judge. If three "Reds" are defined, then the maximum number of points is 24; if four "Reds are defined, then the maximum is 32 points; and so forth. The maximum can be achieved by performing each "Red" successfully (1 point apiece) and then following each "Red" with the "Black" obstacle, which is worth 7 points each time it is performed successfully. So the maximum points possible in the opening sequence is 8 points times the number of "Reds". The maximum point value of the closing sequence is always 27 points, which is the sum of the Yellow, Green, Brown, Blue, Pink and Black obstacles (2+3+4+5+6+7=27). Therefore, the maximum possible score in snooker is defined by the sum of possible points in the opening and closing sequences. For a course with three "Reds", the highest score possible is 51 points; with four "Reds" it is 59 points; with five "Reds" it is 67 points. Typically, a course will only have three or four "Reds". The number is determined by the judge's course plan. A qualifying score for USDAA title is a minimum of 37 points. Qualifying placements must also be earned for title certification purposes.”

You see what I mean. Calculus is probably a breeze compared to Snooker.

If the rules of USDAA classes are not confusing enough, the titles one can earn in competition will be sure to freeze the most nimble of brains. Perusing one website, I try to determine what letters our dog has a chance of lining up behind her name if she manages to win any class. The number of titles available convinces me that if Honeybun just shows up at the event, she will probably receive a titled award; something along the lines of Honeybun A.I.O.P. (arrived in one piece).

This is a partial list of titles an agility dog can earn, and this list is just in USDAA competitions:

AD

Agility Dog (USDAA)

VAD

Veteran Agility Dog (USDAA)

VAAD

Veteran Advanced Agility Dog (USDAA)

VMAD

Veteran Master Agility Dog (USDAA)

VS

Veterans Snooker

VJ

Veterans Jumper

VG

Veterans Gambler

VPD

Veteran Performance Dog

AAD

Advanced Agility Dog (USDAA)

MAD

Master Agility Dog (USDAA)

SM

Snooker Master (USDAA)

GM

Gambler Master (USDAA)

PM

Pairs Master (USDAA)

JM

Jumpers Master (USDAA)

ADCH

Agility Dog Champion (USDAA)

If we choose to enter Honeybun in AKC or UKC or NADAC contests, even more titles await her. I have innocently entered this world thinking it will be a nice relaxing and fun way for Asherel and her dog to bond. I can see now that it will require hours of study just to figure out which box to check on the application for her first agility trial.

Her last Handler Class finally arrives, and Laura sets up a Novice course, complete with jumps, tunnels, and weaves. Asherel hands me the leash as she walks the course. She performs little pirouettes as she visualizes whether she will be doing front or blind or rear crosses, and she points to the jumps in the same manner she will be cuing Honeybun. This unselfconscious behavior in and of itself is worthy of a few letters after her name, in my opinion. She is the only one in the class who has never entered a single event, never done an obedience class, and never gotten an AARP card. I am so proud of her.

She sits her little dog down when it is her turn to do the course. Laura announces the event, and calls out “Ready?” as though this is a bona fide trial.

Asherel calmly walks two jumps away after telling Honeybun to stay. Honey sniffs the grass while waiting, hoping to uncover an errant meatball. She is still sniffing when Asherel shouts, "OK!"

Like a shot, the little golden darling explodes over the first jump. She flies across the next two, and then dashes through the tunnel. The lady behind me says, "Look at how she is so eager to follow Asherel's commands!" I smile at her, recognizing the kindness intended with her encouragement. Next the weave poles. Admittedly, they are channel weaves and are opened so that they are not in a straight line as they would be in contest conditions. Instead they are zigzagged only slightly, but I am still amazed as Honeybun weaves through them, her front feet skipping, and doesn't miss any. Over another jump and through the tire jump. A beautiful front cross maneuver by Asherel, and Honeybun streaks over the aqua jump, wraps around to the yellow jump, and then with Asherel shouting "Go!" she crosses the finish line with no faults (at least none that my untrained eye could see.) The class applauds as Asherel shovels the meatball rewards in Honeybun's gaping jaws.

As we all gather to hear Laura's final words of wisdom, she reminds us that we need to attend our first contest with the mindset of the end goal. Don't enter a starters or novice class with the intent of just winning a novice class. Always look ahead to competing for the end goal, and work with the dog in every contest class with that goal in mind. Never let the dog feel you are disappointed or reprimand her but keep it fun and exciting, and encourage the dog so she will want to enter trials for many years to come. Anyone can qualify in a novice class… but the reward is moving up to the harder classes.

Not *anyone* can qualify, I think. For one, I am pretty sure *I* can't. Secondly, I remember the wild swamp dog we snatched from the doggy gas chamber. That dog could not have qualified, not then. I sneak a look at my daughter who is tossing meatball scraps to Honeybun while Laura gives us our marching orders. Keep the end goal in mind always - both you and the dog want to love what you are doing for a long time to come. The process is more important than the result. I smile. That goal has been reached.

As we head home from our last class, Asherel jumps into her seat and spritely chirps, "Mom, she did so good! She is so proud!"

"How can you tell?" I ask.

"Look at her! She is smiling!"

I glance in the mirror. I don't see a smile, but I do see long confusing forms we need to fill out and entrance fees, and hotel stays to schedule. And I still don't see ribs.

It is 97 degrees, and there are still at least 300 piles of poop to go. Asherel and I have computed that with thirty dogs defecating two times daily, that means there are 420 piles of doggy doo each week at Last Chance Rescue. It has been over a week since the last clean up, and while Arvo helps Malta and Will erect the new dog fence, Asherel and I are assigned poop detail. Malta has put out a plea to all the board members to come to "help erect the fence day". We have come, being promised burgers and beer as reward for our hard work. We pull in to the empty driveway. Will and Malta are already working in the sweltering sun that strikes the ground with harsh slabs of molten heat.

"Where are the hordes?" I ask.

Malta barely glances our way. Will shrugs. Despondency may be knocking at the door. So we are the work force. I had told Malta we could spare two hours, since I try to keep my hard working husband's weekends free.

"Not me," answered Malta, "I don't get weekends off so neither does Will."

I detect some bitterness. Frankly no one should be working manually in this heat. I don't blame anyone for not showing up.

The dogs mill around us briefly as Asherel and I enter the sun bath, but even their attention-starved bodies cannot bear to be in the direct sun for long. They languish under the porch, tongues a mile long and watch us.

Asherel is noble, silent in her suffering. Sweat pours off of both of us. It drips steadily from the end of my nose. If there is anything worse than an hour of shoveling poop it is doing so in 97 degree hot sunshine.

Finally, every mound we can find in our growingly incapacitated state is shoveled, deposited in the green rank container, and scoopers put away.

"Ready for water and peach break?"

Asherel nods mutely. Her cheeks are bright red. We sit in the shade guzzling our drinks, when Malta walks by with her nail gun.

"We'll be ready for our next job in a minute," I say, "Do you have a job in the shade?"

"Wimps," she mutters.

A little dachshund stands nearby at the fence, watching us and barking.

"Hush Hotdog!" screams Malta.

He continues barking, a little happy face beaming inexplicably in the stifling miasma.

"You notice he never shuts up?" says Malta, pausing to wipe her face in the shade.

"I did notice," I agree, "But he certainly is a happy little dog. Is he new?"

"He's a boarder till Wednesday," she says, sipping from her gallon size cup, "He's one of our adopted dogs."

Hotdog looks spritely at each of us, then happily begins wagging his stubby tail and barking again.

"He was about to be euthanized when we rescued him," continues Malta.

I nod. It is the story of nearly all the dogs there.

"He bit the humane society vet."

"That would do it."

"He was being examined in the intake room."

I nod, watching the happy little dog. He doesn't look like a vicious dog at all. He had been very happy for us to pet him when we were back there scooping poop.

"He was being examined in the same room as the bodies of the euthanized dogs."

I stare at Malta. She cannot be serious.

She nods, taking out a cigarette, the poison of choice to cover a shield of smoke over the images that fill her life.

"At the humane society? They examine the dog in a room with dead dogs and wonder why it bit?"

The appalling evil sickness of that makes me want to gag.

"Happens all the time at that humane society," she acknowledges.

I ask which one, and ask if this is common knowledge.

"Of course not," she replies, blowing a stream of smoke that obscures her face as it stalls in the dead sultry air.

The next evening is the on-line board meeting. I have come to dread those meetings because we are usually presented with a litany of rather discouraging news along the same lines- too many animals, too many needs, not enough time, and WAY not enough money. I always feel inadequate, and that any input from me falls so far short of what is needed that it is disdained. Our family is nearly always over-budget each month, and has to draw on our retirement funds. I am determined this year to try to change that, so we can't be a large funding source for the farm. The physical work there is very demanding, and especially in the hot sun, as we have discovered, beyond my capacity to endure for any meaningful length of time. That evening after our hot day of work, I "watch" a dog show on TV with Asherel. While there in body, in mind I am unconscious, passed out on the couch for three hours. I never nap, and sleep is difficult, so know the day of 97 degree oven conditions has felled me. Asherel wakes me up to watch the terrier group. I open an eye long enough to see the group announced, and then the next time I awake, the dog show is over. No, I cannot be a significant source of physical labor for the farm, either. I am not strong enough, nor are we close enough. I can't drive two hours on a regular basis to help them.

Even our work with Sadie has plateaued and it is clear that to successfully train her, she needs daily and regular work. Once or twice a month of bribing her to stick her nose in a halter is not going to do it. At the board meeting, Malta updates animal news with the dispiriting announcement that Sadie will be put on "horsy Prozac" so that they can halter her and provide needed vet services. It feels like my failure, though I had known from the start that our limited ability to get out there would be unlikely to produce overwhelming results.

Sometimes one's best is not enough. Sometimes despite doing all one knows to do still leaves the goal just out of reach of clutching fingernails. If my best is not enough, do I just give up? I think of our journey with Honeybun. My best was not enough then either. I doubt I would have made it without Malta's not so friendly kick.

The board meeting continues with Malta asking for ideas, and reminding us with each suggestion that she and Will cannot do any more themselves. Any idea has to be implemented by the board. Asherel and the dogs wait for me, leashes jangling. The meeting has been going on over an hour now, and shows little sign of ending. It was supposed to be a short one, and I have promised my family a walk. I tell the group I need to skedaddle, but leave the chat room open so I can read what happened while I am gone.

I know Malta is discouraged. The wretched economy has slammed their donation base as well as their sound system installation business. They are fighting for their farm's existence and all those animals that depend on them. Dispirited, I know my pittance is better than nothing, but I am running on fumes of faith. Then, out of the stagnant doldrums, I have an idea of organizing an art show with entry donations, and dream of thousands of entries. It could work. I will work out some details and run it by Malta. You never know unless you get out there and try… and Someone sent me the idea. Someone will send the result too.

Dear Heavenly Father,

It is easier to have faith when you leap with a parachute. But most of faith is a free-fall. Of course, I know that you are standing at the bottom with infinitely open arms, but still…

I pray for Malta and all the struggles she encounters every day. I don't know how she cannot be crying buckets of tears every waking moment.

I have a sense we are nearing an end of our journey. I probably shouldn't say that, since inevitably, you take the occasion to revisit lands I have no interest in seeing again. I often didn't enjoy them the first time… However, I trust that whatever happens, it is with your eye upon us. May we trust in your goodness, knowing that you have brought us this far safely, and ultimately, you will see us safely Home.

Amen

CHAPTER 16

Fulfillment and Redemption

The week before Honeybun's agility trial, both Asherel and I are increasingly distracted. Asherel reads her school books, but this normally gifted student cannot seem to answer a single question about what she has read. I go to my yearly doctor exam, and hand them my insurance card, my mind dwelling on packing lists for the three day trial in Chapel Hill. There is a long silence, and finally I glance at the receptionist.

"Is this your name?" she asks politely.

I look at where her long red fingernail points. It says "Honeybun". I have handed her our USDAA registration card. The lady next to her leans over and quips, "I don't think we accept that breed."

A few days before we are scheduled to depart, we decide it would be wise to do a brush-up private lesson with Deb. I call Deb to remind her she had said long ago that right before we entered our first agility trial, she would help us prepare. I ask if she will let us know if Honeybun is really ready for the trial, and I warn Asherel that if Deb feels it would be a disaster, we won't go.

Stoked with a baggie full of ham, we happily return to the first agility teacher Asherel ever had, and excitedly enter the field. The door clicks shut on a house of barking dogs as Deb emerges, and she directs Asherel to follow a specific sequence of jumps. I am buoyant with expectation as Honeybun has come so far in the year since Deb first met us.

"Show us what you got!" she exclaims.

Asherel removes Honeybun's leash, tells her to sit, and marches a few steps from the first jump.

"Okay Honeybun! Let's go!" she calls.

Honeybun glances up and sniffs the grass.

"Come on Honey!" entreats Asherel. I am developing a stomach ache.

Honeybun saunters slowly over and smells the jump. Deb looks at me.

"That's what she's going to do at the trial," she warns.

Asherel finally convinces Honeybun to jump and do the sequence. Honey trots slowly, looking around, sniffing at grass every so often, and finally lumbers over the last jump.

"Normally she flies over the jumps," I claim weakly. *I don't even believe myself.*

"All dogs that are new to a place will act just like that," Deb consoles, "Until they understand and get used to going to new places. They are all stars in their backyard." (Aren't we all?)

She sets up a second course and tells Asherel to try that one. She encourages her to "walk it" first. Asherel walks it once, and then claims she is ready. Honey is a little peppier, but around Jump four, Asherel is confused, and cannot remember the course.

"You needed to walk it more than once," admonishes Deb," Walk it once to learn it, once from the dog's point of view, and then keep walking it until you can close your eyes and still see it."

As she sets up to do a third course, Asherel walks the course diligently and Deb tells me, "She really is probably not ready for this. She doesn't have the handling experience."

"Should we cancel?" I ask, knowing that will disappoint Asherel, but so will her dog refusing to do a single jump.

"No," answers Deb slowly, "If your expectations are just to go, have fun, learn what it is like.... and don't expect to win or even qualify, you should go. And she *looks* good- in good running shape."

Well that is nice, but this isn't a beauty contest we are spending mega bucks on hotels and entry forms to attend. Still, I have not been led this far for this long, overcoming so many hurdles to be waylaid now. It is not pride propelling me anymore. It feels curiously like a calling, a destiny, a task that must be completed not for my check list… but for my soul. And an audience of one eyed, three legged, discarded misfits of which I am an unworthy member are waiting and holding their breath to see if redemption is truly possible. Besides, I can't get my entry fee back now…

The third run is better, and Asherel makes some good handling decisions. However, it is with humbled, and lowered expectations, we head home. Asherel is surprisingly not discouraged. She feels that this is how Honeybun will learn and tells me that she definitely feels we should still go to the trial. Some kids waste money and lives on drugs, fancy clothes, and makeup. My sweet child wastes money on a little dog doing happy things in fresh air, and sunshine. It is expensive, but I suspect of value I cannot begin to estimate.

Despite some reservations, I pack for the trip. Two days before, I have the bag of dog food and bones for the trip on the table in my room, ready to load in the car the next day.

Busily working at the computer, I glance over to see Honeybun lying on her bed with the bones, still in their plastic wrap, in her mouth. Laughing, I take them from her and run to my room. She has not ripped open the dog food bag, but it is on the floor. She follows me in and stands near as I replace all the food in a large bag. Lucky wanders in, hearing food package crinkling sounds. Suddenly Honeybun turns on him, a deep growl rumbles from her throat, and she crouches about to pounce. I scream and lunge at her, and claw her down into the almost forgotten "dreaded roll". She lies there, then goes limp in submission, and I remove my "claws".

As if a disinterested, novice dog on the unfamiliar course is not disturbing enough, now I have to wonder if latent aggressiveness is reemerging. I know that she is hungrier - the cost of getting her in "running shape". Still, food has not triggered aggression in a long time. Deb mentioned that most aggression she deals with is never obliterated; only managed. Are we just managing aggression? What will happen when the hungry dog is loose on the agility field, and all the other dog owners, pockets bulging with tenderloins, and rival consumers are lining the fence like a buffet? I refuse to give in to discouragement. These setbacks are blips on the radar. We will go and we will do our best, and when we return, we will smack the whip at any and every growl. If lifelong vigilance is required, then lifelong vigilance is what I will give. I only regret that I have but one life to give to my dog... well, not really, but I do feel like I should start marching and singing an anthem of some sort.

Since good news always comes in threes, the next morning, Matt calls from college. He has just been to the infirmary and diagnosed with Swine Flu. It is a mild case, but he needs to be isolated. The doctor says he can either go home, or stay in his house at school, but only if friends are around to help him - bring him food and whatever he might need. He has surgical masks to wear should he need to leave his room, but classes and activities are out for at least a week.

This is the final straw. Maybe the set back *is* more than a blip. I tell Matt we will come to get him as soon as I can find someone to watch Asherel as she should not be in the closed car with him for five hours, with his contagion. Very worried for my son, knowing swine flu can be deadly, I am horribly dismayed that we are so far away. However, Matt insists he does not feel bad, and has a very mild case, and feels he might be better off just staying where he is. He will call if things get too hard, or he feels worse. After a long conversation with the college doctor, it is decided that for now, Matt is better off resting and isolated in his room at college. We will go to the trial, but I know we might be called away to retrieve my sick son. That actually puts us three hours closer to him anyway should he need us. My own head aches with fatigue and worry, and my throat tingles the way it does before I get sick. This Agility trial that had seemed like such a fun idea is not shaping up to be the glorious end of our story that I had hoped. That night I spend more time than usual in prayer.

The day that Asherel has worked towards for so many hopeful years finally dawns. On the drive to the trial, Matt calls. His fever has broken, and he is feeling much better. Is this an omen of the sun breaking through the worrying fog of recent events?

We are among the first few people to arrive at the trial fields. Two or three other groups are setting up their canopies and crates. I pull in and ask where we should set up, telling them we are rank beginners and cannot even figure out this relatively simple task. A helpful older man points us to a shady spot across from the ring where all our events will take place. As soon as we unroll our $10 garage sale canopy, we know we are in trouble. We have forgotten a hammer to pound the stakes into the drought hardened soil. Nonetheless, we sweat and strain and try to erect the tent. About four temper tantrums and an hour later, Asherel agrees we are not going to succeed. A new group arrives to prepare their site near us and I ask if they might possibly have a hammer we can use. They do. So our canopy is successfully erected and we set out our chairs and table and crate. The club owner walks by and introduces herself.

"For newbies, you sure have a pretty fancy set up!" she exclaims. She obviously doesn't know my father, who taught me that the first thing one should do when entering upon a new endeavor is look the part, get the equipment, and worry about the skills of the activity later. If you can't *be* good, at least *look* good. Honeybun sits on one of the chairs in the frilly satin bandanna Asherel has made for her just for the trial. An aura of competence surrounds us, sitting under our huge canopy in our fancy chairs, obscuring the sobering reality that we are clueless.

However, I admit to her that we are actually pretty nervous and scared, and if she has any advice, we are eager to hear it. I am surprised by how many people are so eager to help us, so gentle and forgiving of our lack of knowledge. Perhaps blustering my way through life is not the best tactic. Admitting weakness seems to bring out the best in others, not the carnage I expected.

We walk around the fields so Honeybun can sniff, hoping she will get her sniffing quota completed before the trial begins in the early morning the next day. We meet several people, and quickly ply them for information and advice.

Everyone is very encouraging as soon as we explain this is our first trial, and that Asherel, not me, is the handler. Our $10 garage sale canopy only falls down once. It is double the size of anyone else's canopy. I feel conspicuous, and not just because our dog is wearing a satin white bandana and looks like she is going to a wedding.

Having done all we can to arrange our little corner, we head to the hotel. This is the real excitement of the adventure for Asherel. She has never been to a hotel with Honeybun, and she is gleefully anticipating all the new adventures, like riding the elevator with her dog. A lot of time and expense could have been saved had I known this was the big draw. We tug the sleeper sofa into position, and Honeybun quickly settles on that as her bed. As usual, when it is bedtime, Asherel pulls the covers up over her pampered dog, tucks her in, and Honeybun closes her eyes. Her huffing snores assure me she is not overly stressed by her new surroundings.

At way-too-early-o'clock, we head back to the field in the morning, first in line to be measured. For the first three trials, Honeybun will have to be measured at shoulder height to determine jump height. The judge is a kindly Santa Claus type, and when we tell him this is Honeybun and Asherel's first time at a trial, he is solicitous and oozes geniality. I am nervous about how Honeybun will respond to a stranger touching her with the strange unfamiliar measuring apparatus, but steak tidbits overcome a multitude of sin... and keep her attention while the judge does his measuring.

"Piece of cake," he tells me, "You have done well preparing her!"

"It's just the food," I laugh, "She'll do anything for food. But thank you. I appreciate your kind words."

Polly, the dear lady from our club who had emailed us earlier in the week to tell us she would be there at the trial, and happy to help, looks over the course map with Asherel and they discuss strategy. There are fifteen jumps arranged in roughly a figure 8 pattern. In Agility work, the handler is the key to the dog's successful navigation of the course. The handler has to assess both her path to best cue the dog, and the dog's path to run under the time limit and give the best chance of not knocking the bar off the jump. The goal is to run the course with no jump faults (knocked bars, refusals, missed jumps, or jump out of sequence) and with no time faults. Dogs at varying height levels are allotted corresponding time allowances to complete the fifteen jumps. That time varies depending on the complexity and length of the run, but is roughly forty seconds overall. Asherel's goals are more modest than most. She just wants Honeybun to jump, and not sniff, and not go after any dog or human with malice aforethought.

Her class is blessedly the first of the day, so we don't have long to freak out.

The judge calls the contestants of "Performance Jumpers" class to "walk the course." Asherel hands me Honeybun's leash, and hurries onto the field with the flurry of others. She is the only child handler. Polly enters the field a few minutes later, and I see her walking and discussing with Asherel. I feel a flood of gratitude to this recent acquaintance, willing to sacrifice her own preparation to help Asherel. Is kindness suddenly being introduced to the human race… or is it possible I have just missed it?

As the minutes tick by, other handlers leave the field one by one. Asherel remains, walking it over and over, pointing at each jump successively, until only she and one other handler remain on the field. The judge calls out that time is up, and Asherel with one lingering look back, is the last handler off the field.

She returns for her dog, and stands in line, waiting for her name to be called. I balance my camera on the fence and hold the video camcorder. It is shaking like a leaf. Something must be wrong with this camera's stability controller.

Honeybun's name is announced. They enter the field. Asherel tells Honeybun to sit and stay, and removes the leash. Honeybun looks bored, and sniffs the grass.

"OK! Go jump!" calls Asherel. Not exactly like a bolt of lightning, but not as slow as a slug either, Honeybun canters over the first three jumps. She pauses near the fourth, and Asherel has to re-cue her a few times, but then she complacently decides to play along, and jumps, tipping the bar over. The rest of the run is clean, no other jumps down. She finishes, and lets Asherel leash her, and comes happily trotting towards me. I fall to my knees and stuff her with sirloin goodies.

"That was great!" I trumpet to Asherel, who is breathlessly nodding.

It is far better than what we had expected after her performance at Deb's.

Asherel works as a leash runner volunteer for the next hour, and I take Honeybun for a long walk. My joy is a waterfall of delight splashing across all those hard stones of struggle over the past year, burying them in cascades of exultation. This may sound over the top, but I am remembering the impossible creature she had been and the troughs of despair, the hopeless desire to throw in the towel. The little dog prances next to me. I think she knows something momentous has just happened.

When we return, Asherel finishes her volunteer job, and we settle down to watch the other classes. I meander over to the barn where the scores are posted. I have no idea what any of the scores mean, but want to see if Honeybun has come in last.

I find her name, but there are several numbers written on it, none of which make any sense. A kind man asks me if he can help me, as I must have looked confused. He tells me the number on the upper right is Honeybun's time, and then he shows me how to determine the course qualifying time. She is four seconds over, which is admirable for her first ever agility run, he assures me. Then he shows me how another number indicates the number of jump faults. Just one jump fault, a five point deduction. The next number is the combined time and jump faults, which is how the final standing is determined. Finally, he points to a number circled in the center.

"And this means she won second place."

I blink.

"She gets a ribbon?" I ask tremulously.

"And a toy," he adds smiling. He shows me where the honor system self serve ribbon and toy box is. I hurry over glancing at Asherel in the distance, who is quietly holding her dog on her lap and watching the class in progress. Hiding the ribbon behind my back, I breeze over to Asherel.

"Oh, one thing more I need to tell you…"

She looks up, and I pull the ribbon out, "You won second place."

Asherel is struck silent for a moment, but then her face shatters into a million happy smiles. She shows the ribbon to Honeybun, who promptly begins to eat it.

Day Two, we get to sleep in a little later, since Asherel's class is not until late morning. We arrive well in advance of her class nonetheless, on a hot sunny day. Honeybun languishes in the heat, panting, and surveying her kingdom from my chair, which Asherel appropriates for her. By the time her class rolls around, we are all hot and enervated. Honeybun's tail, normally a sprite flag seems limp, wilted in the heat. Asherel again walks the course the full ten minutes. This course includes a tunnel. I park myself at the same place along the fence as the day before.

When Honeybun's name is called, it all starts well, but as she rounds jump four, a little wide, she notices me beside the fence. She pauses, and then trots over to me. Asherel remains surprisingly nonplussed by this defection, entreats her to return to the business at hand, and with a brief look back at me, Honeybun seems to shrug her shoulders, and leaps the next jump. At the tunnel, she blazes in, but is a bit long time coming out. Asherel later informs me that our little dog had decided to stop and clean her bottom in the tunnel. She speeds over the last few jumps, and tips the second to last bar. All in all, it is a good run, with again just one down bar.

Again we are euphoric. Lowered expectations have a way of making life a pleasant surprise. She has obeyed Asherel, but for that fleeting and understandable desire to visit with me. She is probably a little slower than yesterday, but still not embarrassingly so, and only one jump is knocked down. We praise her and feed her treats, and are grateful to end the day with again not being disqualified for unseemly teeth marks being left behind on dog or human. When the scores are posted, we are astonished to see she places second again. She is nine seconds over time, but having only knocked down one bar still ahead of the competition. Asherel ties the ribbons on the crate proudly. Honeybun gobbles the treats and seems unfazed by our lavish praise, though she appreciates the extra goodies.

That evening, as I walk her at the hotel, I wish we had only signed up for two of the three days. I am exhausted with little sleep, the early mornings, the hot days, and the stress.

While she has come such a long way, she could certainly revert to what she had been in those early days in this new chaotic environment. We have been warned that under stress, many dogs do revert to earlier behavior. We have had a wonderful experience, she has done far better than hoped already, and I am wondering if it would've been better to dash away while we were still not in a hospital or jail.

The next morning we are again the first class of the day. I am awake from 4 a.m., and finally trudge out of bed around 6:00. Honeybun is still snoring. Asherel is huddled deep in the covers. It all seemed like such a good idea, in theory, this dog agility business. I long for my peaceful quiet unhurried mornings of a typical weekend. However, by 6:30, we are all up, breakfasted, and ready to go. I pack our things, check out of the hotel, and we drive into the rising sun, long shadows stretching across a sleepy world.

However, the agility fields are abuzz with scurrying course builders and dogs being walked and stretched. Asherel pours over the course map which she snatches as soon as we arrive. She has only a few minutes to scrutinize it before she is called to walk the course. This one is the hardest of the three days, with a "pinwheel" array of jumps midway through the course. This tight circle of four jumps challenges the handler to be very precise in her cues, and the dog has to pay close attention. It is very easy to miss the jump sequence as the tendency is to follow jumps that are in a straight line from each other.

If Asherel is nervous, she does not show it. She walks the course, again with Polly advising, but Asherel has already determined what she needs to do to help Honeybun stay on course. Polly confirms her decisions. For the third day, she is the final handler to finish walking the course when time is called, memorizing her intended path over and over again.

Honeybun is the fourth dog up. This time, to ensure that I do not distract her, I hide near the Judge table behind the starting line. Honeybun won't see me until she heads for the last jump. I am too far off the fence to film, so decide just to enjoy and watch this one. Honeybun was a full nine seconds over the time limit yesterday, so I know she has no chance of qualifying. This run is just gravy on our feast of happy triumphs. However well she does today, we will be content as she has already exceeded our expectations and garnered two totally unanticipated ribbons,

A dog comes off the course and marches by Honeybun. From the back up, he looks just like Lucky - same golden tan, same wild terrier explosion of hair. His much shorter legs are dachshund length, but even I do a double take, wondering what Lucky is doing here and who has absconded with his legs. Honeybun apparently thinks it is Lucky too. She swings her head around and begins tugging at her leash, straining to reach the dog, wagging her tail. She has ignored the other dogs the whole weekend. It is clear she thinks Lucky is here, her brother, her friend. She wants to say hello. I thought dogs have a great sense of smell. Surely this dog doesn't smell like Lucky. If anything needed to convince me that Honeybun has developed a love for Lucky, this does…but her timing stinks. This is not where her attention should be placed at this moment.

The judge calls Honeybun to the field as she continues to strain after Lucky Lookalike. Oh lovely. All hope of her attention on Asherel is gone, and now she is in danger of leaving the field as soon as the leash comes off.

Asherel commands Honeybun to sit and stay as she removes the leash. I cringe as Honeybun turns to look at the Lucky-like dog, but she remains seated.

"OK, Honeybun!" summons Asherel, "Go jump!"

If I were not standing there watching, I would not have believed what happens next. Honeybun rockets forward and soars over the first three jumps. As she enters the pinwheel, she gallops without pause over all four. Coming out of the pinwheel, she has a brief moment of confusion and looks to

Asherel who is already re-cuing her. She barrels to the correct jump, tail streaming behind her in the funny backward curve. As she tears over the next jump, one ear up and one ear sideways, I am holding my breath. She is jumping cleanly so far, and she has never gone so fast. I might be watching a miracle! Asherel twirls through her handling maneuvers and points expertly at the next jump. Honeybun's attention and focus never wavers. The faux-Lucky dog is clearly forgotten or perhaps she is showing off for him. Jump thirteen is left in her wake and she turns for the final two jumps. Asherel is smiling.

"Go Honey, go!" she trumpets as the little dog clears the final line of two jumps.

I erupt, along with the crowd in a cascade of applause. She has not touched a single jump, and she was fast. Is it possible she qualified? Will she get a Q after her name, the first, I hope, of many letters of redemption?

We shower her with mounds of treats, and some rib bones we have saved from dinner last night as we return to our chairs. Never had we envisioned this sudden and complete transformation. Now we sit tensely, both of us pretending we are not watching the barn where they will post the scores. The club owner walks by and holds her fist up to Asherel, "Great run!" she calls.

Several others come by and tell Asherel what a magnificent run that had been. She is still catching her breath, and her pink cheeks shine brightly like jewels. Many of our new friends come by to congratulate her on a fine run, knowing this is our first trial.

Finally we see them tack the score sheet to the barn wall.

"Come on," I say, "I will show you how to read all those numbers."

The adults milling around the score sheet smile at Asherel as she approaches, and part to let her near. A nice lady, Susan, who sat near us over the three days tells Asherel to find Honeybun's name.

"Where do I look?" she asks. Susan helps her find the name.

"See, here is her time....30.91. The qualifying course time is 31 seconds, so she made time. And no deductions for down bars, so she had 0 deductions. Here is her place."

Asherel peers closely at the number, circled in red.

"Honeybun won," she says softly, with a quivering giggle.

"And this Q here," I say smiling hugely, "Means she qualified."

Asherel gathers Honeybun in her arms, and lifts her up to see her score. Honeybun sniffs, but is unimpressed as it is clearly not edible. We trot over to the ribbon table to collect a blue ribbon, a purple qualifying rosette ribbon, and a special beef jerky treat for all qualifying dogs. At last, thinks Honeybun, an award I can really sink my teeth into!

The indomitable Asherel smiles the whole drive home, and I am bathed in the aura of her unquenchable love of all creatures and the long standing dream realized that she refused to relinquish. I call my parents as we drive, and rave about the little dog and my triumphant daughter. While recounting the weekend heroics, a smell begins to slowly percolate through the car. Asherel glances at me, her brow furrowed. The stench intensifies until we are enveloped in deadly, noxious fumes. Asherel and I look back at Honeybun, innocently gazing out the window. We punch open the windows gasping for the fresh air that comes tumbling in. Honeybun has secured yet another triumph. She has finally expressed those troublesome anal glands on her own.

"Look Mom," says Asherel, when we can breathe again, "She is happy!"

"How can you tell?" I ask.

"Look at her. She's smiling!"

I scrutinize her in the rear view mirror, and I see what Asherel sees. She *is* smiling.

I email Malta that evening, as we all sit contentedly, blissfully at home.

Honeybun is fast asleep in my closet, one of her favorite spots. She disappeared there when we arrived home, and has not emerged since. Becoming a champion is apparently exhausting.

Malta writes back, "*Aren't you glad I yelled at you in that email long ago? Who would ever have thought a last chance dog would win first place*?"

I knew that Malta, more than anyone, would understand the significance of that win. It is not just a ribbon to Malta, any less than it is to us. It is a crown of redemption, placed upon the silky head of a dog left to die. It is all the more sweet that she's been led to her throne by people like us, such bewildered ignoramuses Malta is forced to work her transformations through. If we could do it, really, anyone could. God and a dog just would not let me fail, no matter how hard I tried. If He calls, you, it is best to Heel.

"You should write this all down," Malta tells me, "It might inspire someone else who is ready to give up."

And so I have.

Dear Lord,

To Him who is able to do immeasurably more than all we ask or imagine, according to His power that is at work within us, to Him be the glory in the church and in Christ Jesus, throughout all generations forever and ever.

Thank you.

Amen

The End of the Story

When AKC changed the rules in 2010 such that mixed breed dogs could enter their Agility Trials, Honeybun and Asherel went on to compete in AKC. Within a year, they had earned the title, Honeybun, NAJ, NA. (Novice Agility Jumper, Novice Agility Dog). She consistently placed in the top three of her classes in earning those titles.

Honeybun continues to compete and has earned legs towards her Open Agility Title as well. Every time I look at Honeybun, I remember that the impossible is sometimes possible, never give up, and God can work miracles in the places you would never expect Him to be.

About the Author

Vicky Kaseorg has written her entire life, but this is her first full length published book. Vicky is a professional artist, mother of three children, whom she has homeschooled for the past 20 years, art class teacher, and board member of Hollow Creek Dog and Equine Rescue Farm. She and her husband and youngest daughter reside in North Carolina where she is working on books two and three.

Portions of the sale of this book will be donated to Hollowcreekfarm.org

Vickykaseorg.weebly.com

Vickykaseorg.blogspot.com

Hollowcreekfarm.org

Cover photo of Honeybun by Veronica Kelso

Back photo of author and Honeybun by Asherel Kaseorg

Made in the USA
Charleston, SC
05 August 2011